The Queer Parent's Primer

A Lesbian and Gay
Families' Guide to
Navigating the
Straight World

Stephanie A. Brill

Foreword by Kate Kendall, Esq.

New Harbinger Publications, Inc.

Publisher's Note

This publication is designed to provide accurate and authoritative information in regard to the subject matter covered. It is sold with the understanding that the publisher is not engaged in rendering psychological, financial, legal, or other professional services. If expert assistance or counseling is needed, the services of a competent professional should be sought.

Distributed in the U.S.A. by Publishers Group West; in Canada by Raincoast Books; in Great Britain by Airlift Book Company, Ltd.; in South Africa by Real Books, Ltd.; in Australia by Boobook; and in New Zealand by Tandem Press.

Cover design by Blue Design
Edited by Jueli Gastwirth
Text design by Tracy Marie Powell

Library of Congress Card Catalog Number: 00-134864
ISBN 1-57224-226-4 Paperback

Printed in the United States of America

New Harbinger Publications' Web site address: www.newharbinger.com

03   02   01

10   9   8   7   6   5   4   3   2   1

First printing

For Colleen—
You are my love.

Contents

Foreword

Kate Kendell
Executive Director
National Center for Lesbian Rights

I have been a lesbian parent in two different worlds. In the early 1980s my then partner Lori and I were raising our daughter Emily in Ogden, Utah. In our large circle of friends and family we knew only two other children who were being raised in a lesbian- or gay-headed household. There were few resources for and even less public conversation about lesbian, gay, bisexual, and transgendered parents.

As we enter a new millennium, I am a parent all over again. My partner Sandy and I are raising our son Julian in "queer ground-zero" San Francisco. The issue of LGBT-headed families is front and center in public discourse. Resources abound. It is into this fertile landscape that Stephanie Brill's *The Queer Parents Primer* lands with a big splash. A thin novella this is not, and it is a tribute to the depth and breadth of our parenting that this is so. When many of us came out a generation or two ago, we were led to believe by the dominant cultural messages that being queer and being a parent were mutually exclusive—but this is no longer the case. We are parents in record and growing numbers, and this book covers the vast territory of issues that being queer and a parent present. Brill deftly navigates the most practical issues, such as parenting agreements and second-parent adoption, and the equally critical but often overlooked issues of religion, spirituality, and schooling. *The Queer Parent's Primer* comprehensively addresses our opportunities for celebration of our families and the unique challenges we face.

As lesbian, gay, bisexual, or transgendered parents, I think we have a special and sacred chance to not only be loving, nurturing parents but to instill in our children an understanding of the pain of discrimination and injustice and to foster a desire in them to be agents of change. Brill seems to agree, as *Primer* addresses the societal challenges faced by queer parents not as roadblocks, but rather as "teachable moments" for both our children and a society sometimes still ignorant or even hostile when it comes to LGBT-headed households. *The Queer Parent's Primer* is testament to our visibility, our role as agents of social change, the still groundbreaking nature of our families, and, most essentially, the sheer joy of being a parent.

Acknowledgments

I would like to thank all of the queer parents who have come before me for leading the way with their love and bravery. I deeply appreciate all of the parents and children who have shared their lives and their stories with me.

Special thanks to the founding members of the New Village Charter School—I am a better person and parent for our journey together.

Heartfelt thanks to Kate Kendell of the National Center for Lesbian Rights (NCLR) for doing invaluable work. Thank you for taking time to speak with me and to write the Introduction, you are an inspiration! Thank you to Chris Hwang at the NCLR for your clarifications. My appreciation to Charlotte Patterson and the work she is doing to research our families. Thank you for your time taken with me.

Thank you Jueli Gastwirth for being such a kind and thoughtful editor. You have made the writing process a joy!

Special thanks to: Kim Toevs for helping me over the years to clarify my thought and vision; to Robin Winn for helping me to know myself; and to Jim Otis for friendship and great talks.

I would not be who I am today without the love and support of my circles of family. My extended family, especially Lisa Arellano, and Terry Boland for your love, friendship, and confidence in me. My parents, Laren and Jesse Brill, for their love and dedication to growth. And most importantly my family—Colleen, Gitanjali, and Namaya—you are the loves of my life who inspire me to be the best I can be.

And always, my eternal gratitude to the Divine Mother.

Introduction

Our families—queer families—are far from homogeneous. They consist of men parenting alone; women parenting alone; men and women parenting together; single parents; adoptive parents; biological parents; gay, lesbian, bisexual, and transgendered parents; multiracial, multiethnic, multicultural families; mixtures of all of these; and many more. There is no one face to a queer family. Thus our community has the opportunity to totally reinvent what family means to us, who is in our family, how we would like to go about having children, and how we would like to go about raising those children. This sense of freedom is exhilarating and liberating; it is also often overwhelming.

The late 1990s has brought gay parenting into the mainstream public eye. This positive visibility, in part, can be attributed to queer celebrities, such as Ellen Degeneres and Melissa Etheridge, being out about their sexual orientation. Star appeal has led to glitzy coverage of Hollywood actors and rock star lesbians dining at the White House. Famous lesbians are now commonplace in mainstream magazines.

More lesbian and gay people are choosing to parent now than ever before. There have always been lesbian mothers, but thanks to the ever-increasing acceptable routes to having children, many openly gay men are choosing to parent as well. The gay community is actively busting the antiquated myth that we must choose between parenting and being gay. As the gay population claims its right to raise children, many political and religious hot buttons are pushed.

With the Religious Right taking on family values as its dominant theme, there is much attention focused on gay families. It is ironic that, in part, due to the attention the Religious Right is giving to gay parenting, more and more people are coming to see it as an option. It's also becoming more common to see versions of our families represented on television sitcoms and in the news. This visibility is giving courage to gays and lesbians who long for children, but who have been immobilized from taking the step to become parents due to internal and external homophobia.

The paths to parenthood and the configurations of family have broadened so much for all people that it has naturally opened doors for alternative families as well. American heterosexual women are choosing to parent much later in life. The resultant infertility epidemic has created more readily available alternative treatments to having children. Alternative insemination, surrogacy, egg donation, and adoption have all become much more popular routes in the past ten years to having children. The face of "family" is rapidly changing. Women are choosing to parent without partners. A significant number of children are raised with absentee fathers or in families headed by grandparents. This reconfiguring of families is making it easier for LGBTs both to create families and to live openly as queer families.

It is difficult to determine how many children are raised in nonheterosexual households. General estimates range from tens of thousands to millions. Unfortunately, the situations we could be tracking, such as same-sex adoptions and second-parent adoptions, are not being calculated. Some gays and lesbians create family, some people come out after having children, some gays and lesbians date and partner with existing parents, and some queer identified bisexuals have children. There are also sometimes commonly extended coparents in gay families, donors who have relationships with their genetic offspring, and gay men who parent with straight single women.

Because there has been no standard for how we are *supposed* to create our families, there is no standard as to how we *do* create family. Some resemble traditional families in roles and makeup, yet many do not. Some gay parents are coupled, some are single, some are in group parenting situations. Some families live in one household, some in multiple households. Some children are not of the same ethnic or racial background of any of their family members. Some children are adopted; some have a genetic link to one or more of the parents who are raising them. Some children are raised by female parents, some by male parents, some by female and male parents, some children have transgender parents, and some have one or more intersex (i.e., having both male and female genitalia) parents. Our families are quite diverse.

Issues of whether gays and lesbians should be able to adopt, legally marry, and legally raise children continue to be addressed in most of the states in America and in many countries worldwide. States are looking to set precedents regarding our families. Unfortunately, in conservative states, that has meant gays and lesbians commonly have lost their children. In fact, many gay and lesbian families have lost custody of their children to known abusers (*Bottoms* v. *Bottoms* 1995). The implications of such rulings are breathtaking. At the same time, however, other states are actively passing legislation to secure legal protection for our families.

Other cases that are being tried in courts across the country are brought about by our own families. Unfortunately, many lesbian parents are not acting in good faith toward their ex-partners during times of separation. There have been numerous cases brought to court where the biological or legal mother refuses to allow the "other" mother to have joint custody or even visitation rights to their child. This trend is appalling. We are causing homophobic precedent to be set because we are acting in a homophobic fashion. Why are we currently unable to honor the love, intention, and actual parenting of our partners as valid? Why are we choosing to defer to biology and law when it is convenient? We need a serious wake-up call on this issue. If we want our families to be recognized as valid, we must recognize them as valid, and not just when the mood suits us. Through abominable breakup behavior we are doing a disservice to our children and ourselves. Because it takes such tremendous effort for us to have children, our families are always intentional and, therefore, always created from love: Let's reflect that love in our parenting.

The Queer Parents' Primer addresses the specific issues that gay parents face because they are gay. It is a practical guide. You can read this book when you are in the trenches of parenting; you can read it when you are considering parenting, or when you are in the process of becoming a parent. This book also will help educate friends, family members, and others who care about you. Although it cannot cover every parenting issue, *The Queer Parents' Primer* tries to address the most common concerns. The book offers specific suggestions, and includes examples of how other families have responded to similar situations.

The book also provides guidelines and reflective questions that will help you create personalized responses to situations you and your children will encounter as a direct result of your sexual orientation. The approach will help you clarify your desires. Clarity gives us courage and strength.

Throughout the book you will find self-reflective exercises and journal entry suggestions. While reading the book, you may want to use a special notebook or journal especially for these exercises and to record thoughts and ideas as they come to you. Journal writing can help you to deepen your access to your thoughts and feelings, thus making it a beneficial personal discovery tool. If you are reading the book with a partner or coparent, it is usually best to each have a separate journal that you can share from if you wish.

It is a challenge to write a book that can apply to people in all parts of the country. Locations where there are gay centers, such as the coasts and in big cities, are in many ways light-years ahead of the more conservative areas of the country. Each reader will be different with regard to how "out" they are and how far they are willing to push themselves and family members. The book will try to address this scope. But, just like any civil rights movement, we need vision and grassroots action plans. Hopefully, this book will inspire you.

Although *The Queer Parents' Primer* may seem political at first glance, you will find it's actually quite practical. As queer parents, the personal is political. You have chosen to parent from a place of great love. This is personal. The ignorance you will encounter on your child-rearing path, how you respond to such ignorance, and the manner in which you teach your children and others is political. Yet parenting is practical; it is an integral part of our day-to-day lives. Becoming a gay parent takes great courage. My hat is off to every one of you for following the path of love, the path of pride.

A Note on Language

There is no language to describe our families that makes everyone comfortable. In this book, I use the terms: gay, gay and lesbian, LGBT (lesbians, gay, bisexual, and transgender), GLBT (gay, lesbians, bisexual, and transgender), and queer interchangeably. If I am using the word "gay" to refer only to males, I will make that clear.

PART I

The Path of Love

1

Establishing and Celebrating Your Family

Honoring and Debunking Biology

Our families are unique and special. We are families created from love and intention. It is very rare that a gay family is created by accident. We are all courageous, strong individuals who are willing to face the cultural expectation of heterosexuality with the love we have for one another, for ourselves, and for our children. Although there are many differences in the faces and natures of our families, we have courage and strength in common. If we didn't, none of us could have made it this far. This is a deep, cultural connection.

In many ways our families are no different than other families around the world. There are, however, significant differences. Language, social and legal structures, and religions support most heterosexual families. In fact, most cultures are designed around the nature of these families.

Queer families do not experience this. Certainly we experience pockets of support, but not one of us could honestly say that society was created around nurturing our families. This is not necessarily negative. In fact, it allows us tremendous freedom to create unique families that are meaningful to us. We are not typically compelled to conform. However, it is a stress to have to create and define yourself and then, at times, defend your right to exist as a family.

Queer families are often compelled to protect their sanctity. Because heterosexual parenting is still the only socially condoned family structure, LGBTs must do a lot of work to define and protect our families. It is important that we celebrate, acknowledge, and nourish our choices and our family constellations. There are many levels to this: You must find inner Pride and cultivate it; you must also face the practical realities of how you are going to describe your family and what words you will use, and how you will present your family in public and to your family of origin.

This chapter will help you to explore the practical issues involved in establishing and celebrating your family. It will also help you to find clear and affirming definitions for your family. Even if you have been a family for many years, it is helpful to review these topics to see how affirming your responses are and to examine whether there are family titles or responses you might like to shift to more accurately reflect your family. This chapter is especially helpful for families who are just forming and for families who are re-forming.

Finding Language to Suit Our Families

Because our families are unique, they do not often fit readily into the language available to us, at this point in time, to describe familial relations. Nonetheless, language plays a very important role in how families and each family member is viewed and acknowledged. Language holds much power and the appellations that we choose for ourselves can have far-reaching implications. It is important to make the time to create descriptions that are both clear and affirming, and to review your choices and the language you and your family currently use.

Sometimes we acquiesce to the current limitations of language without exploring the potential implications this may have on our family and on our own sense of belonging and self-esteem. As the face of family is continuing to change, words are being redefined. There is plenty still left to do. Much of the common terminology used in gay families is taken directly from heterosexual- and biology-based models. Words such as "artificial insemination," "nonbirth mom," and "coparent" are socially accepted terms, yet, when examined, are actually affronts to the authenticity of our families. We can easily replace "artificial" insemination with insemination, we can replace "coparent" with parent (when referring to equal primary parents), but with what do we replace "nonbirth mom"? Biology is still equated with ownership and superiority. Language is established in relation to culturally accepted precedents.

The language of family creates a hierarchy that is crowned by the biological connection. The subsequent terminology honors the biological connection as superior to all other connections by defining only relationships of biology as family.

Biological superiority is an outdated concept. It is necessary to both honor and debunk the biological connection. This can be a fine line to walk. A place to start is to first ask yourself who is in my family?

Who Is in My Family?

Words have power. When choosing language for your family, it is best to start by asking yourself, "Who is in my family?"

A person will usually answer this question differently at various points of parenthood. When you ask a very new parent who is in their family, they might readily list their baby/ newly adopted child, and their family of origin. Regardless as to whether they are partnered or have other parents for their child, many new parents list only biology and baby.

Yet if you ask an established parent, they will list their partner, their child's other parents, and any relevant extended family members, be they family of choice or biological family. It seems that the comfort of claiming nonbiologically related family members becomes stronger as you parent longer. When family has become less of a concept, and is a day-to-day reality, it becomes more difficult to defer automatically to biology.

Obviously there can also be an element of internalized homophobia involved in your response as well. Time, familiarity with being a family, and love truly help to wear down internal homophobia. We all know, however, that it isn't always that easy. Chapter 4 is dedicated to addressing the issues of coming out as a parent on a day-to-day basis.

Chosen Family Members

Who is in my family? This is not necessarily an easy question to answer. Our families are based as much on the bonds of kinship as they are on the bonds of biology. Our families are often like tribes or clans. In many of our families, no one is biologically related. This does not make us any less a family. Love and commitment to one another is what makes a family. Because our families are not solely defined through biology and marriage, there is a distinct element of choice available to us. Choice is powerful. Choice can also be overwhelming. Fortunately, family can evolve over time. Relationships can deepen and new family members can be added. However, if there are people in your life and your child's life who you would like to mark as different and significant, then it is important to claim them as family. As a family member they will require a name and a title, but to receive such appellations, they must first be acknowledged as part of your family.

Exercise

In your journal, respond to the question, "Who is in my family?" Write freely and see what you say. Ask yourself if any of the people you have listed are more "family" than others? How comfortable are you in claiming each family member? Could you reference each member in all conversations? If not, who is excluded from your comfort zone? Why?

Is there a different sense you hold about people who are biologically related to one another than with family members who are not related by blood? Are people who are legally married (heterosexual) more family than people who are partnered? Do the responses to these questions reflect how you would like to feel about family? Have you gained any insight into yourself?

Many people are surprised to discover that even though they are gay and have nuclear family members, family who are not biologically or legally related to one another, they still regard biological connection as somehow more valid. It is easy to see that queer families continue the stigma that families with adopted children have carried for a long time.

When you are clear about your subconscious biases, you can work to make sure that you do not taint others' views of your family unknowingly. It is easier to choose ways to accurately present your family when you are aware of choices you might make that would unconsciously undermine your truest intentions. It is just another way of uncovering internalized heterosexism and patriarchal influences.

Choosing Names and Titles

Claiming family members is not a light decision for most people. In relationships where there are two primary partnered parents, the decision to claim a friend as an "official" family member often requires discussion. It is easier for this to be more fluid and less defined when you do not have children; you know whom you love and who is important to you without having to attach a title to that relationship. However, when children enter the picture, everything becomes more complex because your family or families of origin are automatically assured titles of familial distinction, whereas your chosen family is not.

So it becomes important to ask yourself, and your partner, if you have one, "Is Monique actually someone I/we want to be called 'Aunt' or is she just a good friend?" Once you have selected who is family and who is not, then you will want to have some clarifying conversation with your friends to confirm that they too feel like family and would be honored to carry the appropriate appellations announcing their role as a family member.

Each person in your family needs a name and a title for appropriate familial recognition. Utilizing such language is important and validating for your child and is necessary for societal acknowledgment of shared family bonds. It is important to take the time to explore this concept thoroughly. Sometimes it is appropriate to claim titles and terminology that have, in the past, only referenced biological relationships. Sometimes it is appropriate to create new titles and appellations to describe our relationships.

Parents

What would you like your child to call you? If no one else had any input at all and society would completely accept and fully acknowledge any choice you made, what would you choose to be called? Most of the men I have spoken with answer with some form of Dad, Daddy, Papa, and Poppa; the women answer with some form of Mom, Mommy, and Mama. However, many of those same people are not called by their preferred name. Why? In almost all families, without exception, I found that if there is a parent who is biologically connected to the child, that person lays claim to the most socially and culturally accepted title. Likewise, in families where there is only one legal parent, as in the case with most adopted children—at least at the start—the legal parent claims the most socially recognized title.

Why do we continue to let biology or the rulings of a homophobic legal system take precedence in areas where we look at ourselves as equal parents? How can we ask people outside of our families to recognize our roles as equal and yet in the inner workings of our families repeat the same discriminatory behavior? Usually our choices of appellations and the potential impact of those choices are not fully examined ahead of time.

Of course, if you are in a relationship where one of you considers yourself a parent and the other does not, then working out titles is somewhat different. In your situation, there frequently is one Mom or Dad and the other parent is called by their name or by Aunt or Uncle. Also, in the case of families who choose to stay closeted to their children, there can only be one Mom or Dad.

Many people, however, confuse the person who is to be the primary parent in the child's early years with somehow being more of a parent. For example, if Marcy is going to stay home with the baby while Lonnie continues to work full-time to provide an income for the family, Lonnie is not less of a parent. She is simply not the primary parent. In heterosexual families, a father who holds a full-time job so that the mother can stay home with the baby is not considered to be less of a parent. His parenting rights, roles, and responsibilities are not questioned simply because he holds a job and the mother does not. Much to our fault, however, and the added fault of our society, our families are often regarded as such unless we assert ourselves otherwise.

Thus, do not make a choice of family appellations and titles based on who gave birth, who adopted, or who spends more time in the throes of parenting. Take the time to work out names and appellations that feel right. If you and your partner have both always wanted to be called Mama or Daddy, is there a problem with that? If you determine that there should only be one Mama or one Daddy, how will you decide who gets the cherished name? Examine how you make these decisions so that there is not resentment.

There are differing approaches to selecting the name that you wish your child to call you. Some people feel very strongly that a child can only have one Mom or one Dad. If there is more than one primary parent, then one of them must use a name or title that would in no way indicate a mom or dad relationship. Some two-parent families are not comfortable with the idea that they could both be called the same thing or they think having two daddies or mamas would be confusing to the child, so they choose a specific name for each parent. These parents usually decide on these names ahead of time and only refer to themselves and each other by that name. For example: Daddy and Poppy, or Mama and Mommy, or Mama Rosa and Mama Julienne, or Mommy and Momma, Daddy and Dooda. It is these situations that often, when unexamined, give preference to one parent over the other—usually the biological parent or the primary parent.

Some parents hope to avoid any confusion by being called "Daddy Martin" and "Daddy Joshua." If you wish to be called by a parental title, however, this is not a good choice. It seems that very early on children will choose to shorten it to the distinctive terms and you will end up being called Martin and Joshua. Although some parents do not mind their children calling them by their first names, and some parents actually prefer it, many parents feel like something important is missing when their child stops calling them Mom or Pappa.

Many Jewish women in the Bay Area choose for the child to have a Mommy and Ima (Hebrew word for Mom). Many of these same families do not use Hebrew at any other time. It is most frequently the mother who did not give birth who is called Ima—a name recognized by most non-Jews as a name in a foreign language.

Confusing Titles

When talking to a child, it is most common for them to be asked questions in reference to their mommy. Seemingly innocuous conversation at the park, for example, such as: "Who is your mommy?" or "Go get your mama," for the young child, only references the mother who goes by that title. The young child with a mommy and an ima will easily answer, "My mommy is at work today" or " My mommy isn't here right now, my ima is." Although truthful in response, the choice of appellation for the parent allows a child to state that her Mommy isn't here right now even though she is at the park with one of her two female parents. Your choice of names, although effective inside the home, can serve to unintentionally displace one of the parents outside of the home.

Some families wait until the child chooses names for each parent on its own. In these families there is usually more fluidity in the words by which the parents refer to themselves. Eventually a child settles on a name, and, most commonly, parents will start to refer to themselves by that name as well.

Untraditional Moms and Dads

Some gay male parents choose to be called Mom and some lesbian parents choose to be called Dad. The parents I have met who switch the expected gender of parental titles do so because it feels right. They may be a very butch woman who can relate perfectly to the idea of Dad, but cannot even imagine being a mom. Or a man who is not going to forgo the title of Mom because he has always considered himself to be deeply maternal and now finally has a chance to mother. I do not need to tell you that when you do a gender switch it is bound to push many people's buttons. That, however, is not a good enough reason to not hold the title that is most natural to you.

Choices of the Children

And, of course, no matter how much you would like to be called a certain name or title, your child will end up calling you many different things during childhood—some you will cherish and some will make you cringe. A dear friend of ours went through a silly phase where she called one of her dads "Papa Poo Poo" and one dad "Daddy Donut Face." Unfortunately, this particular phase lasted for two years.

Establishing Titles for Donors and Other Family Members

It is important to discuss with all coparents, donors, and other family members what you would like them to be called and how you would like them to reference themselves. These conversations are important as people make assumptions that can end up causing confusion and misinterpretation of your family. Be creative with the titles and names you come up with. I've met one family who calls each family member who is not related by blood "Special," so the children have a "Special Doug" a "Special Grandma Pat" a "Special Katherine," etc. . . . and that is how they introduce them: "This is my Special Gregory." When people ask questions, the children reply that they have a whole family of Specials, and that makes *the children* feel special.

Gaining clarity as to who is in your family is important. Queer families usually emphasize a chosen relationship as being equally as crucial as biological connections. If certain family members are chosen members, it is important to introduce them as family to your biological family and to your friends. For example, if your child has an Uncle Billy who interacts with your family of origin at social functions, it is best to introduce him as Jamie's Uncle Billy rather than my friend Billy. This instantly establishes his role.

Donors

It is important to become as clear as possible about what each person's role and title is to be in your family. For example, are you going to refer to your donor by name, as Anthony, or will you bestow upon him the title of "Uncle Anthony," as you said you wanted him to have an uncle role in your child's life? Will it be common knowledge that he is the donor, or would you like to have the option to reveal that information as you see fit? Can he reveal that information as he sees fit? What terms would you like for him to use when he is not with you?

I have heard so many stories where women discover that their donor has been referring to himself as their child's "Dad" wherever he goes. This can often cause feelings of confusion, anger, and resentment for parents who do not consider their donor to be a parent. The donor on the other hand simply did not think that "Dad" meant more than donor; he was just proud to have helped to create another human being and was spreading the word.

Likewise, if you choose to refer to your donor as "Dad" even though you do not consider him to have a parental role, it would be much easier for him to prove in court that he has an emotional bond to the child if he were ever to sue for custody.

Coparents and nonprimary parents who usually live outside of the main home of the child have chosen a variety of appellations. Some are the traditional Mom or Dad, some are called Uncle or Aunt, some are on a first name basis, and some get creative and invent titles, or the children invent titles that stick. I heard from one family in Georgia. That the dads are both called Dad, but the surrogate, Jennifer, who is also a coparent, is called LuLu. Go figure.

The Question of Last Names

When a child is born or adopted you have the chance to provide it with any last name you please. It does not have to be a name that is in any way related to your own. If you plan to change your child's last name at another point in time, the process is a bit more complicated, but definitely doable, for a fee.

It is important to choose a last name for your child that will honor and celebrate your family. Last names have traditionally served to connect and identify family members. Most queer single parents choose to give their child their own last name or to create a new last name for their child. When you are partnered, or when their are multiple parents who are all considered equal, the decision of the last name becomes more difficult.

I think that if you are partnered, careful selection of a last name for your child is essential. It is salient to make sure that the name chosen does not serve to displace the nonbiological or nonlegal parent—the parent who has the most challenging role from the start. Many biological parents do not realize the potentially negative and far-reaching implications of using their own last name when they are parenting with a partner who is not biologically linked to their child. Doing so serves to reinforce and emphasize the superiority of the biological or legal connection to everyone, including the child. Sharing a last name emphasizes the connection between child and parent while inherently leaving out the other parent. It is a clear message. As attached to your last name as you may be, giving your child the last name of the biologically related parent is the least desirable choice for queer families. With this in mind, there are three preferred choices.

Hyphenated Last Names

One choice is that you could hyphenate both of your last names. Many parents resist this choice because they don't think that their names sound nice together or that the name would be too long. Get over it! It might not sound wonderful, but who would pick their own last name if given a choice? Some parents hyphenate their children's names and not their own, and other parents choose to hyphenate their last names as well so that all family members share a common last name.

Creating a Last Name

If it truly is too long then you can move to the next choice of creating a name. This name can be a word of significance or it can be a shortened combination of both of your last names. One family I know had the last names of Brinner and Cook. They did not want to hyphenate so they combined their last names into the name Brook. People resist this choice because no one else, except possible future siblings, would share this last name. They also resist this choice because it seems too alternative. Either change all of your last names to the one of choice, or choose to celebrate the beginning of a new tribe.

The Nonlegal Parent's Last Name

The third choice would be to give the child the nonlegal parent's last name. The resistance to this choice is usually that it will leave out the biological/legal parent. This is not true; the biological/legal connection of parent and child is the most time honored in our culture and is in no way dependent on sharing a last name. On the other hand, by giving the child the nonbiological parent's last name, you are very clearly sharing the message that you are all a family. This message is strong to both the child and the courts.

In families where LGBT men and women are parenting together, the subject of last names can be even more confusing. If the child has a home that is primary with a single or partnered parent(s) in it, then the discussion is usually the same as above. If there is no primary household or primary parent then three choices seem to be most common. The first is to create a new last name. The second is to give the child the last name of the parent who is least likely to maintain custody in a court case. The third is to give the child the last name of the parent(s) who is biologically related to the child.

I was a single mom when my daughter was born. I chose a last name for her that had meaning for me, but was not my last name. When I partnered and my partner gave birth, we gave the new baby the same last name as her older sister. Having them be able to share a last name solidifies their connection to one another. We do not have plans to change our last names to match theirs, but if we have more children in our family in the future, those children, too, will share a last name with their siblings. The only hassle is that there are three last names in the family, but that is the case for most of us—and really, it is not that big a deal.

As the subject of names seems to push many people's emotional buttons, choosing a name as far ahead of time as possible is a wise choice.

Presenting Your Family to the Public

Once you have selected a name for yourself, or the child is old enough to have found one for you, as gay parents you have the second responsibility of finding language to neatly describe your family and your relationship to the child.

Once you establish who is in your family, you realize that each of you needs a name and a defined relationship. Take the example of Jose. Jose is the single gay dad of Alejandro. Alejandro was adopted through social services. He knows and has lived with his biological mother, though she does not see or raise him now. But to Alejandro, he has a father, Jose, and a mother in his family. He also has a very special surrogate mother.

When Jose was in a single parents' support group he met Sherry. Sherry is a straight single mother of a daughter named Claire. As Sherry and Jose got to know each other they became very close and decided, over time, to coparent both of their children.

The question arose of how to refer to each other. They finally decided that the children would be half siblings. Although that word does not technically describe their connection to each other because they are not biologically related, it is a relationship that others could understand, as it is a term that had meaning. Alejandro calls Sherry "Aunt Sherry" and Claire calls Jose "Uncle Jose."

It became quite clear that they needed a way to reference each other to family, friends, day care, etc. Jose would say, "This is Sherry. Sherry helps me raise Alejandro and I help to raise her daughter, Claire. Alejandro calls Sherry 'Aunt Sherry.' I consider Claire my stepdaughter, and the children see each other as half siblings. Claire and I are not dating. We don't plan to. I am gay."

Although this is a mouthful, Jose and Sherry both learned that it saved a lot of time and prevented a lot of assumptions to set it all out for people. Learn to be comfortable identifying yourself, your role in your child's life, and your referred title. This will ensure that people do not make their own inaccurate assumptions about your family. It is also important that you become comfortable describing the roles of the other people in your family. For example, will you be able to adequately explain the role of your coparent, donor, or ex-partner in your child's life without practice?

Exercise

It is very valuable to practice saying out loud responses to typical questions that you are asked about your family, and to practice introducing yourself and your family. By doing it out loud, you can not only rehearse the words that will be most empowering, but you can also be comfortable saying them. Another benefit is that you will be able to monitor what your body language is communicating. It has been said that people respond more to what your body language is communicating than to the words you are actually saying.

For example, practice the responses to the following:

- "Now tell me, who's the real dad?"

- "But won't she get confused having two moms?"

- "How can a lesbian raise a boy?"

- "Who's eyes does he have?"

- "Where did you get this child, I mean you're gay so how did this happen?"

Remember that it is important to set appropriate boundaries as well. Practice ways of telling people that it is rude to ask such a personal question. By asking yourself these questions ahead of time they will seem less invasive and you are less likely to be taken aback or to become angry when the questions are posed.

This exercise is also helpful to do with your partner, if you have one. This way you can both make sure that you are comfortable with the answers you are giving and that if asked a question at the same time you will give similar answers. This is important. While at a restaurant with their three-month-old Nathalia, her moms, Dedra and Sarah, were asked "Who's baby is this?" by their server. They both answered at the same time. Dedra, who had given birth, said "My baby" at the same time that Sarah said, "She's both of ours." Not only did this confuse the server, but it led to a large argument about how anyone was going to validate them parenting together when they do not present as a family.

When children are not biologically related to each other it is necessary to find language that works to describe their relationship to one another. When two existing parents get together and form family, the children often use the term "step" sibling to describe the children's relationship. Some people just use the term sibling, i.e., brother or sister, to describe the relationship two children in the same family have to one another, whether or not there is any biological connection. Commonly it is extended family who want to recognize biology as the only valid relationship. I strongly encourage you to educate your family on this matter so that they treat all of your children equally. This can be done by statements such as, "Our children are raised as sisters. They do not question their sibling relationship. When you only reference Jackie as your grandchild, they become confused. Whether or not you like my choices, I would like you to use language that is supportive of the children." Or, you can say, "Please refer to both of my children as your grandchildren. When you introduce Jackie as your 'granddaughter' and Amanda as 'Jon's partner Jack's daughter,' you undermine the unity of our family. These differences in language are important to me." It is for the sake of your children that you must assert this maxim.

There are collective queer households that raise numerous children, but the adults do not necessarily consider themselves to be in the same "family." The young ones, nonetheless, have a siblingesque relationship. One family I know coined the term "queerbling" to define such relations—queerblings being children who are related to one another in some queer fashion or another.

Who Is in My Child's Family?

Now that you know how *you* define family and what *you* would like to call each family member, how would you feel if your child defined their family differently? "Who's family am I defining?" is a relevant question to ask yourself. Your child might have a different definition of who is in their family than you do for yours. For example, you may not consider your partner's ex-wife (the biological mother of the child) to be in your family, yet she is your child's mother and a key person in their life. Or you may not consider the next door neighbor who watches your child, or your child's best friend, to be a *family* member, but your child might.

If you extend the realm of family to include people who are not biologically connected, be careful not to then resort to biology as it suits your fancy. Your child may claim chosen family members as well. This is especially true in families where there is a donor or a surrogate. Many parents do not consider their donor or surrogate to be a part of their family. However, many children do, especially if they know that person. That is not to say that the child would consider their donor or surrogate to be their dad or mom, but simply a member of their family.

My daughter, when she was three, decided that a dad was some-one who fed her and would lie down with her until she fell asleep. Thus, although I considered her to have a biological father, but no dad, she felt she had two dads—our housemate and my father (that was awk-ward!). We had two very different definitions of our family for a number of years. This was our experience of family until our family structure changed and grew and we each changed our definitions. Currently we hold more closely aligned views of who is in our family—but they're not identical. We each have various family members who are not in the other's family.

Family can be evolving. Variance in definition from family mem-ber to family member is natural in queer families because so many of our family members are members by choice. It is important to encour-age a strong sense of family for your child, while at the same time allow-ing for a certain amount of fluidity. If you teach your child that love and commitment are all that it takes to make a family, then you must antici-pate that your child will hold you to your word. Thus your understand-ing of who is in your family and your child's understanding of who is in their family may differ.

Family of Origin

Although we have been emphasizing the role that chosen family mem-bers have in our lives, it is equally important to examine the roles that our biological family members have in our lives. This next section will explore some of the variety of experiences that GLBTs have with their families and some creative suggestions for handling your own situation.

Telling Parents about Your Decision to Parent

It is an interesting turn of the circle that draws each of us toward our own parents when we ourselves become parents. Most people feel a poignant need for their parents to accept their choice to parent, whether or not their parents have accepted their sexual orientation. Even if your parents are deceased or are not in contact with you, for whatever reason, the poignant need for them when you become a parent usually remains. It is because the need for our parents at this time is so great that it can be so difficult to tell them of our plans. We want our parents (and, for many, it feels like a primal need) to love and accept our choice to parent and to give their approval and support of us at this transformative time of life. Many GLBTs are afraid that they could not bear the rejection from their parents.

As a result, many GLBTs put off telling their parents for as long as possible. It is not unusual for women to wait until pregnancy has progressed or even until the baby is born to tell their parents. For adoptive parents, it is not unusual to delay informing your parents until the adoption has gone through. The internal logic often is, "If they see that there is no changing my mind, then they will have to accept my decision." From my experience, this approach backfires more often than not.

The Sooner the Better

The earlier you tell your family of your plans to parent, the more time they have to adjust to the idea before the baby or child is actually here. Many families need this adjustment period. Often, the news that you are going to become a parent produces many mixed feelings. If your parents are still having a difficult time accepting your sexual orientation or your choice of partner, the added notion of children can be a lot to integrate. The difficulty for many grandparents-to-be is that your having children often necessitates *them* coming out. Coming out is hard, and when you are not the one who is gay, it can seem even more difficult.

It is out of respect for your parents that I truly feel you should tell them as early as possible. If you delay telling your parents, many will feel hurt, snubbed, and left out. When you delay, they then feel like you don't trust them. They have to integrate that painful feeling with the additional feelings that they might have about your decision to parent. It can be difficult.

Providing your parents with books on queer parenting and giving them local Parents, Friends, and Families of Lesbian and Gays (PFLAG) contacts and Internet resources will help them to not feel so alone. Try to accept that it may take your parents some time to come around. For many parents it is harder information to integrate than your initial coming out.

Acceptance and Timing

Parents react in many ways to the idea that their gay child is going to become a parent. Some people have the fortunate and appropriate response from their families of being excited about the news of your desire to parent. I have helped many women to get pregnant who say that their mothers have been pushing them to get pregnant for years—as soon as they heard it was possible for lesbians to have children. The younger the women, the more accepting their parents tend to be. It is truly a treasure to meet queer parents who say that their parents have always been supportive of their sexual orientation, their partners, and their choice to parent. This should be the norm. Our parents should be proud of us and the love we share and bring forth. Unfortunately this is not the case for everyone. Yet, as our visibility increases it will more frequently be the response.

For some parents, it becomes easier to accept *you* as a parent because you are participating in a part of life that they can understand. Although it is nice to finally have the support of your parents, it can often feel bittersweet if it is only through becoming a parent that you're accepted as a person.

Take Maria, for instance. She had come out to her family when she was sixteen. Her family threw her out of the house in response to the news. When she turned twenty her father died and her mother started to write her letters. They continued to share news with each other through letters and eventually weekly phone calls. When she was thirty, Maria married Carmelita. Her mother was invited, but did not attend Maria's wedding, although she did send a gift.

However, when Maria told her mother when she was thirty-two that she was pregnant, her mother—whom she had not seen in seventeen years—flew into town the next weekend. Her mother visited four more times during the pregnancy and came out for the birth. Maria, Carmelita, and their baby, Machi, recently visited Maria's mother's house. It was Maria's first visit back in nineteen years. Maria says she feels very happy to have her family back and to have her partner and son recognized as family, but she can't understand why her mother could not accept her before she became a mother. The pain of the acceptance has felt overwhelming at times. She finds herself full of rage toward her mother while simultaneously feeling grateful to have her back again. She says she would much rather have her mother in her life than not, but it is definitely a mixed blessing.

Stating Your Intentions Clearly

How you tell your parents is up to you. It is important, however, that you are clear about what you hope their reaction and their roles will be. If you do not tell them, it is much harder for them to do what you hope they will do. Their failure to rise to the occasion in the ways that you hoped is often not from malice, but, rather, from ignorance. Simply informing them that you are becoming a parent is not enough; you must clearly state what you want.

Don's parents said they had accepted the fact that he was gay, but did not want to meet Don's partner, Zach. This was due partly to homophobia and partly to racism. Don is Caucasian and Zach is African-American. Don decided that writing to his parents would be the easiest way to break the news about adopting a baby. His family was one that did not speak openly of personal matters, and he thought that having a conversation would be very uncomfortable for his parents. He wrote the following letter:

> Dear Mom and Dad,
> Zach and I are adopting a baby together. We are so thrilled to finally be able to become parents! We are hoping that you will also be thrilled to become grandparents. Zach's parents are not alive, so you will be the only grandparents our child has. I know that you have never welcomed us into your home, and you know that I am still hurt by that rejection. But I am hoping that you will come to visit us and your new grandchild when our adoption comes through. Our child will be African-American. If you feel that you will be able to accept that our child has two fathers and that both our child and one of his fathers is black, then we will be thrilled to have you as grandparents. If you are still unable to accept Zach, then painfully there will be no place for you in our lives. We hope the adoption will go through in about six months. We are eagerly awaiting your reply.
> Much love,
> Don

Don and Zach waited for about two weeks to hear from Don's parents. One day, Zach answered the phone and Don's dad said, "Zach, let us know when the baby is born, we'll catch the next plane." Don and Zach were stunned. It turns out that in the two weeks time after they received the letter, Don's parents had met repeatedly with their minister and had come to realize that love and acceptance were more important than anything else. Although the first few visits were a little tense, the grandparents have really warmed up to being in the presence of Don and Zach together—with a little help from baby Sasha.

Birth Announcements

Sometimes your parents will want to tell your extended family members and friends about your new baby or child. Frequently, however, one of the most daunting things for grandparents is to feel obliged to tell everyone when they are still trying to figure out what to say. Many LGBTs did not find it necessary to come out to their extended family and friends of the family until they had children. Often, that leaves a lot of people to come out to!

Many families handle the dispersing of this information through birth announcements. You can easily come out to a large number of people through sending birth announcements. Birth announcements are especially effective if they include a photo of the whole family. That way, there can be no misinterpreting of names to make it seem like you had the baby within a heterosexual relationship. Of course, if you are a single parent this does not help you to come out, but it does assert the fact that you are a single parent and are proud of it.

Helping Family Members Process the News

Communication and understanding is often all that it takes for ambivalent family members to come to a place of acceptance. If you can, allow for dialogue and questions from your family members. Some of us have the skill and patience to help our parents and other family members through their journey to acceptance of us. Others of us are not up to that task. It is a personal choice; no one is obligated to help their family members through their homophobia.

If you do decide to help your parents or other family members process their reactions to your choice to parent, be sure to set and to maintain a healthy set of boundaries. It is OK for them to have their questions and concerns and to express them in a respectful manner. It is not OK for them to be mean, cruel, or disparaging toward you, your partner, or your child. In the event that they cross that line, you must, out of self-respect (and gay Pride), assert the boundary and remind them that you expect to be treated with kindness and respect. If that is not possible, then tell them you must disengage from the conversation until they have reached a place where they can again be respectful.

The most common concerns of well-meaning family members are that you are being selfish, you are ruining your child's life, your child will be gay (and that would be a tragedy), you are shaming the family, and, even, that you are ruining your parents' lives and all that they have lived for. If you are not up for processing with your family members, perhaps you have a sibling who would be willing to help the others through their homophobia. In any event, try to supply them with books and other resources to hopefully hasten the process (see References and Resources sections for recommendations).

If Your Parents Reject You

Some parents simply will not accept that their gay children have the right to become parents. Or they will not accept that your partner's child is your child too. This form of rejection is deeply painful and can feel unbearable. Some grandparents come around when they see their grandchildren, but some do not. Grieving at a time when you are experiencing great joy is very difficult. Avoiding this is another reason why it makes sense to tell your parents before the baby or child arrives. If they are going to disown you and your child, then you have a chance to grieve before your child is here. It does not reduce the pain that you will feel, but it allows the initial blow to not compete with your initial bonding with your baby or child. It also allows your parents more time to come around, should time be all that they need.

If your parents do reject you, it is easy for your self-esteem and your confidence to plummet. This is a good time to enter into therapy, join a support group, or to intentionally partake in other forms of self-nurturance. Do not let the lack of support from your family weaken your commitment to parent. If your parents threaten to take custody of your child then the situation can become much more serious. For advice on this subject, please turn to chapter 11, "Protecting Your Family."

If Your Family Doesn't Accept Your Partner

Jo and Sandy are a good example of how having children can change what is and is not acceptable, both for you and your family of origin. Sandy had always been very close to her family of origin. They have never accepted or approved of her lesbianism, but they all love each other dearly and talk at least once a week. When Sandy partnered, her dad's side of the family and all of her siblings were courteous to Jo. Sandy and Jo attended all family functions together.

Disturbing as it was to Sandy, she would acquiesce to her mother's born-again Christian homophobia and not bring Jo with her on her visits to her mother. This was her only concession to her family's homophobia. However, when Sandy got pregnant everything changed. Sandy's closest sister decided that Sandy could no longer have any contact with her children, Sandy's nieces. She said that her "abomination would corrupt them." Then Sandy's dad berated Sandy for having a child "out of wedlock." When Sandy said that she was planning to marry Jo that very spring, he said that Jo was no longer welcome in his home.

Sandy's family was shattering. She tried to visit her dad without Jo, but it did not feel right. Her mother had told all of her friends that Sandy was going to be a single mother. Sandy felt totally betrayed. All of her life her family had been most important, and now that she was having a child they were deserting her.

Sandy tried repeatedly to talk to her family members and to get them to support her in her pregnancy and in her choice to marry Jo. She was not heard. The pain of this was consuming their pregnancy and creating undue stress on their relationship. Finally, in couples counseling, they decided upon a solution. Sandy and Jo sent out a letter to all relevant family and friends describing their love for each other and their excitement about the arrival of their new baby. They also made it clear that until their family unit was accepted and respected, they would have to withdraw from the circle of people who meant so much to them, their family. They said family had always meant love and respect and they were hurt and disappointed by the response of their family regarding the great joy in their lives. No one returned their letter. That last communication was three years ago.

Sandy spent many months in counseling grieving the complete loss of her family. She said it felt like everyone important to her other than Jo was killed in a car accident. The only difference was, really, they just no longer loved her. It tore her up, but she was not willing to settle for partial acceptance. They needed to honor her family; it was not negotiable.

There are times when you decide that it is worth putting up with a certain amount of homophobia in order to stay connected to your family of origin. However, you do not need to give in to their homophobia altogether. For example, Kaplan and Charles were raising their baby, Palmer, together. Kaplan's family was fully aware that they were gay and were parenting Palmer together. Kaplan's family was planning a large family reunion in honor of his grandmother's one hundredth birthday. His grandmother was coming all the way from Wales. All of the family was coming to celebrate this big event. Kaplan and Charles were very excited that everyone, especially his grandmother, would get to meet Palmer.

Two weeks before the reunion celebration, Kaplan's parents said that Charles was not invited to the event, only family was invited. They were afraid that coming out to the grandmother on her one hundredth birthday just might kill her then and there. This led to long, heated phone arguments. Kaplan's parents would not budge. Kaplan did not know what to do; he could not imagine going without Charles, and he knew this was a once in a lifetime chance to see his whole family together.

Charles and Kaplan came up with a compromise that they could live with. Charles, Kaplan, and Palmer flew to the reunion. They got a hotel room together. Although Kaplan did go to the celebration dinner alone with Palmer, he attended all of the informal gatherings where his grandmother was not present as a family with Charles. He ate many meals and went to a ball game with other groups of family members. Although his parents were not pleased with this, Kaplan felt like he respected the family's wish to not come out to the grandmother while still honoring their own family sanctity. It was a compromise that worked! If they had not done so, they never would have discovered that there were two lesbians and one bisexual male cousin in the family. No one had ever come out to one another until Kaplan started the ball rolling.

If Your Family Does Not See Your Partner's Child as Your Own

It can be difficult for your parents to recognize as their grandchild the child that your partner gave birth to or that you adopted. It is very painful when your family does not recognize you and your child. The claim is that because you do not have a biological connection or a legal connection through marriage or adoption, then the child is not yours. Most grandparents would never react that way if you were heterosexual and were adopting a child. They feel that they can use the cultural supremacy of the biological connection and the legal system to defend their homophobia.

Many grandparents come around when they come to visit and they see that you are indeed a parent. Witnessing your day-to-day life with your child is irrefutable proof of your parent/child connection. However, some parents refuse to even meet the child.

For example, MayBeth partnered with Joanne. MayBeth had been out to her family for many, many years. Her family would not let any unmarried couples sleep in their house. So whenever MayBeth and Joanne went to visit they would stay in a hotel, as would her siblings who had relationships with people to whom they were not married. Other than that, her parents accepted her homosexuality as long as no one ever mentioned it directly. MayBeth had been bringing Joanne home for the holidays for years and everyone in the family warmly welcomed her.

When Joanne gave birth, MayBeth was shocked to hear that her parents did not consider Jonah to be their grandchild, and they had no interest in meeting him. This came as such a surprise because they had heartily congratulated Joanne at the news of her pregnancy. In all of their phone calls during Joanne's pregnancy, they would ask about her and seemed very interested. MayBeth and Joanne had been so pleased by their response. It made the rejection that much harder.

MayBeth was heartbroken and felt totally invalidated by her parents' lack of recognition of her child. It made her status as nonbirth mom seem second-class. To her complete surprise, however, when MayBeth completed the second-parent adoption and was able to become a legal parent to Jonah, her parents threw a party for her. They were suddenly very excited to be grandparents. They met Jonah when he was eighteen months old, which was how long the adoption process had taken. In their Christmas card to the family, MayBeth's parents mentioned that MayBeth had adopted Joanne's eighteen-month-old son, Jonah.

MayBeth was once again hurt and told her parents that she had not adopted Joanne's son, but that they had planned, conceived, and birthed Jonah together. MayBeth and Joanne were both Jonah's parents. Her parents would not give on their perspective. MayBeth and Joanne decided to compromise and accept the fact that this was going to be the approach of MayBeth's parents and that there was nothing they could do to change it. It was more important to them that Jonah know his grandparents.

When Jonah was seven years old, MayBeth's mother made a comment to Jonah that threatened to start a large family fight. They said to Jonah, "Isn't it so nice that MayBeth adopted you so that Joanne would not be a single mom?" Jonah was silent for a moment and responded, "Isn't it nice that Grandpa adopted MayBeth so that you didn't have to be a single mom?" MayBeth's mom said, "Grandpa didn't adopt MayBeth, he's her father" and Jonah responded, "Well I guess I am lucky! MayBeth is my mom and my dad. She put the sperm in my other mom just like grandpa put the sperm in you. Having two moms is the best! MayBeth didn't need to adopt me, she was already my mom. But since they couldn't get married she decided to adopt me instead. I am sorry you didn't get to have two moms, Grandma. Maybe you wouldn't be so confused if you did!" After that interaction, MayBeth and Joanne realized that Jonah was doing just fine standing up for himself.

Choosing Not to Come Out to Your Parents

Most GLBTs who become parents have been out to their families for a long time before they have children. However, there are many GLBTs who have never had the courage to come out to their families. There are a multitude of benefits to living an out life, but when and to whom you come out is always a personal choice.

Some GLBTs choose to tell their parents that they are having or adopting a child, but omit the fact that they are gay or that they have a partner who will also be raising their child, if that is the case. They do not come out about their sexual orientation because they feel stuck between a rock and a hard place: either they come out and, in so doing, they lose their family, or they don't come out and are able to keep their family of origin in their life and in their children's life while living a lie.

It is an incredibly difficult decision to make. Of course, some people choose not to come out because they are afraid of a total rejection that might not actually happen. However, it is paramount that you consider the longterm when you decide not to come out to your parents, yet you *do* decide to tell them that you are a parent.

Ooops—They Weren't Suppose to Find Out That Way

If you are out everywhere in your life but to your parents, they will find out at some point in time. Take Maggie and Nancy. Maggie and Nancy decided to adopt a child from China together. They live in Arizona. Nancy was not out to her parents. Her parents thought that Maggie was her best friend and roommate. Nancy's parents live in New Hampshire. Nancy's mother went with Nancy to China to pick up their new daughter and helped to deliver her safely home to Arizona.

Over the months, Nancy's mother would espouse how fortunate Nancy was to be living with Maggie. It was almost as if she wasn't really a single mom after all. Nancy would take their daughter to visit her parents and Maggie would come along "to help out." Maggie would stay in Nancy's parents' guest room. Although it felt terrible for them to be living such an elaborate lie, Nancy was convinced she would be disowned and felt she could not bear that.

When their daughter was ten months old, they ran into Serene, a childhood friend of Nancy's, in the grocery store in Tucson. Her friend turned out to be a lesbian as well and came over for dinner that night. Nancy and Maggie did not even think to tell Serene that they were closeted to Nancy's family. Well, Serene called her mom and said, "Why didn't you tell me Nancy is a lesbian raising her child with her partner? I thought you said she was a single mom?" Well, one thing quickly led to another and Nancy was confronted directly by her parents.

This was not how Nancy had planned to come out to her parents, but she would not lie when pointedly asked if she was a lesbian. Although her parents eventually came around to accepting Nancy and Maggie into their lives in order to have a relationship with their granddaughter, it was not easy. Nancy's parents did not know whether it was harder to have a lesbian daughter, or harder to have a daughter who lies so blatantly to her parents, or to have been so embarrassed as to have found out from a member of the book club that Nancy was a lesbian and that Maggie was not her roommate after all.

The Impact the Closet Has on Your Own Family

When deciding to not come out to your parents, you may also want to consider the impact this decision has on *your own* family. If you are partnered, it can cause tremendous stress on your relationship. This is especially true if there are family visits that involve leaving your partner at home or claiming that they are your roommate. But almost more importantly is to consider the impact your decision will have on your child as your child gets older.

By remaining closeted, you are asking your child to lie for you. That is very serious. If you are partnered and you ask your child to pretend that they are being raised by a single parent, you are asking your child to negate their own parent. You are requesting that your child shroud their family in shame and secrecy. You are saying that your parents are more important than their parents, that your need to lie is more important than your child's need to tell the truth, and that living in your family is something that needs to be hidden. If you are single and you ask your child to keep you closeted, you are saying that it is not OK to be gay. All of these messages are damaging to self-esteem and to a healthy sense of Pride in your child—not to mention yourself.

You must ask yourself, is it worth it?

Celebrating Our Families

Because queer families are a special blend of love and biology, our children have a wonderful opportunity to develop fresh ideas of families right from the start. This requires a specific intention and teaching by example. By not conforming to the assumed heterosexual, biologically dominant, culturally accepted model of family, we are encouraging our children to think broadly.

Although they are growing up in so-called alternative households, our children themselves, by definition, are not alternative. If we are able to instill healthy values, however, that embrace love and commitment to one another as the defining features of family, then we will raise a generation that rejects the existing confining models of nuclear family.

There are many situations you can utilize to help widen your child's definition of family. For instance, if you see a billboard of two men playing basketball with children, you can easily say, "Look at those gay dads playing with their kids." Or when you're reading storybooks to young children you can change the titles of the family characters to include coparent, donors, adopted children, gay families, and transgendered people. The families you enhance don't always need to look like your family; the purpose is to continually broaden the models presented to children so that they view a wide variety of family structures as "normal."

As our children age we can question their choice of family representation in their creative writing, and we can point out the heterosexism in literature. My daughter came home just the other day with a coloring book. We were looking at it together and I told her how nice the book was. She was very excited about her new acquisition. Then I said, "I notice it is a very heterosexist book." She responded, "Yeah, I just saw that as we flipped through all of the pictures. But that's OK, some people are heterosexual. And anyway, just because someone is supposed to be a girl or a boy doesn't mean that I will color them as a girl or a boy. You can't always tell just from looks, you know."

2

The Foundation of Healthy Parenting

Bringing a baby into your life is one of the most powerful, life-changing experiences that will ever happen to you. Babyhood is the time for laying the groundwork for the rest of your parenthood. It is a time filled with an unaccustomed blend of extreme joy, awe, love, amazement, intensity, and physical and, often, emotional exhaustion.

There truly is nothing comparable to the first year of life with a new baby. In many ways it does not matter if it is your first baby or your fourth, everything in life must change to make room for a whole new person. When it is your first baby, however, your entire orientation to life undergoes a complete overhaul. For the first time ever, someone becomes more important than you.

Becoming a Parent

The transition to becoming a parent is not always easy or smooth. It is nothing short of all consuming. Basic transformations happen to every new parent. Without awareness, it is easy to try to resist this natural process by attempting to stay in control—striving to maintain your life the way it was. The whole first year of parenthood is a transition. Your baby will grow amazingly during this year and so will you. How you grow will differ according to your role in the baby's life. However, it is safe to say that who you know yourself to be at the beginning of the first year will not be the same person who finishes the year—you will have become a parent.

The first year of life is like parental pregnancy—providing time for you to metamorphose into a parent. During the first year you are growing yourself. When you have parented for a year, you are fully gestated. The art of parenting begins at this point, and you now work to refine and improve yourself as a parent. It is imperative to acknowledge this period of parenting gestation in the same way that it is important to focus on a pregnancy. Babies are born much stronger and healthier when pregnant women focus on nutrition, receive prenatal care and sufficient sleep, and reduce their exposure to toxic environments. The same is true for you. The strength of your parenting can be directly influenced by the amount of nourishment and attention you provide yourself during this crucial first-year period.

Because babyhood is a time of such rapid growth and change, it is essential, if you are partnered, to make sure that you not only grow as individuals, but that your relationship grows as well. Statistics show that up to 50 percent of heterosexual couples break up in the first two years of parenthood (Ahrons 1994). It is safe to assume that queer couples have at least as high a statistic and probably higher. Our relationships are rarely honored or socially recognized, and our parenting rights are not guaranteed. There are no institutions set up to support our families in making it through the transition to parenthood. These factors can exponentially increase the stress factor during this time of life. To avoid becoming a statistic, it is valuable to give thought to how you are going to nourish your relationship through the changes that come with parenthood.

Nourishing a primary partner relationship while parenting can require both focus and attention. Making your relationship a priority is essential. Prioritize time alone, couples counseling, going on dates (without the children), having fun, and making love. Sharing a joint commitment to clear communication and to keeping the spark alive will help to carry you through the transformations of parenthood.

Identifying and Developing Your Parenting Style

Much of the challenge of this first year is learning to *identify* and *develop* your parenting style. To identify your parenting style, it is helpful to identify the style of parenting in which you were raised. If you are partnered, it is valuable to explore this both individually and together. If your child will have additional coparents, this is a good topic for a family meeting during which all important family members have the opportunity to discuss and share their personal parenting experiences.

How you were parented directly affects your subconscious. Your inner messages are influenced by how you yourself were raised. You are most familiar with these parenting styles, and you will naturally resort back to them in times of stress. Parenting as you were parented, or speaking to your children the same way in which your parents spoke to you, despite any intentions to the contrary, is much more likely to occur if you have not examined your upbringing.

To be a conscious parent, it is important that you identify how rules and expectations were communicated to you while you were growing up. Then you can intentionally choose how you would like rules and expectations communicated within your current family and what parenting style you would like to maintain with your own children.

Exercise

Find a quiet place to answer the following questions. Write the answers in your journal, or take the time to answer them out loud with someone who will simply listen. Use these questions as a starting place. Allow yourself to explore further questions that naturally arise.

When you were a child:

- How were you spoken to?

- Where did you sleep?

- How was conflict handled?

- What kind of discipline was implemented?

- Did your parents enjoy being parents?

- Did your parents spend much one-on-one or family time with you?

- How were rules and expectations communicated?

- How did family members speak to one other?

- What things were not said?

- What was missing from the environment?

- How did your parents handle stress?

When you have answered these questions for yourself, examine the information. Notice what the themes are. If you are parenting with others, share what you have learned. Encourage your coparents to do the same. Usually the information is quite insightful and will help you to understand one another more deeply and to become more equipped to parent together. This information can indicate how *you* will parent in times of stress. With this insight into your upbringing it becomes easier to differentiate between how you were raised and how you would like to parent.

Next, look at your answers to the questions above and see which qualities and approaches you would like to repeat and which you would like to replace with another approach.

For example:

As a child, I knew when I did something wrong because my mother emotionally withdrew from me. I would know I had done something that did not live up to her expectations when she spoke to me in a cold and courteous tone.

This is something I do not wish to repeat in my parenting. I realize from this exercise, however, that this may be a challenge because I currently repeat this very same behavior with my partner. As a parent I want to clearly and directly communicate my expectations to my child. When she does not live up to them I hope to be able to lovingly remind her of my expectations.

Or:

My grandparents raised us. They were always so patient with us. They would spend endless hours teaching us new skills. They never seemed to be in a hurry.

I hope to emulate them in this particular aspect. I am finding it hard to have patience with my baby. When I feel like I am at my limit I actually pretend I am my grandmother and I find a calmness inside of me I can't find on my own. This is a quality of my grandparents that I definitely want to repeat.

Or:

Family Upbringing	Desired Parenting Style
harsh words	gentle and supportive
spanking	time-out?
slept in my own bed	same
everyone fended for themselves	feeling of family

The information that you gather from this exercise often points to areas of parenting you had not thought about yet. It's also a helpful way of noticing any glaring differences in the approaches to parenting that may exist between coparents. These differences should be addressed early on.

It can be quite helpful to refer to this list whenever you feel you're not parenting in your highest fashion. Examining your past is one way to start clarifying the kind of parent you hope to become. More on this will be covered in chapter 3, "Conscious Parenting."

Universal Challenges

Being aware of universal parenting challenges can help you to grow more smoothly during this often-rocky time. Even if you're accustomed to personal growth, there is nothing like a child to speed up the process. If growth and change do not come naturally to you, then it is all the more important to notice what the most common themes are so that you can learn to identify your resistance as it arises.

Trying to Maintain the Status Quo

Keep an eye on your tendency to want to continue life as normal. Life is irrevocably different. This can be scary because you are uncovering your new life day by day and adults are "supposed" to have themselves together. Nonetheless, keep in check the desire to mold your baby to your life. Allow your life to change. Becoming a parent involves making room for your child. This is what creates family and your new life as a family.

Parents often strive hard to not let themselves be consumed by their baby; the American way is grounded in a (sometimes false) sense of independence. Trying to maintain a fierce sense of independence is not conducive to early parenthood. Nonetheless, new parents commonly try to fit a baby into their full and complete lives, instead of allowing the baby to reveal to you, its parent, its particular set of needs and its natural rhythm. This approach to parenting can lead to depressed parents and to a rushed and jangled baby.

If you take the time to learn from your baby its nature and individual rhythm, and try to honor that as much as possible, you will have a happier baby, and thus you will be a happier parent. It takes courage and patience to surrender to an *ever-changing* daily routine, and, with a baby who is growing and changing, the routine *is* ever-changing. Courage, patience, and faith are a few of the most valuable qualities a parent can develop.

The Power of Love

The love that you feel for your baby is life changing. It is so huge that it can be overwhelming. It might be hard to imagine love being stressful—until you have experienced it. Having so much love flowing toward you and from you to the cutest little being that ever lived is like nothing you have experienced. It will rock your world and cause you to question everything in it. In a way, the life changing elements of baby love are very similar to first coming out—wonderful, terrifying, beautiful, and tumultuous.

In the face of this love, some people become very afraid of losing their child and become irrationally afraid of the world; others become terribly afraid of losing themselves and try hard to not bond with their baby. Others wonder if their parents loved them this much and they find a new respect for their own parents. Some people deeply feel the lack of love they received as a child. These feelings all can help you to become a better parent. The balm of love can be very healing. But it's not always easy medicine!

Identity Crisis

Many people try to avert the identity crisis that comes with parenting by staying very busy. This is simply an avoidance tactic—the identity crisis of new parenthood is inevitable. Just let it happen and watch who you become.

You'll probably feel like you don't know who you are anymore. You may even question your right and your competency to be this perfect creature's parent. You will ask yourself endlessly, "How will I ever fulfill this all important job?" All of these questions and emotions can stimulate feelings, deep-seated perhaps, of personal inadequacy.

The key is to allow yourself to recreate. If the feelings are too strong, or you feel lost, stuck, or scared, it's probably a good time to seek counseling or to join a facilitated new parents' group. The intensity of this time passes, but for some it can be more consuming than for others.

Adoption: After Your Baby Comes Home

Whether your adopted baby is a day old or ten months old it is important to regard their homecoming as the beginning of your postpartum period. This will help make the transition to parenthood and family more smooth for all of you. Because you didn't have the opportunity to bond with your baby for nine months before birth, it's crucial that you take ample time in the beginning of your life as a parent to establish that bond.

Things will differ according to your particular child and to the age of your baby, but resist the tendency to try to fit this ready-made being into your life. Take the time to bond that you would if you were the one having to recover from giving birth. Can you arrange to take the automatic four to six weeks that new birth mothers are given?

Immediate Postpartum

Perhaps the time of greatest adjustment is the postpartum period. Postpartum simply means after birth. Although it is not a defined period of time, it is *at least* six weeks.

The arrival of the new baby is never quite how it's imagined ahead of time. Usually we hold blissful images without much thought to how our days actually will be spent. Postpartum is often very time intensive. For most, sleep deprivation begins in the first week. Waking up to feed and rock your baby, and to change diapers, are all part of the daytime and nighttime routines. You are now on a twenty-four-hour clock. Babies don't often note the difference between the middle of the day and the late hours of the night.

New Dads

There is no difference between a man's and a woman's ability to nurture and care for a baby. There is, however, a significant difference in the way that men and women are socialized around babies. This can leave men feeling less prepared for parenting. Some gay men believe they are not supposed to express any feelings of inadequacy because it would indicate to others that they should not be a parent. This fear is supported by the culture's supposition that every child needs a mother. A more accurate statement is that every child needs to be loved. When you are a fumbling new parent, it can be challenging to resist gender normatives and to claim your right as a man to parent. This feeling eases as you become more comfortable and you become internally certain that your child is not fundamentally lacking simply because you are not a woman.

The Biological Mother

During postpartum, there is a dramatic difference in roles if one of the parents gave birth. Because the birth mother is physically recovering and healing from the labor and birth process, she requires a lot of personal attendance. She is also hormonally affected during this time. These hormones are a mixed blessing: although they can cause an emotional roller-coaster ride, they are also responsible for producing your lovely new baby and for making the milk perfectly designed to feed them.

It is important to make a distinction between the shared parenting you had envisioned and that will eventually occur, and the actual reality of the initial postpartum period. In the beginning, if the birth mom is parenting the baby, the baby will naturally feel closest to her. This, of course, is intensified if they are sharing a breast-feeding relationship. A number of studies have also shown that breast-fed babies are more psychically connected to their birth mothers through this breast-feeding relationship (Chamberlain 1998).

Remain Flexible

It is quite common during pregnancy that women plan with their coparents the practical elements of their life; yet, when the actual experience arises, they discover their choices were based in theory and in actuality do not feel appropriate. It's important to be flexible in the first weeks and months of parenthood. You cannot predict the nature and the needs of the baby ahead of time nor can birth mothers anticipate the depth of their attachment and connection to the baby prior to birth. This is a bond that must be honored. Painful as it is for the other mom or coparents to handle, in the beginning, the birth mother's relationship truly is primary.

Honor the Biological Connection

If you are in a family where the birth mom is a parent, it's a good idea to allow particular space for her feelings. This is not to ignore the needs and desires of all the other parents, but to recognize that her needs are frequently of a different nature in the first few months. Hard as it may be for the nonbirth parents to honor the body-based connection of the birth mom and baby, it is essential that you learn to do just that.

Examine and Communicate Feelings

The exclusivity of the birth mother/baby connection can feel threatening. The reaction of wanting to deny or override the body-based connection that you do not share usually stems from feeling threatened. However, if you both acknowledge your feelings about this connection and share your feelings with your partner or other coparents, you open up space to talk about your feelings. When your feelings are heard and accepted it becomes easier to acknowledge and appreciate the unique bond between birth mother and baby. The desire to regulate or interrupt their connection is thereby naturally minimized.

When the hormonal connection is not honored and a woman feels forced, threatened, or coerced into fulfilling predetermined expectations, it can cause tremendous amounts of stress. Let me give you an example.

I know a woman who was partnered with a woman; they had two dads/coparents who lived in a separate house. During pregnancy they drew up a parenting contract. In it they had decided that the birth mom would breast-feed for six months, and starting at six weeks, the baby would spend the night at the dads' house once a week. Also in the first three months, each dad would bring the baby to meet his out-of-state family. When the baby was four months old the birth mom would go back to work and the baby would be placed in in-home day care. The only way that changes could be made to this contract was during a family meeting by majority rules. This is what happened:

After the baby was born, the birth mom discovered that she loved nursing. She loved the closeness of the baby at her breast and felt like nursing was sustaining the baby in a way that was difficult to articulate. She said, however, it felt as if it was feeding both of their souls.

Starting at two weeks old, however, the other mom wanted to feed the baby with a bottle so that she could share in the feeding and the closeness. The birth mom felt this was not right—maybe later, but not yet. After multiple fights and allegations from her partner, she gave in and let her partner feed the baby from a bottle with her expressed milk.

When six weeks came along, the baby was not sleeping in her own room yet as planned; rather she was in bed with her moms. Yet, according to the contract, it was time for her to spend one night a week away from her mothers. The baby was nursing one and a half hours throughout the night. The birth mom called a family meeting and said that she was not ready for that length of separation and felt the baby was not either. Her partner did not share these feelings. She was looking forward to sleeping alone with her partner without the baby. They had not decided that the opinion of the birth mom held special significance, and thus the majority ruled.

Before she had adjusted to having the baby gone one night a week, it was time for the baby to see the in-laws with her dads. These trips entailed the baby being separated from her moms for two three-day trips. The nonbirth mom felt fine about this; the birth mom was completely torn up. This felt heart-wrenchingly wrong to her. She started to become depressed. Things were just not happening the way she had envisioned.

When it was time to go back to work she was not ready; it was the hardest thing she could imagine doing. Then, to make matters worse, instead of finding an in-home care provider as agreed on, the family decided it would be too expensive and overruled the birth mom's opinion again in favor of a group care situation. The day care selected was too far away from her work for her to be able to nurse at lunchtime as she had planned. When seeing her sorrow over all of this, they decided she must be suffering from postpartum depression and told her she needed to take antidepressants.

She did not want to take antidepressants because it would mean giving up nursing, but they insisted, and declared that her feelings were going to interfere with her capacity to parent. Because of their pressure the birth mom went into therapy. In therapy she quickly realized that all of these decisions felt entirely nonconsensual. She called another family meeting and tried to get the other parents to realize that she was depressed because her intuition was being disregarded and replaced with a majority rules attitude. She requested that her feelings be taken more seriously and expressed that the original arrangement was not working for her. Once again her suggestions were not agreed on and were overruled. That was the last straw, she'd had it. Within two weeks of this meeting she took the baby, moved out, and went into hiding.

As much as this story may seem extreme, it is not. I have heard numerous versions of the same story. There are a number of issues touched on in this story, not the least of which being the disregard for the birth mom's unique relationship to the baby. Although the depth of this relationship continues, it is highlighted in the first year of life. This connection is a built-in human survival mechanism. When it is constantly overruled or ignored the situation is dangerous.

Allow Relationships to Develop Naturally

Flexibility is the key. There are birth moms who may have felt comfortable with the arrangements in the example. There are other families that would have heard the birth mom more clearly and been willing to adapt to her needs. When following the path of love, try not to feel threatened, and allow time for love and relationships to develop in their own ways.

The tendency to disregard the connection that birth mother and baby share appears to be accentuated in queer families for two reasons. The first reason is that there is so much negotiating of each parent's role prior to birth. This negotiation does not occur in most heterosexual families because the bond between mother and baby is typically accepted. Queer families think of chosen family members as equal to biological members. However, we miss the mark if we completely disregard the power of the biological connection of birth mother and baby. Much as we can redefine family to suit our needs, we cannot ignore the bonds of the newborn baby and mother, if that mother is parenting the baby.

The second reason that the connection of the birth mom and baby seems to be minimized is that lesbians often feel that the baby will have two moms, so why should one mom be "better" than the other. Although at times it is appropriate to disregard biology, the first few months are a time to honor its impact on your family. The intensity of this connection naturally shifts around ten months.

Nursing

A woman does not know how she will respond to breast feeding her baby until she has established a strong nursing relationship. Breast feeding is more than just food, it is very special time. Everyone can be surprised by how much time a newborn spends nursing. It is normal for a newborn to spend most of its waking hours on the breast. The time between feedings gradually lengthens as the baby grows. Most parents-to-be can not anticipate how they will feel about breast feeding. The feelings that arise may surprise you.

Unfortunately, many nonnursing parents feel threatened and left out by the apparent completeness of the nursing relationship. It is a bond that they do not share—it is an exclusive connection. Although all fathers have been left out of this relationship and felt displaced for a long time, queer families seem to be hit by this even harder than heterosexual families. In fact, I have noticed in my midwifery practice that it is quite common for a woman's female partner or their male coparents to start pressuring her to stop nursing much earlier than men pressure their wives. It is valuable for the nonbiological mom to examine her feelings about nursing, as it is often jealousy and feeling unneeded that trigger the pressure to wean.

Introducing a Bottle

Having the birth mom begin to express some milk that coparents can feed to the baby via a bottle can alleviate some of the stressful dynamic of breast feeding. Feeding your baby with a bottle provides all parents time to hold the baby in their arms and sit quietly for extended periods focused exclusively on the baby. This sacred time seems to serve a triple purpose of equalizing the parenting relationship, allowing more opportunity to integrating yourself into the role of parenting, and providing you with uninterrupted bonding time with your baby. Although this can help to establish a meaningful feeling of self-importance for the nonbirth parents, be aware of the following considerations.

The Breast Can't Be Replaced

Nonnursing parents should resist the urge to feel like they have the right to feed the baby. Resist the urge to replace your partner's breasts by always offering or insisting on feeding the baby even when your partner is present. This urge often comes from insecurity; parenting choices are best made from a place of what is best for the child, before looking at "what is best for me?"

I have seen many nonbiological moms' zealousness to feed their babies cause nipple confusion and actually lead to an abrupt weaning for which neither birth mom or baby was ready. Likewise, be wary of introducing the bottle too soon. If this occurs, the baby can become confused and choose the bottle over the breast. Waiting until the baby is at least five weeks old will cut down on this risk.

If you choose to breast-feed and bottle-feed the baby, it is valuable to talk together about what the role of the bottle will be in your family. Are there certain times when it will be used? For example, will you use it only when the nursing mom is not present? Will you decide to use it for one feeding in the night?

Remember, to maintain your milk supply you must pump every time you miss more than one feeding!

Many people start with the bottle during the week before the birth mom must go back to work, if she is returning to work in the first six to twelve weeks. If she is not going to be working during that time, many people pump anyway just to have more freedom.

It is important to note that many breast-feeding moms choose not to express their milk at all. It simply does not feel appropriate to them, whether or not they thought it would prior to giving birth. Also, some babies do not like bottles and will prefer to drink from a cup.

The World Health Organization and the American Academy of Pediatrics recommend that all babies breast-feed until they are at least one year old (American Academy of Pediatrics 1997; World Health Organization 1995). They feel strongly that this is what is healthiest for the baby. Because this is so, it truly pays to examine any tension you may feel about the nursing relationship.

Nonbirth Mom Nursing Too

Some nonbirth moms may want to nurse their baby. There are multiple possibilities for how this can work. This can be done if you have lactated previously in your life. Or, you can bring milk in by religiously pumping your breasts multiple times a day. It can also be done through a supplemental device that attaches to your breast and is filled with breast milk. Some people dry nurse their baby for comfort; that is, they nurse the baby even though there is no milk in their breasts.

If you are a nonbirth mom and are nursing the baby, it is important to have an honest conversation about why you are doing this, and when it will be right for you to do so. Even if you do begin to lactate, your breast milk should be regarded as supplemental, and not the primary food source for the baby. The milk you have will not be sufficient to provide adequate nourishment. This may be different if you are currently nursing a baby. In that instance, you are more equipped with the hormones in your body to produce high quality milk.

Perhaps the most appropriate time for this kind of nursing is for comfort. However, like with bottles, you need to be sure that the baby does not develop nipple/breast confusion. It is vital that the baby receives the milk made for it during the immediate newborn period; it is full of particular antibodies and nutrients not available in breast milk of other periods. After that time, you can explore sharing the breast feeding in ways that seem best for baby and for you.

Nonbirth Parent Pep Talk

The first few weeks to months of new parenting is very, very hard for nonbiological parents. It helps to know this and it helps to remember that this phase is time limited. It is deeply challenging to feel like you have lost your partner after she gives birth. The bond of birth mom and baby is so intense in the beginning it can be hard to have a strong sense of where you fit in to your own family. Likewise, because your role is not culturally understood, well-meaning people treat you like an afterthought, as if you did not just become a parent as well. One mom stated it clearly; she said she feels like she is the one expected to clean up after everyone while friends and family bask in the glow of her partner and the baby.

Do not become discouraged. When you feel inadequate or left out or jealous, try to identify it as such, rather than project it onto the birth mother by implying or stating things like she is spoiling the baby, or that she must not love you anymore. Within a matter of months, you will have established a relationship with the baby that is meaningful to both of you whether or not you ever give the baby a bottle. Practice seeing the beauty of their relationship. Honor their closeness. Let the love be contagious.

Parenting Roles in the First Year

As with all of the adjustments to parenting, identifying, defining, and accepting your role as a queer parent in the first year can be an emotional challenge. As a primary parent, being in such demand can be completely overwhelming. Yet, as a nonprimary parent or as a donor, you can find yourself questioning if there is even a place for you at all. Once you have clarified your role, however, it is easier to relax into it and to accept—know that your baby's growth will bring about change naturally.

The Primary Parent

Will your child have a primary parent? A primary parent is the one who spends the most time with the child. The primary parent has the strongest bond with the child. A child may have multiple primary parents if each parent spends equal amounts of time each day with the child. However, there is frequently a parent who nurtures more instinctively than another and, when all other things are equal, children will create a special bond with that person. If the birth mom is raising the child, she may or may not be the primary parent. If your time with your child changes year by year or season by season this may not be relevant terminology for your family.

It is useful to recognize if your child does indeed have a primary parent and to honor that bond. Acknowledging this relationship is particularly helpful when exploring the potential impact your choices as adults may have on your child. For example, although your baby will be affected emotionally if any parent goes away on a business trip, most especially when they are very young, it will be affected more significantly if it is the primary parent who leaves. Knowing this can assist the other parent(s) to prepare for such a trip accordingly.

Nonprimary Parents

If you are jealous of the primary parent because you consider yourself an equal parent but feel excluded by the added intensity of their bond, there are a number of approaches you can take. One is the test of time. Toward the end of the first year and definitely into the second year your child will be developmentally ready to widen their bonds and be reaching out for you. In the meantime, however, scheduling as much time alone with your baby without the presence of the primary parent will help you to strengthen both your bond and your parenting skills. Allowing for plenty of alone time for the two of you will allow your baby to become much more comfortable with you. Likewise, try to arrange to take one day a week off from work to be with the baby, or to alter your work hours so that you can spend more time with your baby. The more time you spend alone with your baby, the more confident you become as a parent. This confidence allows you to feel secure in your role as your child's parent. If you can manage to do so financially, seriously consider taking the second year of your child's life off from work or go to part-time. Resist the temptation to fall into traditional roles, unless it feels comfortable to you.

Parents Outside of the Home

As a coparent living outside of your baby's home, it is not always easy to determine what your role is in the first few weeks or months as a parent. This is especially true if the birth mother is raising the baby and is nursing. It can feel awkward to know that you have become a parent and yet have not spent much time with your child. Your role will unfold over time. Having patience and maturity helps immensely during this phase. Becoming clear on how much time you would like to spend with the baby is the first step in negotiating the arrangements. Even if your baby may not be ready to come to your house for some time, make an effort to bond with the baby in their own home.

If the other parent(s) are more primary, it is common for you not to spend much time at all with the baby in the first two months. This time is being used for the primary parent and the baby to become used to each other and establish their bond. Don't worry! The baby will still love you and bond with you whenever you are able to spend more time together.

Donors

Much is the same as with coparents. If you are to have an "uncle" or "aunt" role in the baby's life, you will have to wait for the baby to grow for that to develop. Let the parents know how you would like to be involved. Navigating babyhood as a donor can be confusing for everyone as you all are trying to discover what your role is exactly. For example, Michael, a donor in Arkansas, has this to say:

> I felt excited when I got the call saying she was born! I was at work, and didn't feel like I could shout "I am a donor!" to my coworkers. I wasn't allowed to see the baby until she was nine days old. That was really hard. I had to manage my feelings of disappointment and entitlement. I knew I had an "uncle" role, but I wanted to see if she looked like me. For the next few weeks I was trying so hard to respect their privacy. I only called every other week. It hurt my feelings that they never called me. I found myself distancing from the whole thing. Then when they called me at twelve weeks to see why I wasn't seeing the baby and was I still interested in being her "Super Uncle" I felt totally confused.
>
> I see her now about one time a month. I will see her less frequently as she gets older because she won't be changing so fast. This is the only way I can keep up with her. I feel the communication between the adults is improving. Being a donor is not easy! I am not sure what my role is and I don't want them to think I am forcing myself on them by wanting to clarify so often, but this first year has been a total whirlwind.

Sleeping Arrangements

Deciding where your baby should sleep requires some thought. As with all parenting decisions, it is a very personal choice. Many families who originally believe that the baby will sleep in a cradle or in another room end up with the baby in their bed. Others, who plan to have a family bed where everyone sleeps together every night, discover that they can't get any sleep with their children in bed with them.

Queer parents have expressed concern and fear about both choices. Although some parents say their sexual orientation does not influence their decision about where their baby should sleep, this is a place where internalized homophobia and fear of outsiders' homophobia can run strong. Some parents do not realize to what extent fear influences their decisions. Although it does not change the situation, it is uncomfortable to accept that parenting truly is affected on the most basic levels by the fear of people trying to take your children away or drawing unwanted attention to your family.

Sleeping in a Separate Room

Although some queer parents desire that their babies sleep in a separate room, they fear that the natural, although loud crying will raise the neighbor's homophobic suspicion that unhealthy relations are occurring behind closed doors. For example:

> I wanted to be perceived as the perfect family by our neighbors, to not give them any reason to say that gay men shouldn't parent. Yet when our baby cried at night, I imagined what they thought we were doing to him. I had such urgency to get him to stop crying that he probably cried louder because I was being so tense. We ended up with him in our bed. It was not an intentional choice, and I felt guilty about it, but it was the only way he would not cry.

The Family Bed

Although some queer parents feel that sleeping with their children is more natural, they can be faced with the fear of outsiders perceiving their family bed as a form of sexual abuse. For example:

> I really wanted my baby to sleep with me, it has always seemed most natural, and certainly many cultures around the world view it as a normal part of life. But I thought that because I am a single lesbian raising a son, people might think that it was incestuous. I know straight parents can also fear the opinions of others, but they have society to support their right to parent and their right to privacy. It feels like all your rights to privacy in your parenting go out the window when you're a dyke. I decided to let him sleep with me, but only during the first year. It was a compromise decision; it didn't feel right to me, but then nothing did.

The truth of the matter is, unless someone actually observes you sleeping, no one truly knows how or with whom anyone sleeps. The proverbial neighbors will have many thoughts that may or may not include where you sleep. Babies cry in the night for many reasons. Where you choose to sleep and how you choose to parent during the day as well as the night are personal decisions. Who you choose to share these decisions with may be a different matter. You may end up feeling good about your decisions and simply not sharing them in environments you think will not be supportive. Or you may try to educate those around you about why you chose the approach that you did.

How you choose to raise your child can spark heated debates, but, ultimately, you have to parent in the ways that seem most natural and appropriate to you.

Sleeping at the Coparents House

Some families with multiple parents plan for their child to have more than one home. Because every family and every child is unique, the time when your child is ready to sleep away from its primary home also is unique. Here are some rules of thumb: If the baby is still nursing through the night, and not taking a bottle, they should not sleep away from the nursing mom until she either weans at night or is ready to try it. Many families I have spoken with have waited until the second or even third year for regular sleepovers.

It's good not to arrange a sleepover until the nonprimary parent(s), whose house the baby will be sleeping at, has had time to thoroughly bond with the baby, and the bond is mutual. Likewise, the parent(s) should have proven capable of caring for the baby for extended periods of time, as a sleepover can involve more than eight hours with the baby not only awake, but unhappy.

If parents with separate homes feel like it is taking too long for sleepovers to start, they need to examine what the desire for a sleepover means to them. Often parents don't feel like they are truly a parent until they care for the baby at night. This is a big milestone, yet it might not come in the time you had hoped, expected, or been promised. A milestone that usually comes first is caring for the baby for a morning, and then having the baby for a whole day. Once a parent outside of the home, or any parent for that matter, feels comfortable being with their baby from morning until night, then the parent and baby are probably ready for a sleepover.

Plan to Take Time Off from Work

If you read this book prior to having your baby, please consider that one of the most worthwhile ways that you will find to establish a connection to your child is to take as much time off after birth as possible. This goes for all parents who live in the primary home of the baby. For parents who do not live in the baby's primary home, it is good to talk with the primary parents as far ahead of time as is realistic to establish what your role will be in the early days and weeks. If your position involves spending a lot of time with the baby, were you to be available, then arrange to take time off as well. If the imagined role for you is bigger when the baby is a little older, save your vacation and sick time so that you can be available at that time or if someone is needed to stay home with the baby when they are sick.

It cannot be emphasized enough how valuable taking extended time off can be for bonding with the baby. Arranging for this time off can take courage: Insist on parental leave and paid time off. Push the envelope and insist on equal rights for our families!

Returning to Work

After having a baby, there are many ways to arrange your work life so that you can spend more time with your baby. Think creatively about your options. For long-term bonding, you could arrange for each parent to work part-time so that each parent can have quality time with the baby. Likewise, some families can afford for one parent not to work. In fact, many parents discover that it is more affordable for one of them to stop working and to not put their baby in day care at all. Try planning your work life to reflect your parenting goals.

If you must return to work after having a baby, going back is usually a heart-wrenching experience. It can be especially challenging if your partner is still home with the baby. Remember that it may be an option for you to bring the baby to work. Some families choose to rotate with whom the baby goes to work, e.g., one day at Daddy's office, two days at Pappa's work, one day at home with Daddy, and one day at day care.

Maybe no other employee has brought their baby to your workplace. You could be the first. Your new priorities as a parent may encourage you to push the envelope. Can you ask to work a day a week from home? Asking for these circumstances may mean coming out at work even more. Do what will be best for you to feel like you are parenting in the ways that are most important to you. Surviving and feeling good about the first year of parenting requires that you pay attention to your intuition and be creative.

You Might Be Surprised

Many parents are surprised by the backseat that work takes in comparison to the new love of their life. This can be part of the transformations that occur in the first year. People, who once considered work the focus of their lives, find themselves trying to figure out how to become a stay-at-home dad or mom.

Likewise, some parents who planned to take an extended leave from work are surprised that they can't wait to return. This impulse, although certainly authentic for some, can be a desire to escape from the new and deeply profound set of emotions and responsibilities that come with parenting.

For example, one family decided that Jim was to be the primary parent. He was going to stay home full-time for the first six months. During the second six months each parent would each work half-time so that both dads could bond with the baby. When the baby was a year old it would go to day care full time.

At four months, however, Jim was offered a great new job. Jim wanted to take the job so they had to reevaluate their child care situation. They decided that the other dad, M.J., would arrange to stay home full-time for three months. Then when the baby was seven months old, they would send him to day care. This worked for them, and the baby remained in day care from seven to twelve months of age.

When their son was a year old, M.J. realized he could not work full-time with his baby in day care. Being away from his son was making him depressed—a role reversal of what the couple had expected. Their finances would not change significantly if M.J. moved to part-time work and took the baby out of day care for the other days. Many parents find that spending more time with baby becomes such a priority. Because child care is so expensive, reevaluating work and lifestyle goals often leads parents to spending more time with their baby.

Relationship Issues

A few of the greatest changes in your life as a parent include a lack of downtime, a shortage of money, exhaustion, and the twenty-four-hour-a-day nature of your life. These challenges can be very stressful on a relationship. In addition, parenting triggers many old feelings and while you are working through these, whether intentionally or in a less aware fashion, you are often not as emotionally available and present for your partner.

There is a unique stress in queer relationships, especially highlighted during this first year, in that one parent is *legally* responsible for the baby and the other usually is not. Although in some states second-parent adoptions and other forms of legal parenting agreements are available before or within weeks of birth, this typically is not the case (see chapter 11, "Protecting Your Family"). This is particularly challenging for the nonlegal parent because the amount of love pouring from your heart is tremendous and it can feel like it will be taken away at any time. This fear and tenuous standing can enhance an already stressful situation and relationship. It is valuable to recognize and honor the nonlegal parenting status and to intentionally foster styles of communication that validate equal parenting.

Rule of Thumb for Committed Couples

If you are in a committed relationship and you plan to stay together for the long haul, a good rule of thumb is to not seriously consider breaking up until you have been parents for at least one year. Secure this time as a safe zone, and realize that, if you are like most couples, you will deeply question how and why you are going to stay together. You'll question yourselves many times in that first year, especially in the first six months. By creating a safe time zone, however, you allow yourselves the freedom to go through awkward phases and to feel distant from one another while having trust that you will feel connected again in a matter of months. If, after a year, it is still necessary, then you can discuss the future of your relationship.

Clear Communication

When you are partnered, it is essential that throughout your relationship you continue to nurture the connection that brought you together in the first place. This requires clear communication. It is also imperative that you keep the lines of communication clear with coparents and donors who may not be your life partners, but, from now on, are your partners through life. Clear communication will not only make life easier and more enjoyable for you, but it will model healthy patterns for your child.

Using specific communication formats can be particularly helpful in this first year of your baby's life. Many parents have found that it greatly benefits their relationship to continue these practices throughout parenthood, as they are quick avenues to feeling connected. This is vital in early parenthood when there is so little quality time as a couple.

Many people feel that communication exercises are too contrived. When done correctly, however, they serve a great purpose. When practiced regularly, creating committed time together where you are dedicated to keeping communication clear serves to grow your love. It can feel like a joint spiritual practice. These exercises are useful in times of tension as well.

Connection Exercise

Arrange to spend one-half hour together that will be uninterrupted (turn the phone and beeper off). Face each other in a sitting position. This exercise has three parts to it.

Part One

Spend time looking silently into each other's eyes; you may touch during this time if it seems appropriate. Feel your body and breathe deeply while you notice your partner. What do you feel when you look at your partner? Just look at the person with whom you have chosen to walk this part of your life. When you have settled in to your body and can feel both yourself and your partner, take some moments to notice your heart. Does it feel open, free, contracted, protected? Take some time and breathe from your heart. Just breathe your heart open while looking deeply at your partner.

When enough time has passed, close your eyes for a few moments and take in what you have just experienced.

Part Two

Next have one person speak from their heart about what they appreciate and are grateful for in the other. This can be simple statements, such as, "I am so grateful that you clean the bathtub" to "I am grateful that you stay with me and support me through times when I feel scared and overwhelmed." Allow your heart to speak whatever comes up. Try not to qualify what you say, such as, "I am grateful that you clean the tub, I just wish I didn't have to climb over your clothes to get into the tub." When you have run out of things to say in that moment, it is the other person's turn.

Spend a few moments with your eyes closed taking in what you have heard and experienced during your exchange.

Part Three

In the last part, have one person go first and express the following: what they are bringing to the relationship at this point; what their vision is for the two of you; and how they are trying to foster that vision. For example, "I am trying to create a more beautiful home environment that reflects our love. One way I am doing that is by trying to keep up on the laundry." Or, "I am supporting you in this time when you are processing your childhood abuse by loving you so dearly. I am trying to show you in as many ways as I can that I love you and am here for you."

To end, spend a few moments with your eyes shut breathing in everything you have exchanged. Allow everything to find a place to live inside of you. Allow it to enliven you.

When the exercise is over you can turn the phone back on and go through your day.

Clues

Some people feel safer and their minds are more relaxed if they decide ahead of time who will go first. It is sometimes nice to either use a five-minute egg timer, set a portable timer, or make a tape that has a bell every five minutes. If you want to go past the timer at any point you can, but it sets a nice structure to the exercise. Some couples like to schedule a regular time each week to do this exercise.

Heart Share Exercise

Another lovely exercise that only requires ten minutes, but can serve to keep you connected and current with each other's inner processes, is called a heart share.

A heart share involves each of you being in a physically comfortable position. Many people find that this is best done lying next to each other, but not touching. One person goes first and, for five minutes, speaks what is in their heart. The other partner is not allowed to respond or comment. If something is not making sense, however, you can ask for clarification. When the five minutes is up, the other person takes five minutes to express what is in their heart. Be careful not to respond to anything said in the first share.

The information said in a heart share is sacred. Unless you ask for permission, you are not to refer to what was said; it is a communication from one heart to the next. If something is burning, you can ask permission to discuss it, but respect if your partner does not choose to.

This exercise is a nice complement to the previous connection exercise as it can lead a couple to feel more connected with what their partner is feeling and thinking.

Fighting

During the first year of parenting, especially during the first few months, it is common for parents to fight and to experience more overall tension. There are a few reasons why learning to fight well becomes important. One, when you combine hormones, sleep deprivation, new roles, and a lack of sex, not to mention any of life's other stressors, people tend to fight poorly. New parents often resort to arguing styles that are less mature than their usual communication methods. What you say to each other will be received more deeply in these states and yet it is common for delivery to be much less tactful.

How problems are addressed and how decisions are made—rather than what actually is decided—is crucial to sustaining positive feelings in a relationship. When conflicts are resolved in a positive manner, it's easier for all emotions to flow more freely. When the conflict resolution process is not completed and resolution is not reached, it becomes harder on a relationship to express love freely. Your child learns from your ways, and develops their self-esteem from the home environment you create. Early parenthood is often very fertile ground to help you identify communication patterns from your family of origin and, therefore, to choose which, if any, you would like to repeat.

Patterns of ineffective communication can be passed down for generations. Effectively communicating with other family members is not a luxury, but a basic emotional need. The overall atmosphere of a family is directly related to whether communication facilitates or inhibits conflict resolution. Attention to family atmosphere is crucial as living with high and consistent levels of tension can not only lead to divorce, but is thought to be the single largest contributing factor to maladjustment in children (Peterson 1996).

There seem to be three themes which people most commonly argue about in the first few months of parenthood. These are time—alone, together, with the baby—money, and sex. There is a shared experience in most families that there is never enough of these three things. Although it is true that there may indeed be shortages of these valuable resources, it is quite possible that these fights are also serving as outlets for the stress of not knowing who you are anymore, not knowing when you will regain a solid sense of yourself, and not knowing when the initial ordeal will end, if ever.

It is common for threats to be made during arguments. In fact, all of the families that I interviewed experienced fights where the "legal" parent threatened to leave with the baby—acting as if the baby was more theirs than their partner's. If we cannot have our parenting rights secured, we must live by our words. If you have made or adopted a baby together, you are both parents. Honor this intention, even in fights. It is good policy to make custody threats off limits.

Couples counseling can also be quite effective as you can learn, with guidance, new manners of addressing and resolving tension and conflict. Although in times of high stress many people do not resort to using exercises, it is nonetheless a good idea. Trying to adhere to a structure is always safer, especially when less healthy patterns have been triggered.

Unfortunately, this is also a common time for domestic abuse to surface. As GLBTs, we are often reticent to seek help in these situations, because we feel that there are no resources for us and that if anyone else found out, our children might be taken away from us more easily. This is not reason to stay in a violent relationship.

Sex

Whole books can be written on the subject of sex and parenting. Sex is a vital and important component of life. In fact, unless you are celibate for spiritual or other chosen reasons, it is a necessary part of life. Whether it is with yourself, or with your partner, sex needs to be integrated into your life for you to feel balanced. This does not mean that it needs to be on a daily or even weekly basis, and, believe me, for most parents in the first year of parenting, it is not. However, it is important to try to keep your sex life alive, especially when you are in relationship with someone.

That said, most parents do not have much sex in the first ten months of parenting. So if you do, consider yourself fortunate. This lull seems to be somewhat shorter for families who adopt their children. Gay men appear to have a significantly shorter lull in their sex life than lesbians do. This, at least, is in part due to the fact that for women who have given birth it can take months to completely recover on both a physical and emotional level.

For all parents, one of the big changes in your sex life can be the lack of time. Long gone are the luxurious Sunday mornings, for example. Sex usually becomes "catch as catch can." When the baby is young, that can be ten to twenty minutes together. In fact, it usually ends up that when you are hoping the baby will sleep (i.e., when you are in the mood), the baby will not sleep. When the baby decides to take a longer nap, you may have to drop everything and get down to it. Countless parents have said that regardless of the sounds they are making, their baby wakes up just before or else during orgasm! Thus, many people end up arranging child care in order to have sex. This, of course, takes away the spontaneity, which is the second big change in most parents' sex lives.

Do not forego a satisfying sex life simply because it seems too hard. These are small obstacles to which you can adjust. Many people find that they have more time for masturbation than for partner sex. While you are working the partner thing out, keep masturbating, it keeps the sex vibes alive.

A last note, if it has been ten months and you have not had sex, go ahead and do it. The longer you wait, the harder it becomes to do. Many feelings set in: shyness, lack of confidence, contentment in being asexual, fear, etc. Just know that, like any other form of exercise, it only takes practice to get back in shape.

A special note to coupled lesbians: Do not let parenting deaden your sex life. Professionally working with the lesbian population for a number of years, a "dead sex life" is one of the most frequently used excuses in lesbian divorce after children. Make the time; even if you are not "in the mood," usually your body will take it from there and you will be happy that it did.

Family Meetings

It is very valuable for all people parenting together to meet regularly to reflect on how things are going. This can be used as a time to evaluate schedules, discuss developmental shifts in your baby, establish unified or at least compatible parenting approaches, and more. If you hold a family meeting while the baby is present, make sure that everyone is able to participate equally and is not distracted by the little one. You may want to arrange child care.

It is not always necessary to arrange a formal structure when there are only two parents who live in the same home. However, even in smaller families, structure is often helpful. A structured family meeting becomes essential, however, when there are multiple parents or participating aunts/uncles/friends who regularly spend time with the baby. The needs of the family will structure the meetings. Some people choose to have a facilitator, some families record notes from the meetings in a special binder to reference in the future. You may wish to set a fixed amount of time for the meetings or to meet until everything is addressed.

Acknowledgment and Appreciation

Family meetings are a good time to address concerns. Because it is a forum in which concerns will most likely be regularly raised, it is also an excellent time to set up an appreciation practice. Parents can all too quickly resort to criticism and forget to acknowledge and appreciate one another. The family in its entirety, as well as its parts, needs nourishment. Sometimes a modified version of the exercises in the relationship section (earlier in this chapter) is helpful. Have everyone verbally acknowledge appreciation for each other. Then take it one step further and say what you are learning from each other. When this is done toward the beginning or the end of each meeting, then whether or not there are challenges to discuss, everyone is being nurtured as well.

For single parents, calling together the people who support your parenting on a semiregular basis will help you to build and then to solidify your community. If your circle does not provide child care for you, this meeting may serve a different purpose than a family meeting, although it can serve as a structure to nurture you as a parent.

Friendship Circles

You will notice that when you become a parent your friendship circles usually change. This is because being a parent becomes your primary identity. Sheri Pies (1988) wrote an entire book documenting that parents feel their primary peer group to be other parents with similar philosophies. Many people find that their gay identity falls into second place and that their identity as a parent takes precedence. Fortunately, at this point in time, the two are more able to go hand in hand and you can identify as a gay parent.

Honoring Your Parenting Style

Many people let outsiders influence their parenting decisions. Part of becoming a parent during the first months and years is distinguishing your parenting style. Deciding when and how to compromise what feels right to you is very personal. If you find you are altering your style of parenting dramatically from what seems natural to you, examine that tendency. Is it necessary? Could anything be changed to give you more freedom in your own home and mind?

Remember, in order to walk the path of love, it has to be a path of Pride. Take Pride in who you are, in who your child is, and in who your family is.

3

Conscious Parenting

Parenting comes more easily for some than for others. This in no way means that "natural" parents deserve to be parents more than those who have to work harder at it. Instead, it means that some people enter parenthood with practice, experience, and an automatic affinity to care for and oversee the development of a little person. The ability to be a loving, respectful, focused, attentive, and nurturing parent is a goal; for most, it is not the starting place. Conscious parenting develops over time and, with attention and focus, it is available to us all. When we are parenting in a way that feels "right," when we can be connected to ourselves and to our children, then we are walking the path of love.

Inner Work of Parenting

This chapter emphasizes the inner work of parenting. It is through paying attention to our own inner worlds—to our own responses and feelings—while simultaneously nurturing and caring for our children, that we learn to parent consciously. As parents, we must learn to cultivate an inner dialogue that allows us to examine ourselves, our responses to our children, and the requests of parenting.

If you already practice self-reflection, it is certainly easier to be a self-reflective parent. However, anybody can develop the necessary self-reflective skills of good parenting. Self-reflection requires patience and the ability to admit to yourself that you are not perfect, that you make mistakes, and that it is all right to change your ways as you come into your own as a parent. Those of us who are afraid to admit that we might not be parenting in a way that best supports and nurtures our child are the ones who hold firm to strict ways of behavior. Through examination of our day-to-day interactions and the messages we are sending our children, we are able to grow and refine our parenting.

It can be challenging to not be consumed and overwhelmed by doubts, concerns, problems, and conflicts in our parenthood. The inner work of parenting, however, provides us with skills that allow us to maintain clear perspective on our parenting and to not be consumed by the drama.

The GLBT Advantage

Parenting is a path. It is a large part of who you are and who you will be for the rest of your life. The overwhelming majority of GLBT parents are parents by choice. Our conscious desire to raise children is a powerful motivator. Most queer parents must work through tremendous emotional, practical, and spiritual changes to have or to adopt a child of their own. Thus, although parenting itself is a path, because of the extraordinary amount of constant courage and dedication required, for GLBTs who are out prior to parenting, parenting is also a calling. Being this dedicated to bringing love into the world increases the probability that the needs of each member of our families will be consciously considered with love, focus, and attention. When your child is wanted, you are more likely to treat them with care and respect, regardless of your sexual orientation.

As GLBT parents, we truly do start our parenting from a different place than most parents. When each of us came out, we underwent a radical re-evaluation of everything that was presented to us as a "given," and we quickly realized that there is always choice. In coming out, many of us experienced the world radically transforming itself and opening up possibilities that before were not even imagined. Coming out can transform your entire worldview. In so doing, it often creates a natural side effect of questioning everything, especially that which is handed to us as truth.

Challenging the Status Quo

Thus as GLBTs, one could say that, by design, we are less likely to automatically fall into culturally established methods and means of parenting without first examining their value for *our own* families. We have an innate opportunity to approach our parenting with a greater awareness of the choices available to us. As a queer parent, it is often natural to choose to parent in ways that are authentic to you, whether or not they are mainstream approaches to parenting. We are well equipped to question and examine what feels appropriate to us, to pick and choose from available options, and to create new options when necessary. This built-in ability that practically comes with the territory of being gay is both a gift and an asset.

Develop Inner Authenticity

The inner work of parenting is the key to maintaining your sanity. Part of your work is to learn to cultivate a deep sense of inner authenticity. How each person parents is uniquely personal. Who you are as the best parent that you can be is determined by who you are as a person and what your overall philosophy about life and about children is. It's important to take the time to explore and to listen to your heart about what feels right for you in any given moment. This requires practice and maintenance. You need to tend to your heart and to your beliefs regularly. As you change and grow, which is inevitable as a parent, your philosophies change and grow as well. You will likely discover that you no longer hold so fast to a belief that you once thought absolute. Thus, to develop inner authenticity, you must regularly check in with yourself about what you hold to be true.

For example, in my home I had a rule for my daughter when she was young: No Barbie dolls. Barbie was not allowed in my home. I had very strong beliefs about the misogynist messages that Barbie carried with her and did not want those messages creeping into my daughter's mind. I held firmly on to this rule despite the fact that my daughter really wanted to play with Barbie. Over time, she started going over to other people's homes to play, simply because they had Barbie. She was much too young to understand the philosophy I was espousing, but she was old enough to realize that she could get what she wanted elsewhere. Barbie was a tense place between us.

One day, while I was pondering who and what I was serving by maintaining this hard line, I came to realize that by not allowing Barbie, I was greatly enhancing her presence and influence in our lives. I was ensuring that she, and all of her cultural messages that I did not want, were a daily part of our lives. Holding firm to this rule was doing us all a disservice. So, after years of no Barbie, I lifted the rule. I hoped that in doing so, her mystique would fade, as the no longer forbidden is rarely coveted.

From that point on Barbie was indeed allowed into our home with a few caveats. She needed to be flatfooted—everybody needs to be able to stand on their own two feet—and she needed to be as closely proportionate to real women as possible. We all know that Barbie would fall over from the weight of her breasts, and her ribs and lungs would cave in from how narrow her waist is. The only "Barbies" that met these criteria were Barbie's teenage playmates or children accompaniments. The stipulations of our compromise worked very well. Allowing Barbie into our house ended our struggle, and, consequently, ended Barbie's insidious presence in our lives.

Never would I have imagined that I would have allowed Barbie into my home. And now, so many years later, I cannot imagine that I thought my rule was important enough to have a power struggle with my daughter. I had been holding firm, rather than listening to what was really needed in the moment.

When Our Focus Is Love

Parenting is a fluid reality. Often when we find ourselves holding fast to something, we aren't actually paying attention to the truth of the moment. When you are experiencing struggle, frustration, anger, or you are feeling overwhelmed in your parenting, it is worthwhile to take pause, close your eyes, and listen to your heart. From this place, ask yourself if *in this moment* you are coming from your place of highest love. It is hard to go wrong if you allow love to be your ultimate guide. Ask yourself, "Am I making this decision, speaking this way, doing whatever it is I am doing, while feeling the strongest and truest love I have for my child?" When we maintain our sense of true love it becomes virtually impossible to feel overwhelmed and, thus, new possibilities or answers become more available.

We typically are trained in our culture not to speak directly of the huge, raw, tremendous love we feel for our children. Because of this silence surrounding parental love, asking you to focus on that love when you are in the confusing or challenging moments of parenthood can be discounted as New Age. However, if we all parented while actively feeling our love for our children, we would be a much happier society. Children and parents would feel greater harmony in their homes and this would naturally radiate throughout their lives.

Maintain Flexibility

In each and every moment of parenting, we have a choice about how we respond. You do not need to consistently respond in the same way as long as you are being true to your heart and true to your child. This idea conflicts with many current child care philosophies, which espouse the value and necessity of being consistent. They state that you should draw a line and never cross it for fear of giving your child negative mixed messages.

There is a different way of looking at this, however. Children are incredibly sensitive creatures. They can often be found expressing and mirroring our own emotions. Although it is essential to be consistent with our children, I believe that the consistency needs to be in the internal place we parent from, and not necessarily in our actions. My goal is to always come from a place of great love and ultimate respect for my children. When I speak or act from a lesser place I am being inconsistent (I also feel badly). Being inconsistent does indeed give a mixed message. And yes, I have seen it have a negative effect on my children. So, for my family, if I were to draw a line in the sand about a behavior and never cross over it, I would not be able to stay in a place of love. Circumstances change. If I did not allow for change or recognize change, then my children would grow confused and their hearts would be hurt.

A good example is Margie, a single lesbian mother who was in the process of gradually weaning her fourteen-month-old baby. To wean her daughter, Margie decided to nurse only upon the baby's waking, after nap time, and before bed at night. This was a drastic change from the nursing-on-demand that her baby was used to. When her daughter wanted to nurse at times that were not predetermined, Margie would say "no." Her daughter would start to cry and grab at her breasts. Margie couldn't take this desperation and struggle and she would become frustrated. Sometimes she would leave the room with her daughter sobbing after her. Shortly thereafter, her baby started needing to be held all the time. Her clinginess seemed unmanageable. Margie felt like they were going backwards; she was feeling out of control and frustrated.

When Margie came in for a session regarding what was "wrong" with her baby, I gently asked her if she had explained to her daughter what was happening with the new nursing schedule. She said she had not said anything other than "No, you can nurse at nap time." Then I asked her if she was able to feel that easy sweet connection of breast feeding with her baby during times when she was not nursing, and if they were enjoying new ways of achieving that state of love connection. She said that she had not thought to replace nursing with other connecting activities. She said, in fact, she felt like she had had to withdraw psychically and emotionally from her baby in order to wean her.

I asked Margie how she thought her baby was feeling in response to this dramatic change in both routine and depth of intimacy with her mother. Margie spent a few moments quietly trying to achieve empathy with her daughter's experience. When she did, she started to cry. Margie had not considered how her baby was feeling during all of this. She now felt she understood the situation more clearly. It was no wonder the baby was needing to be held all of the time; she was scared and confused. Her source of love, nourishment, and connection had been taken away and replaced with her mom being frustrated, saying "no," and walking away.

Margie said that her most important goal in parenting was for her baby to feel loved. This did not mean she had to give up her own needs, but that she had to think of her baby's needs as well and honor them deeply in all that she did.

Margie continued to wean her baby, but she stayed connected with her sense of love. When her baby cried, she sympathized. They spent lots of time snuggling and rocking in the rocking chair. They found other ways to take a break and enjoy basking in parent/child love. Margie experienced an immediate shift in her child's behavior. She no longer was clingy and soon stopped crying to nurse. She started coming to her mom for snuggle time with her blanket and a book instead.

Develop and Rely on Inner Resources

It is particularly important to develop and rely on inner resources as a gay parent because we are parenting in the face of adversity. If you do not cultivate a strong sense of who you are as a parent, it's easy to feel overwhelmed, vulnerable, and insecure. Feeling this way can make you feel open to attack. By cultivating a strong inner feedback loop, you develope a strong sense of yourself as a parent. With a deep sense of inner understanding, you are able to claim responsibility for the choices that you make. You claim your autonomy.

Many GLBT parents experience a lack of places where they can receive support in their parenting. There are many times when gay parents do not feel they can get feedback on their relationship or parenting issues from heterosexual parents. They feel that they must hold up a good front at all times to make up for their perceived uniqueness. Often, joining a new parents group or a play group can seem like more work than it is worth if you have to deal with other parents' homophobia. Many heterosexual parents ask their own parents for advice, but many gay parents are estranged from their parents or feel like asking for advice would be admitting failure. This is a lot of pressure. The isolation can be great at times and especially in certain geographic locations. Learning to enhance your trust in your own decisions and your own ability to navigate the challenges of parenting is one of the greatest gifts you can give yourself.

Cultivate Inner Awareness

The goal of cultivating your inner awareness is to find ways to calm the chatter of your mind and to connect with a loving, respectful, nonthreatened place inside of you. If you are familiar with self-reflection, incorporating it into your parenting will come a little more naturally for you. However, you need not have any previous concrete history with self-reflection; inner awareness can be cultivated in numerous ways.

Establishing specific practices can allow you to reach and maintain this state of being more easily. Having a personal practice can greatly ease your road to self-reflective parenting. Some parents practice meditation as a way to calm the business of their minds and to allow for deeper revelations. Some parents practice a martial art or yoga that cultivates a body/mind/breath connection and allows them to feel centered and connected to themselves. Through therapy, some parents have developed self-reflective skills that allow them to identify common themes and issues in their lives that repeat themselves. They have also developed skills to make different choices. Some people use prayer as a way of connection that provides them guidance and clarity of heart. Others have found exercise or time alone in nature as a source of revelation. Cultivating your inner awareness and becoming a self-reflective parent is a combination of developing intuition, strengthening listening and communication skills, and learning to recognize the influence of your own issues.

Nurture Your Intuition

It is through inner awareness that we learn to nourish and refine our parenting instincts. When we honor and follow our instincts, our intuition starts to grow. Our instincts and intuition can then become the grounding post of our parenting. Our deeper selves let us know when we are doing something that does not feel right. But just like any other skill, honing your intuition takes practice. Listening to your intuition means really listening to yourself.

At first, many people justify their worries or fears as their intuition. You might say that you do not let your children play on the slide by themselves because you have this feeling that they will fall. Perhaps what is more accurate is that you are afraid that your child might be hurt and so you're doing everything you can to try to ensure that doesn't happen. This is not necessarily intuition, but a worry that you are coddling.

Likewise, if you interview a child care provider who comes highly recommended and on meeting the person you feel a little nervous and uncomfortable, it is important to self-reflect on that feeling. Is this your usual nervousness at trusting anyone with your child other than you? Or is this your intuition telling you that this person is not the right choice for your child? It is important to take some time to examine the source of the feelings. Worry does not serve us, but perception does. Through self-reflection and honoring the messages you are giving yourself, you will learn the distinction between worry and perception.

In many cultures the skills of intuition, which are simply the skills of paying attention to the subtleties of life, are time honored; a person who does not refine these skills is regarded as having an empty life. Yet, in modern industrial society, so often the development of the rational mind is encouraged above all else. We are not encouraged to listen to "the little voice in our heads" or the nagging feeling in the pits of our stomachs. Parenting, however, must be a natural blend of the rational and the intuitive.

Increased Sense of the Spiritual

When you speak to parents, you discover that almost every parent can identify an increase in spirituality that accompanied parenthood. Not only does this sense of spirituality begin to permeate their whole lives, but often specific incidences occur that lead to this deepening. Because we are so distanced from deep listening to ourselves and others, having intuitive or psychic experiences are often termed spiritual. For example, many parents of new babies report having received very clear messages from their babies about something the baby wants or needs.

That which is termed *psychic communication* becomes commonplace during infanthood when your child is preverbal, only to recede again as the child ages. Likewise, many parents report *knowing* that their child is injured before receiving the telling phone call. Because the parent/child connection is driven by such a pure love, having a child can automatically increase your ability to listen to your intuition. The parent/child connection is so profound that it can bring us to learn new ways to heighten our sensitivities to the needs of our children.

Strengthen Listening and Communication Skills

Becoming a conscious parent requires strong listening and communication skills. We need to be able to hear our children clearly and to guide them to express themselves—their feelings, needs, and experiences—clearly. We also need to be able to speak clearly to our children in ways that are supportive and direct. How we communicate, both with them and with other adults, is one of the most influential models of communication that they experience.

Most of us are not accustomed to taking the time to truly listen to children. Yet developing this skill will greatly assist every other aspect of our parenting. Adults often don't expect to hear something valuable from a child, and, often times, adults think that they know what a child is going to say. They either then do not give the child their full attention while they are talking or they cut them off in the middle. Adults also interrupt children with their own perspective, feeling the need to correct the child without ever hearing them out. These behaviors are ones that most of us engage in to some degree or other.

When we take the time and cultivate the patience and the respect required to allow young people to express themselves, there is a lot to be gained for all involved. When children are listened to, they learn that their opinions and feelings are valid and worth expressing. As they learn to express themselves, they are able to develop the skills required to self-reflect. As adults, when we listen to children, we allow ourselves to slow down. By not jumping in or tuning out, we are practicing a form of meditation. We are in the moment. There are added benefits to being in the moment because we have the opportunity to actively enjoy our child. The love and respect that is communicated when we truly listen to our children is remarkable. We are enhancing their sense of self and their self-esteem when we look into their eyes and give them our undivided attention.

When we do not develop the skill of listening with our undivided attention, or we devalue its importance, we lose contact with our children. If our children know that we will take the time and we have the desire to listen to them, then when they approach their teen years, there is a greater chance that they will not pull away from us. If your method of listening always involves correcting your child, your child may feel like you never listen to them and can feel misunderstood. Needless to say, these children are more likely to turn away from you as they approach adolescence.

Learn to Recognize Your Own Issues

Learning to recognize how your own issues are impacting or even interfering with your parenting is not always easy. It takes courage and time, and often it takes a willingness to review uncomfortable parts of your past. When you strive to recognize the overlay of your own issues onto your parenting, you're taking responsibility for yourself. To parent with this much inner reflection and personal vulnerability is a powerful choice.

It's usually the subtle (or not so subtle) influences of our own issues that interfere with our ability to feel and express love fully. When you're able to discharge the hold that your past has over you, it's common to experience an increased capacity to nourish, love, and care for yourself and all of your loved ones.

A personal issue can have a significant impact on your parenting. Ross, for example, is the single, bisexual dad of his daughter, May. Ross is also a survivor of sexual abuse. If Ross knew one thing about his parenting it was that he was going to protect May; she was never going to have to go through the kind of trauma and isolation that he went through as a child. When May was two and a half years old she experienced a lot of pain in her vulval area. Ross got alarmed. She was hurting a lot, but would not let him look. This was very unusual behavior; she had always let him look at her body. He gave her a bath, but it only seemed to aggravate the situation. He knew that she must have been abused that day at day care. He asked her all sorts of questions to suggest such a thing, but received no confirming answers.

By 10 P.M. he decided to take her to the emergency room to determine if any sexual trauma had indeed occurred. The medical personnel needed to examine her, but she would not let them near her. They eventually decided to sedate her. Under sedation they discovered that she had a minor laceration on her labia, most likely from playing outside. There were no signs of sexual abuse.

The next year she started an after care program. Within a few weeks, she became withdrawn and her vulva became red and irritated. She did not want to go to the program. He assumed the worst. But no matter what he asked her, she said no one had touched her. He called their pediatrician. She said it sounded inconclusive, but if he was at all concerned, he should take her out of the program. He hired a friend to take care of her in the afternoons instead. Her vulval irritation continued. He got so upset that he accused his friend of molesting his daughter.

Less than a week later he found his daughter very actively masturbating. He realized that no one had been abusing her; her irritation was from her own activity. He apologized to his friend immediately. It became painfully clear to him that he was afraid of the whole world. He felt there was no safe place for his daughter to be. His past was creating havoc with his trust that his daughter was safe.

After entering intensive, emotional therapy, Ross was able to start to believe that May was safe in the world. Now, five years later he no longer obsesses about her being abused. He knows that she is at risk, as are all children; however, he no longer thinks about it every day. He has taught her to say "No!" and what to do in difficult situations, but he does not overemphasize this possibility. He feels that the influence of his own sexual trauma no longer has a negative influence on his parenting.

Parenting as a Path to Wholeness

It often becomes clear to us as parents that there are parts of ourselves that have been damaged. Parenting is an opportunity to reclaim our wholeness. When we are willing to self-reflect as parents and own our own issues, we are able to strengthen the relationship we have with our children. If our goal is to live our love, then we must look at the elements of ourselves that hold us separate from one another.

For example, Connie is Luca's birth mom. Julie is Lucas' stepmom. Julie and Connie got together when Lucas was three. Lucas is now nine. Julie and Lucas have always had tension in their relationship. They clearly love each other, but they tend to fight a lot as well. Julie always attributed this dynamic to the fact that she is his stepmom. She also felt that Lucas and his selfishness were to blame for the majority of the arguments.

Recently, however, Julie has tried a new perspective in her parenting. She is trying to see each dynamic in her parenting as a reflection of herself. She decided to look at the tension as an indication of a missing or hurt part of herself.

What she found from this new perspective was that she treats Lucas differently when she is jealous of him. She had never realized how many of the fights *she* actually started. She had never realized that she felt inadequate and jealous whenever Lucas got something she did not get as a child. She was jealous of having a mom who expressed love for him, jealous that he did not get spanked as a form of punishment, and jealous that he had so many toys when she had had so little growing up. She also realized that what she had been referring to as his selfishness, was more accurately his positive ability to speak up for himself, something she had never done as a child and was only just now learning to do as an adult.

Although she had to admit to herself that she was a little embarrassed by both having these jealousies, and then subconsciously picking fights with Lucas, she was able to use this insight. By seeing that she still harbored very hurt feelings inside of herself, she was able to self-nurture and reclaim her wholeness. Amazingly, through this process of inner awareness and self-love, their parent/child relationship quality improved dramatically. Had she not practiced seeing their tension as a reflection of her own pain, she never would have experienced inner healing or the healing with Lucas.

Develop a Guiding Vision

In chapter 2 you spent some time exploring how you were raised as a means of identifying and developing your own unique parenting style. However, identifying how you were raised and what you would like to keep and discard of your upbringing is only the first step in consciously creating your parenting style. The next step is to clarify what your own views are. If you are partnered or are coparenting with others, the third step is to share these views with one another and to develop compatible parenting approaches for day-to-day situations. Clarifying your beliefs will lead you and your partner or coparents to the final step: developing a guiding vision.

Exercise

As you explore the answers to the following questions you may want to write in your journal or talk freely with a friend or partner. If you choose to do this exercise with a partner, allow this to be a one-sided conversation. The goal is to uncover what *your* beliefs are. Many people choose to do this exercise separately and then come together afterward with their coparents or partner to share their findings. Take the time to deeply explore your feelings about each question.

Questions to Help Clarify Your Parenting Style

- What is your view of children?

- What do you believe the role of a parent is?

- What do you believe the role of a child is?

- What is appropriate behavior for a child? How about for a parent?

- What is your style of discipline? Can you imagine exceptions? If so, in what kind of circumstances?

- How do you handle stress?

This exercise can be repeated throughout parenthood. You will find that your answers may often change as your parenting transforms with the developmental stages through which your child grows. Keeping a parenting journal will allow for you to notice the changes in your own perspective over time.

If you are parenting with others, it is important to create a safe environment for sharing your answers to these questions. It can be scary to share a different philosophy with the primary parent because the power dynamic is already not in your favor. It is very important, however, to discuss parenting philosophies and approaches among all involved parents. In so doing, you have the opportunity to reach a unified approach or to respect your differing styles. If you do not share your philosophies with one another, then you are more likely to automatically adopt the style of the primary parent and to feel resentful in the process. This exercise provides you with a map of your current perspectives. If you uncover basic philosophical differences, then you have concrete topics for discussion and inner exploration.

Creating Your Vision

You can use the information you discover from this inner reflection as a springboard for developing a concrete guiding vision.

Practicing this reflection is similar to developing vows for a commitment ceremony. You are generating a spiritual container for your family. When you have a guiding vision, it is easier to self-evaluate if you are acting in accordance with your own vision. It's easier to hold yourself to higher standards if you yourself have created them.

When you have a guiding vision, it's easier to decide how to respond in overwhelming times or when you have unclear internal messages about new phases of parenting. Of course, your guiding vision may need to be adjusted over the years. As you grow as a parent, your vision often grows as well.

Guiding visions can simply be a sentence or an idea that says it all for you, or it can be a paragraph or more that speaks to your philosophy. It is nice to write your vision out and frame it somewhere in your living space as a constant inspiration.

Sample Guiding Visions

- I will honor and respect my child(ren) in all of my actions and interactions.

- All members of our family are treated as equals. Through equity will come world peace.

- My love for my children guides me in all that I do.

- An orderly and respectful child leads to an orderly and respectful family.

- My children are not me; I support them fully in discovering and becoming who they are.

- Do unto others as you would have them do unto you.

Changing Direction Midstream

You do not always have to be right and your child does not always have to be wrong. It's acceptable for your child to be right. It is possible that neither of you are right, or that both of you are right. Although it takes humility, it's important to remember that even if you are in the middle of a disciplinary lecture, you can change your mind and take a different approach to the situation at hand.

You do not have to take yourself so seriously as to think that you need to continue something just because you started it. You might think that it is totally appropriate to speak harshly to your child about her having thrown the ball in the living room and breaking your favorite vase. However, thirty seconds into your diatribe, you realize that you are not treating your child with respect. It is OK to stop your yelling and say, "I am sorry for yelling at you. I am just very sad that my favorite vase is broken. There are reasons for the rules I set. I am upset that you did not follow the rule. And I am upset that my vase is broken. But I always love you, and I did not mean to treat you like you broke the vase on purpose."

This kind of conversation allows room for your child to both feel and to express their feelings. When parents use respectful communication instead of attacking communication, there is more room for your child to safely feel remorse and other feelings. When anyone is being attacked they automatically go on the defense as a self-protective measure. When you are in a defensive stance, it is harder to have authentic feelings. Being forced to apologize never served any child, but being allowed to feel remorse and to develop an authentic heartfelt apology is a gift you can give your child and yourself.

Stopping in the middle of what you are doing or saying and remembering your guiding vision takes practice. Demonstrating that everyone can make mistakes provides strong role modeling for our children. Teaching them that self-correction is always the preferred way of saving face will allow them to learn this skill early. When you think you are too proud to change your ways, you are modeling obstinacy over truth. Is that the message you want to send to your children?

Parenting Challenges

What do you do when you encounter challenges in parenting? Observe how you respond when you are challenged in your parenting. Do you feel helpless? Do you try to find something or someone to blame for your difficulty? Do you take time to introspect and examine the nature of the stress for you? Do you talk to other parents or read books for helpful suggestions? Do you try to ignore the challenge and hope that it will go away? What have you found to be useful in the ways that you respond to stressful parenting times? What have you found yourself doing that feeds the confusion?

There are many challenges in parenting. Some you will face with a partner or coparent; some you will face on your own. Whether or not you are a single parent, many of the challenges of parenting are within you. Being able and willing to look at the situation from as many angles as possible provides you with solutions. Every part of parenting is a phase. Thus it is helpful to put your current challenge into perspective knowing that it will soon pass. When you cannot easily find a solution to the challenge at hand, it can help to spend some time in silence. During this silence or meditation, pose yourself the question, "How can I best serve my child in this situation?" Usually, if you wait, a new answer will come to you.

There are times, however, where the challenge comes from not having the necessary skills needed for a specific phase or element of parenting. It's important not to self-isolate when a challenge is greater than you alone can handle and you really need help. When these situations arise, it can be helpful to register for a parenting class or a parents support group. Contacting your local community center, YMCA, church or temple, psychotherapists, or pediatricians will be helpful ways of identifying the resources in your area. Also, there are numerous parenting support networks online, and a plethora of books on most elements of parenting.

Insecurities in Parenting Roles

An interesting dynamic is both common and unique in same-sex partnered parents. Because there are two moms or two dads, the parents often find that they compare themselves to one another. They can compete for who is the "better" mom or dad or feel insecure that they are not as good a mom or dad as their partner. This is an emotional trap that is easy to fall into, but important to stay out of.

In heterosexual couples, parents tend not to compare themselves as much to one another because it is understood that their roles and approaches to parenting will be different. In queer families, there are no preset cultural assumptions made, so the rules and roles are up to us to define. We usually have to fight internalized stereotypes about what a mom or dad is to do. Just as GLBTs have had to debunk what a man or a woman is, so queer parents must debunk what a dad or mom is.

It may take practice to realize your value as a (nontraditional) parent. Yet, in any two-parent family, each parent has different qualities that they bring to parenthood. This is not based on gender. Inside of ourselves, we need to remember that difference is meant to be celebrated.

Relationship Dynamics

There are many dynamics within any relationship, some of which are life enhancing and some of which are life depleting. Relationship dynamics are not inherently a problem. However, depleting dynamics can have a negative impact on your whole family. This is especially so if you resent the dynamic, but you do not recognize your own participation in it. The word "dynamic" implies a relationship, thus if you do not like the dynamic, the most helpful way of shifting it is to take responsibility for and to change your role. When you personally claim responsibility for changing the dynamic, change will occur. If you choose instead to tell your partner, coparent, or child to change, you continue to deny that it is a dynamic that requires your participation for it to continue. It's most productive to discuss the dynamic you would like changed only after you have decided to alter your participation in it.

For example, Mark and Elly are coparenting their nine-year-old son Harry. Harry spends Sunday night through Thursday morning at Elly's apartment and Thursday after school through Sunday evening at Mark's apartment. They do not tend to see Harry when he is at the other's house, but often they talk with Harry on the phone. Mark was having a problem. He was frustrated because it always seemed like Harry would have lots of homework on Thursday night that was due on Friday. The work was usually assigned on Monday, but Harry would leave it all until Thursday to do. Thursday nights would be long and hard. It was not unusual for Harry to go to bed late, exhausted, and crying. Mark resented having to start their time together every week in a struggle around homework. He resented that he had to be the "heavy." He resented that Elly didn't require Harry to do his homework throughout the week.

Mark had tried talking to Harry about starting his work earlier in the week to no avail. Harry said he could never remember that he even had homework until it was too late at night. Mark had addressed Elly about the problem. This had not been helpful because Elly did not regard the situation as problematic. She felt that Harry was given too much homework and he shouldn't be forced to spend all day in school and then all afternoon completing schoolwork. Mark was becoming really angry. He felt trapped by the fact that neither Harry nor Elly prioritized Harry's homework and Harry's time management.

One day while venting to a friend, his friend suggested that Mark look at what he himself could do to change the situation, instead of what Elly and Harry weren't doing. It was as if a light bulb went off in Mark's head. He hadn't realized he was just as responsible for the dynamic as they were. He came up with a list of things he could change. He could call the teacher and ask her to e-mail him the homework assignments for the week every Monday. Then he could call Harry each night and help him remember to start on various projects. He could go over to Elly's house and help Harry set up a place to study. He could more actively teach Harry study and time-management skills. He could see if Elly would let him hire a tutor for Harry during the first half of the week. He could see if he could switch days with Elly so that he had Harry during the first half of the week.

When Mark realized there were so many options he no longer felt helpless in the situation. He implemented some of his ideas and Harry started to do homework every night, not just Thursday night. After taking action he felt more confident and was able to schedule a time to talk with Elly. Together, they were able to devise an ongoing approach to homework that was a respectful compromise between what each parent thought was best. This teamwork solution most likely would not have been possible had Mark continued to think that this was Elly's and Harry's problem.

Self-Reflection in the GLBT Family

Maintaining clarity within each of our family units is essential. Because our families are self-created, we do not usually have pre-established roles for each family member. Thus we have the power and the obligation to self-define our roles. It is through clear communication within ourselves and with each other, and through heartfelt honesty, that we can nurture and support the bonds within our families. Most families never discuss exactly what each person sees their own role and the role of coparents, partners, and other family members to be. However, when you begin your family from a place of self-definition, it is very helpful to actually go through the process of self-defining!

Exercise

To clarify what the role of each person in your family is, it is helpful to ask yourself the following questions. Truly take the time to explore and create the clearest answers that you can:

- What is the role of each person in your child's family?

- Have you, as adults, clearly defined these roles together?

- Have you already established mechanisms to allow for these roles to change and grow over time?

- Have you established a method for evaluating how parenting as a partnership or team is going?

- Are there ways in which you feel that you or another family member is not fulfilling their role?

- Would you like to address this directly?

Clarifying your parenting style can help to bring awareness and focus to the choices you make every day. When you take the time to explore your beliefs and ideals, it is much more likely that you will become the parent you want to be. Each of the questions explored in this exercise relates directly to our day-to-day interactions with our children. When we know our ideals, we can evaluate our interactions and make adjustments as necessary.

Craig and James are a strong example of how clarifying roles can benefit and deepen relationships. Craig and James moved in together when James' children were three and seven. Both of the children consider themselves to have two dads and they don't seem to make a significant distinction between them. Craig and James feel that they have equal parenting roles in all areas but one—discipline. When Craig first joined the family, he was very careful to not interfere with James' role as the children's dad. He hoped he would come to be accepted by the children, but understood that it can take time. As he had never been a parent before, he deferred to James in most situations. The children quickly welcomed Craig into the family and Craig became an integral part of their lives.

In terms of final decisions and areas of discipline, however, Craig continued to defer to James. James seemed to really need that, because the few times Craig had tried to give the children time-outs James had gotten quite upset. Also, when Craig registered the children for an after-school class at the community center, James had been perturbed that he had not registered them himself. Given these reactions, Craig decided that it would be easier to simply defer to James. However, he also felt like he wasn't being allowed to be a full parent. Craig started to worry that James was going to treat him as a stepparent forever, even though the children did not seem to hold that distinction. This hurt his heart.

Eventually, in couples therapy, the issue was brought up. Craig and James had never discussed the roles they each played as parents or what their ideal family would look like to them. They found this clarifying exercise helpful. It was quite a blind spot for them to not have explored this together because one of their weekly relationship habits had always been to visualize together and to set intentions as to how they would like their lives to be. They would set their goals individually and jointly and then support each other in attaining those goals.

However, they soon recognized why they had not touched parenting as a subject of joint exploration—parenting seemed to hit many emotional buttons. With the help of their therapist, Craig was able to let James know that he really wanted to be a *full* parent in all ways and that to have to hold back in certain areas made him feel like a subordinate. Craig said he really wanted to parent jointly with James and to have a parenting relationship together based on trust and mutual respect.

James was able to say that he felt safe being the one holding the reins and that he had not even realized that he was still the ultimate decision-maker in the family. He too wanted a parenting relationship based in partnership. He was scared to share that deeply, but he did not want Craig to feel subordinate.

From a place of love and partnership they approached making changes that would support their vision and their desired roles. James practiced getting out of the way and allowing Craig to discipline the children when necessary; Craig supported James in this process and tried to resist the habit of deferring to James. Their relationship deepened and they learned new skills to approach their parenting from a more unified place.

Evolving Roles and Relationships in Our Families

Establishing a common vision regarding the roles of each person in your child's family takes time. Often the way things start off is not what they become. A single parent, for example, might start off assuming that they need to work full-time to support their family. Over time, however, they may feel that day care providers are raising their child. So, in clarifying that it is more important to spend time with their child, they decide to cut back to part-time work and to adjust their lifestyle.

Families change and transform and so do our roles in each other's lives. You might have become a parent with a girlfriend or boyfriend who, although not interested originally in being a parent, finds they want more of a parental role in your child's life. You may have a friend who volunteers to baby-sit, who becomes so bonded with your child over time that they become a coparent. You may enter into a group living situation and have to identify and clarify the roles of your housemates in your child's life. Staying clear about what your intentions and desires are for each family member helps to avoid confusion, unintentional overstepping of boundaries, and unmet expectations. It also serves to strengthen your family. This level of clarity can have far-reaching positive affects in your life. When you are clear about roles in one area of life, it naturally carries over to all of your relationships.

Having More Children

Many queer families decide to have more than one child. Here again is an area where our families can depart from traditional heterosexual models. When most heterosexual families decide to have a second child, the same parents commonly raise the new child, or the children will be half-siblings in a stepparent relationship. In the majority of heterosexual families, the children are raised by at least one of their biological parents.

When GLBTs decide to have another child all the questions we had to answer the first time must be considered once more. Women partnered with women who plan to birth their baby must decide who will be pregnant this time. Two or more parent households must decide if this new child will have the same primary parent(s) or not. Partnered parents choosing to adopt must decide who will be the adoptive parent.

Next the questions of biology arise: Will you use the same donor/surrogate or will you use another source? If your children have different known donors, what, if any, will the donors' relationships be with the other children? How will your children feel if one has an involved donor and another does not?

These questions and numerous others present themselves to us when we want to expand our families. It is important to take time to thoughtfully explore the changing dynamics and parental roles a new child will inevitably bring to your family, making sure that your choices feel solid and are aligned with your family vision. The decision to have more children can bring many issues old and new to the forefront. Remember to approach these issues with sensitivity. As we continue to recreate our families we are all tender and vulnerable. It is an excellent time to enter into short-term personal or relationship counseling.

Reaching Resolution about the Origins of Your Child

As GLBT families there is often an element of compromise that was inevitable in the way that you became a parent. As a single parent, it would be nice to be able to create a baby on your own. As gay men it would be nice not to have to depend on women. As lesbian women it would be nice not to have to depend on men to make babies. Using a surrogate mother, a sperm donor, a sperm bank, adopting, or coparenting can all feel like they involve some level of compromise. It is important to work through any unresolved feelings that you have about the origins of your child so that you do not unintentionally or subtly communicate them.

For example, if you did not feel comfortable using frozen sperm, or you will never know the donor and you feel guilty about your choices, you must take the time to explore these feelings and move on. Otherwise, when your child asks you why you made the choices you did, you could find yourself apologizing. Just like a child never wants to hear that they were an "accident," no child ever wants to hear you apologize for your choices in how you became their parent. Your insecurities about the choices you made can undermine your child's sense of self-esteem.

Before your child is of the age to engage in lengthy discussions with you about their origins, practice answering their possible questions. If you detect regret, shame, or sadness in your responses take the time to explore your feelings and to develop new responses. Your child does not need to hear of the compromises that you made until they are old enough to fully understand that you would have done anything to become their parent. A child does not ever want to feel like they were a mistake or a second choice.

Unresolved Feelings about Race, Culture, and Ethnicity

This holds equally true if you have unresolved feelings about your child being inter- or transracial, or inter- or transcultural. Many parents adopt or birth babies from different races, cultures, and/or ethnicities. This can bring up anticipated or unexpected feelings of personal displacement or estrangement from your child. These issues can be highlighted if your family of origin or your community brings any attitudes of racism or ethnocentrism toward your family. The issue is complex and all of the possible intermixing within a family only add to the personal complexities.

Unfortunately racism and ethnocentrism are still quite prevalent and may, at times, have a significant impact on your family. However, when resolving your own issues around the racial and ethnic complexities within your own family, it is often helpful to come to peace with the origins of your child. These inner discussions are often interlinked.

For example, Daphne, a Chinese-American woman is partnered with Shani, an African-American woman. Daphne was to be the birth mother of their children as Shani is infertile. Because of the interracial element of their own relationship, they were already dealing with not only homophobia, but the racism within their own communities. It was not easy to choose their sperm donor. They had two choices of known donors in their lives—one was an Asian-American man who was their best friend from college, and one was a white man who was a friend of a friend whom they did not know well but who was willing. An important part of the decision came down to what ethnicity the sperm donor should be. In making this decision, they had to confront their own internal issues about race and ethnicity.

It was difficult enough that Shani's role as nonbirth mom would not be recognized and that they were both gay women of color. They finally decided that it would be too difficult for Shani to not have any visual resemblance to her child. They ultimately chose a biracial white/black donor from the sperm bank. Although her daughter is much lighter skinned than Shani, she is much darker than Daphne. They feel that they have blended themselves into their child.

Using a sperm bank was not their first choice, but other issues clearly prioritized themselves. After she was born, both moms found that they were embarrassed to say that they had used a sperm bank. One of their friends pointed this out and asked why they had made a choice they did not feel good about. When they heard this feedback on how they were communicating they faced the fact that they were experiencing internalized homophobia.

They realized that they were afraid that others would think less of their daughter because they had purchased the sperm for her at a sperm bank. They feared that people would not think of her as real, or that she would be an outcast because she did not have a father. They felt that people would more easily accept a child of lesbians if there were a man in their lives. Out of this fear came shame about their decision. When they identified the issue, they were each able to find their pride for having created their baby their way. After that, they no longer brought up the sperm bank because it had lost its hold over them. Fortunately for them, they confronted this issue before their daughter started to ask about her origins.

Taking Time for Ourselves

It is vitally important that parents find time to balance all sides of themselves. It is all too common to ignore our own needs as we become so absorbed in the needs of our children. However, if you do not refill the well that supplies your child, then you will not have much to give. Parenting requires endless amounts of physical and emotional interaction. To be able to truly be there for our children with patience and love, we must take time to nourish ourselves.

Nourishing yourself and pursuing personal loves and hobbies is also invaluable modeling. Many modern day children experience their parents as work machines. Showing through example that other things are as important as work and that it is important to pursue your interests demonstrates self-love to your children. This can provide them—and you—with a healthy sense of balance.

Parenting is never what you think it will be. It is so much more demanding and rewarding than you ever imagined. Returning to our sense of love, joy, respect, and fulfillment as a daily practice helps those same feelings to radiate within us and through our families. Being a parent has the potential to be unbelievably fulfilling. When we learn to parent consciously, we experience parenthood as a path of love.

PART II

Our Place in Society

4

Coming Out Every Day

Perhaps the greatest gift that we could leave to our children and to the world would be to have created a more open and accepting society. We must create a culture that embraces and celebrates the differences that exist in our incredibly diverse world. One of the best ways that we can achieve this change is to increase the visibility of a variety of families.

Come Out, Come Out Wherever You Are

As GLBT families become more and more visible, the general population will become more familiar and comfortable interfacing with us. When there are enough out GLBT families, we will become a natural variation of family rather than being seen as an anomaly. When we are closeted, our numbers seem much smaller than they really are. It's easier to create change for a group of people who are willing to be counted. Our children deserve a secure place for themselves; and we're the ones who can best facilitate the changes that will make society a welcome place for everyone. Come out, come out wherever you are—we need you!

Reasons to Be Out

As most of us know, there are many reasons to be as out as you can at any point in your life. It is important to be out for moral, personal, health, and political reasons. You have a right to live your life as who you are. It can be very damaging to your self-esteem to live a life where you feel you have to hide a vital part of yourself from others. When you have to monitor your interactions, and omit important pieces of information about your daily life, it feels like hiding a big secret. As time passes, the weight of the burden of secrecy grows and grows. We do not have to hide or be ashamed of who we are. If we do not share this information with others, however, we act as if our sexual orientation is something worthy only of hiding. As you'll read below, it is doubly important to be out as a queer parent.

Sustaining Your Relationships

The weight of being closeted can actually have negative affects on your ability to maintain healthy intimate relationships. Not only does it require tremendous energy (that could be used elsewhere) to maintain secrecy, but the lack of openness about a relationship can squelch its possibilities. How can you love with an open heart if you are afraid others might see your love? If you're ashamed of your love and feel it should be hidden, how can you foster deepening intimacy? It is common to have stress within your relationship around who is out and who is closeted. The very fact that others do not automatically respect our love for each other is an immeasurable stress on each of our relationships—a stress that the majority of heterosexuals do not experience.

Physical Health

The stress of staying closeted can have negative effects on your physical health. It is now common knowledge that stress can manifest itself negatively in the body. It's also more broadly understood that there is a mind/body relationship. This means that fear, shame, and secrecy can lead to impaired health and even, at times, to illness.

Visibility

The only way to ensure a more open and accepting society is to allow others to know our sexual orientations. Only then will society see our families as normal and something that is comfortable to be around. For people who don't have openly gay people in their lives and have never come in contact with a gay family, there can be many preconceived negative images. However, when your children play in the street with their children, and you feed their cats while they are away, you become the same as any other family. Therefore, many GLBTs feel there is a political obligation to be out. GLBT visibility will lead the way to a more open and accepting society.

It's Doubly Important to Be Out as a Parent

Most parents have dealt with the issue of being out prior to having children. In fact, not being able to come out is a primary deterrent to having children for many gays. Most gay parents are, indeed, out in at least one area of their lives. Many gay parents, however, are far from being out everywhere, and some hide their queer identities from their children.

The reasons to come out and live openly as a lesbian, gay, bisexual, or transgendered person are never so great as when you are a parent. We are the people our children look to to teach them what is right and what is wrong, what is good and what is bad. We have the biggest influence on their sense of self-esteem. If we are not fundamentally comfortable with who we are, how can we expect our children to feel comfortable with who they are? How can we expect our children to respect us, if we do not respect ourselves? How can we instill respect for diversity, if we are afraid to show our own true colors? As parents we want what is best for our children. Thus, having children is often the incentive needed to take the risks necessary to come out once and for all.

Most parents share a common set of important qualities that they hope to instill within their child. As a parent, you most likely want to teach your child to tell the truth. You most likely want to teach your child to feel good about who they are. You most likely want to teach your child to feel comfortable in the world. And you most likely want your child to have a high sense of self-esteem.

If you are closeted, you are living in fear and shame; you are showing that you do not feel comfortable in the world and you are not proud of who you are. When you are closeted, the qualities that you are directly modeling for your child are the absolute opposite of the life qualities you would like your child to know. This double standard is painfully apparent to children. Actions speak louder than words.

When your children are young they are learning about family and meaningful relationships from you. What you model will become their formative memories. It is from this base that they will unconsciously attempt to create their own relationships. Your means of relating will continue to influence your child as they form their own relationships.

Thus, if you are partnered and your children see you showing affection toward one another, and if they hear you use terms of endearment toward each other, then love and affection become normalized for them. Your relationship with your partner is seen as one of family. Or when you date, if your children see you getting ready, and they meet your date at the door, they see it as normal that Daddy dates men sometimes and women sometimes. When they are older, and they have the capacity to understand the full nature of your relationship, it has always been seen as normal to them. When something is normalized from a young age it is natural to internalize it and to take pride in it.

How Closeting Affects Our Children

On the other hand, if you are partnered, but when your children are around you refrain from touching each other and you speak and hold your body in a restricted way, then that is what your child is learning. If you hide the true nature of your partner relationship from your young child, you are affecting their very perception of what intimacy is and you are laying the foundation for their adult intimate relationships. So not only are you not being honest, you are modeling restricted and constricted expression. In effect, your shame is also communicating homophobia to your child. They sense that you feel uncomfortable about something when you are with your partner. They see that although you are emotionally and physically free and expressive with them, you are not with your partner. You may be teaching your own child to be homophobic.

Shame, fear, and secrecy can have a devastating impact on the health of your family unit. Not only is the weight of this burden heavy on your personal shoulders, it is a weight the whole family must carry. It can be too much strain on a relationship.

If you are not out to your children, you are doing them a great disservice. It is an honor to be raised in any family that wants and loves their children. The largest category of parents who do not come out to their children are the parents who come out themselves after they already have children. Having an honest relationship with a child is a priority for most parents. If you are not out to your children, regardless of whether you are actively hiding your sexual orientation from them, you are affecting the depth of honesty available in your parental relations.

Many parents do not reveal their sexual orientation to their children because they are afraid that their children will not understand and may even reject them. The fear of being rejected by your own child can be debilitating. Some parents who are gay from the start figure they will wait until their child is old enough to figure it out on their own. Don't allow it to be your child's burden to figure out your sexual orientation and what is "different" about your family. When parents do not directly discuss their sexual orientation with their child from the beginning, it is difficult for the child to bring it up, especially when they are young. your parent/child relationship may be the only relationship that will continue throughout your entire life. Pay your child or children the respect they deserve and live honestly with them. Ultimately you will be very happy that you did.

Coming Out When You Are Already a Parent

If *you* come out when you are already a parent, the issue of when and whether to come out to your children is certainly more complex. It is relevant whether you have primary custody, whether your sexual orientation is known and accepted by your ex and your family, and what the general state of affairs toward gay people is in your area. It is absolutely worthwhile to hire an excellent divorce attorney if you anticipate this to be an issue. Contact the National Center for Lesbian Rights (NCLR) (see References and Resources) for referrals in your area and pro bono possibilities. Do not let a lack of money stand in your way—there are defense funds set up solely for the purpose of securing custody when it's challenged due simply to sexual orientation.

The concerns about losing custody can be very real and should not be glossed over. Many parents, however, are just experiencing the normal coming out process we all must go through and are simply afraid that others will reject them. In these cases, there is often no actual risk of losing custody; but it can certainly take time to learn to differentiate internal homophobia from a real threat of external homophobia. A good book on the subject of coming out to your children, especially if you came out after a divorce is *The Final Closet: The Gay Parent's Guide for Coming Out to Their Children,* by Rip Corley (1990).

If you are not out to your child, how will you raise them to be accepting and tolerant of all people, including gays? If you don't raise them to resist negative biases and stereotypes, then it will be more difficult when indeed your sexual orientation is revealed to them. If your children have internalized and think they agree with conventional homophobic ideas, they will have to unlearn them as part of coming to terms with you.

Coming Out to Older Children

When you do come out to your older child, because that is when they are adopted into your family, that is when you yourself come out, or that is when you are ready to share this information with them, you can expect a lot of questions. Some of the questions and responses of older children are accepting and inquisitive, such as, "Oh, so that's why Sally always spend the night" and "Does anybody else know this?" Often, however, there are more difficult responses that children have initially before they adjust to the information. Such responses may include:

- That's disgusting!

- Don't come in while I'm dressing or taking a bath anymore, OK?

- If anyone finds out you're queer, I'm going to kill myself. How could you ruin my life like this?

- I can't believe you're telling me this. Couldn't you at least have waited until I left home?

- How am I suppose to live with you now?

It is also common that, unless your children have been raised in a very progressive home that challenges bias directly, they will never have truly questioned the homophobia that abounds. As a result you may have to go through an awkward phase of unwinding their beliefs and gaining or regaining their trust in you. The younger the child, the easier the acceptance process. When you show children that your love for them is not contingent on their blind acceptance of your sexual orientation, they will recognize the support they are receiving and will be more likely to accept you more quickly.

If You Insist on Being Closeted

If you insist on being closeted, it is essential to know that younger children are unable to understand what is a secret and what is not. In fact, most younger children are not able to actually keep a complex secret that involves changing so many regular aspects of their lives. How can you expect a preschool-age child who lives with her dad and daddy to remember that at school and with friends she has to call her daddy "Fred." Not only does she have to change his name, but she has to remember that "Fred" is a "housemate," and "Fred" does not sleep with Dad in their bedroom; he has a room of his own. What initially seemed like asking your child to keep a secret is, in fact, asking your child to create a fantasy world for the benefit of others. As a result, if you want to be closeted, you must be closeted from your children. Young children love to talk and share. It is part of their authentic nature. Knowing that you have no control over what they say when you are not around should help to guide you in what they see and are exposed to. My own daughter is a good example.

In kindergarten one morning the children were discussing breakfast. My daughter, who was infatuated with both carbonation and my new girlfriend, announced proudly, "My mom's girlfriend drinks beer for breakfast every morning!" Now fortunately for us, the teachers approached me with this report. After laughing heartily, I explained to them that my daughter did not know the difference between beer and soda. Colleen actually drank Coke for breakfast every morning. However, had I been closeted, I would no longer be and her teachers could easily have surmised that my daughter was living with an alcoholic lesbian and feared for her safety.

Thus, if you do not want others to innocently find out about your sexual orientation then you must deliberately hide it from your child. You must not show physical affection in front of your child. And you must not let your child see you lying in bed with your date or partner of the same sex. In fact, if you live with your partner, they need to either have their own bedroom or at least a separate bed in your room to perpetuate the illusion.

You must also remember this when you are deciding what your child should call each of you. Do not choose a name that is traditionally a parental name, such as Mom. Instead you must choose names like "Aunt Kate." Likewise, if you do not want your child to answer the neighbor who asks "Where is your Daddy?" by saying, "In bed naked with Uncle Joey," you need to think about these things. You must be very careful about what your child is exposed to even when they are preverbal because they will often talk about it later on.

It is very hard work to live this kind of lie in your home for the benefit of your child. However, if you are absolutely going to remain closeted, then it is essential when your children are young to do the lying for them. It will harm your relationship with them when they discover the truth, but it is the only way to avoid unwanted outings.

Don't Blame Your Child

You may begin to resent your child if you are not out to them because you can feel like they are intruding on your freedom of expression. You or your partner can feel like there is a competition for intimacy and private time. This is common because when you are closeted, you cannot include natural intimacy with your partner in the time you share with your child. In most families this kind of intimacy—such as hugging each other, or dancing together—is effortlessly integrated into family time. Resenting your child can feel awful, and it can also put added stress onto your adult relationship. Unfortunately, most young children are emotional sponges and, thus, can feel that they are not wanted; they just don't know why. This leads to internal confusion and feelings of rejection and shame on their part.

Asking your children to lie for you is serious business. It will affect your relationship and, if done too frequently, will affect their trust of you and their self-esteem—not to mention their attitude about gays.

When you expect too much from your children, they suffer. A child should not be punished for forgetting who it is OK to talk to, what is OK to talk about, or for making a mistake. Asking a child to shroud their life in secrets is asking your child to internalize shame about who you are, who they are, and your family as a whole. If done on a regular basis, it will only backfire.

When Children Are Told
to Be Closeted

As an out family living in a liberal area (Berkeley, California), it is very hard for me to imagine asking my children to be closeted. In fact, I would choose to relocate my family in order for them to be able to discuss freely whatever they chose to discuss and not have to hold a secret.

To a young child, family is life. The identification with family is crucial to the development of self. If the child is told to not tell anyone about their family (the center and source of their life and love), then internal confusion starts to multiply.

I can imagine the fear in which closeted families live when I think of traveling to other countries where you can be arrested and never seen again for being gay. There is much of the world that I would like to travel to with my children. However, we will never go there when they are young because I do not feel it would be safe for us to travel as an openly gay family, and I will not ask my children to closet. Asking your children to closet is asking them to internalize shame, fear, and guilt. It is telling them that you are not OK, they are not OK, and that the world is not a safe place. You are also encouraging them to lie when directly questioned.

As children age developmentally they will be able to understand the potential ramifications of a homophobic reaction to your family. However, children ten and under cannot fully understand homophobia in a way that will not cause them to internalize and personalize it, and to be terrorized by it.

If you are in situations where you are asking your children to closet for you, perhaps you should ask yourself why you are having them do this and if it truly is better than whatever the feared ramifications would be if they were to live openly.

Being Out with Your
Family of Origin

Many GLBT families are out everywhere except to their families of origin. Coming out to your parents may be the most difficult thing that you ever do. Because of the huge—and often realistic—fear of rejection, some people never do come out. This is one of the hardest lies to live. Choosing whether to come out to your parents is a very personal decision. There is no right answer.

Unfortunately, homophobia leads to a fracturing of families. If you choose to remain closeted your child can have grandparents. However, being closeted will also usually require you and your child to openly lie at various points in time. It also denies your family structure and, unless you are single, being closeted undermines the integrity of your family unit. Being out often irreparably separates the grandparents from you and your children. Being queer in a homophobic family can feel like a no-win situation for all involved.

Some people choose to remain closeted and some choose to come out. Others choose to do something in between and refer to their "roommate." If you choose to stay closeted to only your parents, you will eventually be outed by a well-meaning friend who did not realize you were closeted to your folks.

So You Thought You Were Out?

Many parents are shocked to discover the levels of coming out on a daily basis that are required as part of the job description of being a GLBT parent. Even if you have been out for many years, it is nothing like being a parent. The daily level of coming out is definitely accentuated in the early parenting years when you accompany your baby or young child to all of their social events as well as your own.

The state of being associated with needing to come out is uncomfortable. Many people living an out life have not been in this state since they first came out. For some, the last time they experienced this unique set of emotions was many years ago. Thus, it can feel unsettling and disconcerting to have to be in that state again.

Yet, when you are in the grocery store with your baby and the checkout person says, "John, I never knew you were married," your heart can start racing again. How are you going to respond? Are you going to say, "I am not married. In fact, I am gay. This baby is my daughter Samantha. We are not genetically linked. Actually, my partner Greg is the biological father. We are coparenting her with her two moms. Thanks for asking!" Or are you going to say something ambiguous like, "You don't have to be married to have a kid." How out are you going to be in situations where people don't even know what they are asking or assuming?

Exploratory Exercise

Coming out as a parent has many more twists to it than just coming out as an individual. As you journal in response to the following questions, take note of your physical and emotional responses—they can often be revealing. These are important questions to pose to yourself and to discuss with your partner. When you come to realize that omitting the truth can hurt not only yourself but your children and partner as well, choosing to come out can look more appealing.

- Are you going to tell everyone that your partner gave birth and you are now a mom?

- If you are a birth mom, will you take every opportunity to let people know that you are a lesbian whether or not you are partnered?

- When you adopt a child are you going to reference your partner to everyone or let some people assume that you are a single parent?

- If you don't bring it up, why? Is it because you hope to protect yourself or someone else from a potential homophobic response?

- Are you, in effect, closeting yourself? How does that feel?

- When you are partnered or parenting with others how does it feel to not acknowledge the fact that you are parenting with someone you do not always mention?

- Imagine your partner or other parents not acknowledging you, how does that feel?

- If you are a single parent, will you come out to everyone? How will you decide?

Living life openly as who you are has amazing benefits. It can also be scary. The hardest part for most people is the actual act of revealing your sexual orientation—saying out loud that you are gay. For most, coming out is significantly more difficult than living your life openly.

Living an Out Lifestyle

The opportunity to come out arises frequently when you are a parent. Sometimes it is confusing trying to decide when it is important to reveal that you are gay and deciding when it is not needed. Often times, parents decide to come out as a means of protecting their children from homophobic reactions from others. For example, before you sign your child up for camp you call the director, come out, and make sure that the camp is a suitable match.

When your child is a baby, you find yourself coming out to make room for yourself, to create a world that will honor you and your family. It is usually not so much to protect your baby from homophobic reactions of bigotry, but rather for you to acknowledge and respect the family that you have created.

Thus, even though the server at the restaurant did not realize she was asking a loaded question when she said "Now who's cute little baby is this?" if you do not say "both of ours" when you respond, who are you protecting? What are you communicating to yourself and to each other if you cannot acknowledge the sanctity of your family to a perfect stranger? What is the worst response that server could have? Scrunch up her face and say "I see," refuse to make eye contact, decide that you cannot eat in that restaurant? If she does none of the above, but also does not understand what you mean and continues "I bet she has her father's eyes," you can respond, "We have never met her donor," or "Actually she looks nothing like her donor," or "It's funny, she has a lot of features in common with all four of her parents," or something equally suitable to your situation.

Is it worth denying your family to theoretically make someone feel more comfortable? When you are a private person, having to come out as a parent every day can feel very exposing. Try to resist using privacy as a reason to stay closeted. Privacy and shame should not be confused. It is natural to not want to rock the boat. It is also natural to have children and to be proud of your family. In the United States, having a family, having children, is considered to be a big accomplishment as well it should be. Take Pride in your beauty.

Coming out may never feel quite natural to you, but for most it becomes easier with time. Consider this next example. Bobbie and Candace come out on the phone to all service providers who are coming to their apartment. This gives the provider the option to not come to their apartment if they would rather not. Although at first this may seem a bit extreme or shame based, it is not. This started in response to a plumber who came to their house and then kept muttering about "filthy dykes" under his breath while he was working. Their four-year-old was the one who heard these comments because she was so interested in the workings of the toilet he was fixing. She asked her parents what a "filthy dyke" was at bedtime that night and the story unraveled. Committed to never allowing another homophobic person into their home, they now come out on the phone.

There certainly comes a time in your child's life when you stop doing the coming out and it is up to your child to decide whether and with whom they discuss their family structure. However, until they reach that point, there will be many, many times when you will be making the decision. How comfortable you are with discussing your family sends a direct message to your child. If this continues to be an area of discomfort for you, take the time to explore the feelings that arise for you and practice answers to anticipated questions.

Passive Ways of Coming Out

There are multiple passive ways of coming out. You can send holiday greeting cards from your family that include photos. You can refer to your partner or coparents in casual conversation. You can put all relevant family members on religious, school, and athletic team rosters. You can display a family photo on your desk at work.

There are ways to come out that don't leave room for response. These are disclosing statements woven into conversation. Such as, "As a lesbian I am particularly interested in . . ." or "I was at the local gay bar last night taking two-step lessons. It sure is fun to dance" or "I am afraid I can't make it that night, I have to set up chairs at the Male to Female Transgender Conference at that time." Some people feel that this form of coming out is easier and more appropriate than trying to say something that makes a big deal of it. The choice is personal, and both passive and nonpassive modes of communication are effective.

Symbols of Pride

There are symbols that indicate if someone is gay. Although many non-gays do not know these symbols, they are still very useful. The rainbow flag is one of the most widely recognized symbols of gay pride. Children love rainbows and usually take a lot of pleasure in the fact that the rainbow is a symbol of their family. Hang a rainbow flag from your home, or post one in the window of your apartment. Put a rainbow flag bumper sticker on your car. Wear rainbow or pink triangle jewelry. Teach your children gay symbology: point out pink triangles, rainbow flags, etc., whenever you come across them. Children love to feel like they are part of a tribe.

Being Out in Your Home

Your home can be a great source of gay Pride. Your home can nurture, validate, and celebrate your gayness. It can serve as a haven for you and your family, and it can inspire questions and curiosity from others who visit your home. Other people can be passively educated when entering your living space.

Overt Sexual Expression

You may want to consider removing all signs of overt sexual expression from your child's environment. This is important for all parents in our puritan society. However, for gays, who are often seen as perverts, anything that can be construed as pornography can and has been used against us. This means that items such as sexy or graphic books, videos, sex toys, and photographs should be out of sight and reach of children.

For many gays, being out and proud includes being out and proud about sex. You can feel comfortable kissing and snuggling openly, but common sense and our cultural mores dictate that actual sexual activity should be conducted away from the children. Because our sexuality has been so criminalized, many GLBTs have become very open in their homes with sexual artwork and other objects. When you have children, it becomes imperative to try to separate the sexual aspects of being gay from the daily aspects of our lives. Our children need to be surrounded by our culture, but they should be sheltered from explicit sexuality. This is safest for us all.

I know of one family in Arkansas where the dad came out after he had children. His ex-wife was not very comfortable with their children spending time alone with him after the divorce. She felt his gayness would "rub off" on their children. She had primary custody. One day, playing hide-and-seek the children found a graphic gay male sex book in their father's bedroom. They found the images both funny and con- fusing. They put the book back where they found it and the dad didn't know they had been looking at it. He found out about it the next day, however. The children had started talking about the images at dinner at their mom's house. She hit the roof, and had finally found the evidence she needed to go back to court.

Photos, Books, Art Doodads, and More

There are numerous ways to be out and proud in your house that are not explicitly sexual. The changing table seems to be a place that inspires Gay Pride. I have seen photo montages of Gay Pride marches, rainbow mobiles, gay slogans, or inspiring posters hung just where baby can view. I actually think, although probably not consciously, parents are putting these images in a place where they (and their baby) will be able to affirm themselves many times a day.

I have found that having gay photographic coffee-table books pro- vides many opportunities for addressing children's unvoiced questions and voracious curiosity. This is a way that we can help to answer ques- tions from our children's friends.

There are some beautiful gay history books and books about gay families that include lovely photos. Other suggestions of ways to be out and proud in your home are to have rainbow art doodads such as pot- holders or candlesticks, to display photos of your queer friends and fam- ily, and to wear gay friendly T-shirts. Your home does not need to be a commercial for gay identity. But what we have often come to accept as a natural part of us can be intentionally fostered and supported in our children and in their friends who play within our walls through visibility in our homes.

Are You Out at Work?

As with all areas of your life, there is not a "right" way to be at work. However, the only way that GLBTs are going to make progress in securing equal rights for ourselves is to be out and to organize against discrimination. If you determine that it would not be safe for you to be out, then so be it. Certainly the easiest way to be out at work is to come out up front. If you start your job being out and you are hired, then you usually have little to worry about.

Some people have concerns that if their place of work knew of their sexual orientation then they might lose their job or never progress up the corporate ladder. For women, people of color, and other people who are already discriminated against in the workforce, this can be a significant concern. Some people who are out in all other areas of life choose to be closeted at work. They feel that their personal life has no relationship to their work life.

Some people choose to be partially out at work. This means that perhaps a select person or group of people know that they are GLBT. Other people may have shared that they are a parent, but are not out about being gay. When you are a queer parent it is difficult to reveal your parental status while omitting your sexual orientation. Some people do not feel that it is an option to even share that they are a parent because it would naturally bring up questions and they do not want to be forced to tell a lie. Others feel that they may suffer discrimination for being an unmarried parent.

If you choose to be out at work as a GLBT parent, then you will be able to share freely in conversations with workmates, take personal calls more easily at work, and attend work functions as a family. You will also be able to make strides not only for LGBTs, but for LGBTs family rights. For example, insist on or request the same bonding time that heterosexual parents receive when your baby is born or adopted.

Some GLBTs need to remain closeted at work. Until society has become more accepting of difference, there will always be those of us who choose the closet. More and more GLBTs are out at work, which is slowly transforming the entire workforce into a safer place. The trickle down effect, however, takes time.

Unfortunately, if you remain closeted at work then you will always have to actively screen what you mention about your personal life. This level of compartmentalizing is inherently stressful. It requires constant self-monitoring and can be emotionally painful.

Professional Closets

If your place of work does not know that you are a parent, you will probably suffer on a day-to-day level. You will naturally want to share in the discussions of the weekend and of developmental milestones your child is encountering, but you must keep quiet. As you hear other parents speak with pride about their children, your work associates may not even know that your child exists. Needless to say, this can undermine your own sense of self-worth as a parent. In addition, the isolation can become quite extreme. Many parents receive informal support at work. Likewise, if your place of employment does not know that you are a parent, who will be called when your child is sick? What if there is a family emergency? These are the situations in which parents cannot plan ahead.

When you hide the fact that you are a parent, you begin to feel as if you have something to hide. It becomes a self-destructive circle. This form of omission can become lying. It can feel as though you are keeping a very big secret. If anyone finds out, which they inevitably will, they may feel like you cannot be trusted—not because you are gay, but because you acted as if you weren't a parent.

I know a female attorney who is a partner in a large firm. Although she has been an out lesbian inside her firm from the start, she is not out to her clients. She brings her partner to firm holiday parties, but does not have a photo of her on her desk. This originally was not a problem for her because she did not feel that her clients needed to know any personal information about her.

However, when she became pregnant her clients felt free to comment and to ask her questions. Both she and her firm felt that it would not be appropriate for her to come out; she would run the risk of losing very big clients for the firm. They lost one client because when asked if her husband was happy she stammered that she did not have a husband. After that she thought she would avoid prodding conversations by wearing a "wedding" ring. But she was wrong. She heard things like, "Must have been a shotgun wedding, who is the lucky son of a gun" and "I'll have to invite you and your husband out for dinner to celebrate, what did you say his name was?"

The situations she endured could have been included in a comedy, only they weren't funny. After her maternity leave she approached her partners. She said that she was no longer willing to lie about who she is. Omission and privacy protection were fine, but directly lying was not. They all agreed that she should not be forced to lie, and she stayed with the firm.

Coming Out to Parents of Your Child's Friends

Most parents find it is necessary to come out to the parents of their children's friends if those children will be coming to play at your home. The primary purpose of coming out prior to having them over is to prevent any emotionally painful homophobic backlash in the future. Whether to come out as a single, gay parent is always a question. However, children's friendships can be long lasting. If you date, your child may mention that at school or to friends. Word can travel back to the parents.

Likewise, if you do partner in the future, it can become an issue for some parents if they were not previously aware of your sexual orientation.

Depending on the approach to homosexuality in your ethnic, racial, and/or religious communities, you will convey this information in different fashions. Likewise, it can be challenging to know how to approach parents who are clearly from different cultures and communities than your own. When you choose not to come out to someone from a community different than your own, it can be challenging to see where this choice stems from. It can be difficult to differentiate between perceived racism, internalized racist or ethnocentric beliefs, perceived homophobia, and internalized homophobia.

If you choose not to come out to specific parents of your child's friends, try to evaluate why it is that you are making that decision. If you are afraid that if they knew you were gay, they would not let the children play, perhaps you should find this out before a strong friendship develops between the children.

The key in coming out directly to parents is to use finesse. Make sure that you are not providing them with a reason to validate their homophobia. You will want to try out a few ways of expressing this information to find one that suits your needs and purposes.

For example, you do *not* want to say: "I thought you should know that I am gay, just in case you won't want your child to play with someone who has a gay parent."

Instead, you could say: "I thought you should know I am gay. Some people feel strongly about this and for the sake of our children, I want to avoid any difficulties around this issue."

Or you could say: "As a lesbian mother I have encountered some prejudice on the part of other parents. Although I do not expect this to be an issue with you, I want to be sure that you know. If you have any questions about our family, please feel free to ask as I understand you may have some."

Some parents choose a less direct way of coming out to other parents. If you are partnered, perhaps you are both there to greet your child's friend's parents when they come to pick them up from your home. Or when the parents drop their child off you might say, "My partner Jonathan will drive Melinda home to your house at four." Or when a parent telephones you might say, "This is Riva's mother Tamara" and on another day, your partner might say "This is Riva's mother Jane," allowing the sometimes confusing process of deduction to be conducted by the calling family.

If your child is out at school, most of their classmates will mention it at home. Once the word is out, it tends to spread quickly and much of the work of coming out and screening parents for obscene levels of homophobia is already completed, seemingly on its own.

There are some situations where you can prepare a revelatory statement ahead of time. The majority, however, are situations on the spot. There are unexpected opportunities when car pooling, on a school field trip, at the supermarket, at restaurants, when you visit old family friends, the list goes on. For example: You are waiting on the soccer field watching your child's game and another parent approaches you trying to make small talk and says, "Where's your wife today?" or "I saw the way they botched your names on the roster, your husband's name isn't really Michelle, it's Michael, right?" How are you going to respond?

Moving to a New Neighborhood

Whenever I seriously consider moving to a new neighborhood, I literally knock on every door on the block or on the floor of the apartment building and introduce myself. I see who the neighbors are and get a general feel of the area. Although I do not always come out to every person, I definitely get a sense of how comfortable they feel around me. If you do this with your partner, you would certainly get an even clearer sense.

People who are buying their own homes are strongly encouraged to be out to their realtors. This way the realtor can help guide you to gay friendly neighborhoods and also do some of the preliminary investigating for you. Prior to buying a home, it is a good idea to meet your neighbors. There would be nothing worse than buying a home next to an adamantly homophobic person when you could have chosen to live on another street.

When you do move in, it is good to introduce your family to each of the neighbors. You do not have to say that you are gay, just make the rounds on a Saturday and your neighbors will get the idea. As you start to know your neighbors you will want to be sure to introduce each family member to cut down on awkward moments in the future.

When Not to Come Out

Indeed, there are times when it is probably wisest not to reveal your sexual orientation. If you feel that there is an actual physical threat to your safety and the safety of your loved ones then it is usually wisest not to come out. Hopefully these will be situations that arise few and far between. If you feel that you live in a place where your physical safety is truly threatened on a daily basis you should probably examine two things.

One: Why is it that you do not move elsewhere? There are many places where you will feel physically safe most, if not all, of the time. Is this threat of physical harm that you and your child and loved ones live with on a daily basis worth the benefit of living where you do?

Two: Is the threat that you perceive actual? Are you truly in danger? What makes you believe this? Is it possible that you are more afraid than you need to be? Are you using fear of physical harm as a reason to not come out? This is a painful, but important level of self-examination. The threat of physical harm is very real. In places where homophobia is condoned it may not be safe for anyone to know that you are gay. Other times, we hear about violent acts perpetrated toward gays and use them as reasons to stay closeted when the fear is not based on any immediate threat in our own environment.

Like people of color, Jews, Muslims, fat people, people with disabilities, and other openly persecuted groups in our culture, gays, at times, have internalized the fear of harm to such an extent that it is impossible to differentiate true risk from the fear of being harmed. Needless to say, if you belong to more than one oppressed group, the internal process of knowing how to stay safe becomes complex. This is why it is imperative to have a strong and growing sense of Pride and self-esteem.

If you feel like it is not physical harm that you are risking, but other forms of safety, such as job or housing security, you may choose not to come out as well. Check with your work, local and state statutes to see if there are sexual orientation discrimination protection clauses. If there is protection available, then you may be willing to challenge the system should serious consequences to your coming out arise. At times, your life circumstances and the environment you live in will dictate whether it is safe to come out. Only you can be the judge of that.

Pride and Love in the Face of Fear and Hate

The more parents that your child has in their family the more personal relationships to being gay they will be exposed to. This can be a lot to track for a child. Your relationship to being gay, being out, and coming out are no longer exclusively your issues; when you have a child they become group property with your child. So, if there are varying attitudes and levels of closeting with the parents in your family, your child has to try to understand these and learn to negotiate them. For the sake of your child, try to work on and resolve these issues while your child is still young. Dealing with homophobia will be something your child may face throughout their life—dealing with your internalized homophobia is a needless burden.

Taking Pride in who you are is not always easy. At a time when you are feeling good about yourself and self-confident, make a list of why you love being GLBT. Put this list on your mirror, or on your refrigerator, someplace where you will see it on a regular basis. Then, on days when you have encountered a homophobic person or are questioning why you chose to have children in a homophobic world—you can look at your list and remember why with Pride!

5

Raising Our Children with Gender Awareness

It is important to recognize how you choose to interact with gender and how you choose to communicate the concepts of gender to your children. The ideal time to begin this contemplation is prior to having children, but any time that you bring this vital subject to your attention will be extremely beneficial. Gender normatives, that is, what is expected in terms of behavior and presentation of your sex limit and restrict everyone. Gender could be considered the most oppressive of all oppressions because it crosses class, religion, race, and age.

Homophobia can be defined as a fear of people who live outside of the accepted gender normatives. Many of the homophobic acts of violence and taunting perpetrated on gays, lesbians, bisexuals, and transgendered people or people thought to be GLBT is founded not so much in sexual orientation, but in gender presentation. Gays and lesbians who "pass" as heterosexual are generally not targeted as subjects of discrimination. Because violence and ridicule that is directed at people who do not act or look typically male or female starts at a young age, even children become afraid of stepping outside of gender presentation expectations.

It is the stepping outside of the expected gender behaviors that triggers discrimination. Thus, one of the most concrete ways that we can change society and make a grassroots impact on homophobia is by carefully examining the messages of gender that we provide children. To do this it is important to determine how these normatives are communicated and what we can do to open them up, if not get rid of them altogether. Every human who lives within such rigid confines of behavior expectations suffers, not just GLBTs. Sexism naturally arises from rigid gender expectations. The impact of sexism damages both males and females alike.

Teaching Gender Expectation to Our Children

Deciding how to relate to gender in your child rearing can be quite complex. As a gay or lesbian parent, the ways you relate to gender development and communication of gender can be compounded by your sexual orientation. One could easily surmise that GLBT parents would automatically address issues of gender construct and the subsequent confinement of gender with their children. Due to the desire to be accepted by family and friends, however, quite the opposite is more commonly true. GLBT parents often find themselves adhering to societally accepted gender expectations and intentionally communicating these mores to their children. This conformity is usually driven by fear—fear of not being seen as good parents, fear of the child having to carry too much of a burden, fear of undesired exposure and questioning by outsiders.

It appears easier for parents of girls to consider taking steps to encourage their children to step outside of the gender expectations than for parents of boys. This divide seems even greater with gay parents.

Sexism and gender expectations are instilled prior to birth; therefore, to change the world, we need to change ourselves. Gender is such an emotionally charged issue that many people feel better not dealing with it. Touching it, thinking about it, dissecting it, and approaching it intentionally, however, is vital to making changes that will make the world safer for us, our children, and all people.

A child's young years lay the foundation for the development of a strong, confident sense of self, compassion and empathy, healthy attitudes toward people different from themselves, and social interaction skills. Without conscious attention to this development, the institutionalized forms of oppression (sexism, racism, homophobia, etc.) in our society will interfere with our child's maturation. Through attentive parenting we can teach our children how to resist these influences as we strengthen the qualities that will help them to feel good about themselves and to respect others.

Issues That Arise When Gender Is Addressed

Being gay and being a parent is still a non sequitur for many heterosexual people. Heterosexually based gender and parenting roles are ingrained in us from such a young age that anything "other" is wrong. Given this, there are many issues that come up for GLBT parents when they address gender in their parenting.

Fear

Many gay parents feel that their children and their parenting will be much more intensely scrutinized simply because of their sexual orientation. The fear of such scrutiny can lead to a fear of not wanting to rock the "status quo boat" any farther than they feel they have already rocked it simply by having children. Tragically, it is from this place of fear that many GLBT parents make their parenting choices.

In the face of this fear, I have seen many parents set aside what they personally think is important. Their fear is most often that of "what will the neighbors think?" This fear in itself becomes reason enough to acquiesce to the supposed preferences of the "neighbors."

Although fear can be a useful signal of danger, it often is over-indulged. Making your parenting decisions from a place of fear is neither healthy practice nor good modeling for your children. It is much more powerful to make choices that you feel strong about and with which you have resonance. If fear is what comes up for you when you think about stepping outside of what is culturally expected of you, then you are probably working within the confines of internal homophobia.

Internal Homophobia

Homophobia is insidious because it is both outside and inside ourselves. Internal homophobia is the fear of what others might think or of how others might react to us or to our children. Frequently, internalized homophobia has greater impact on our parenting than external homophobia. Unfortunately, oppression continues either way. For most, the fear of homophobia is more debilitating than actually confronting it when and if it does arise.

Many people find that their own self-contained homophobia seems to subtly affect the responses they receive from outsiders. When you question your right to parent, it is easy for others to pick up on that shame and doubt, and reflect it back. Your body language, choice of words, and intonation can communicate your insecurities. On the other hand, in the face of self-confidence, not only is it harder to feel better than someone, but it is less likely that a homophobic response will be devastating. Likewise, when you have reached a level of comfort within yourself about your right to be gay and your right to raise children, you will be less likely to interpret every nuance as homophobia. (If you have not worked directly on this before, it is a good time to either read a book on the impact internal homophobia has on self-esteem, or to enter into therapy with a therapist trained in helping people feel more comfortable with their sexuality.)

Assimilation

The biggest fear gay parents have when thinking about raising their children to not conform to gender expectations is of being accused of trying to "convert" their child to be gay. Whether conscious or not, this is a fear I hear expressed again and again. Consider the following examples.

Two fathers:

> We are trying so hard to raise our son to be "manly." We don't know exactly what that means (laugh), but we don't want him to be called a fag.

Pregnant woman:

> I couldn't possibly dress a boy in pink. Or, for that matter, anything that could be perceived as even slightly feminine. What would the relatives think? I really don't think they could handle it. They don't even think a lesbian should be allowed to raise a boy.

Mother:

> My ten-year-old daughter wants to cut her hair. She has shoulder-length hair, she wants a crew cut. I don't know what to say to her. I am stalling. We live in a small town, you know? People will assume that I made her cut her hair. They'll think I am trying to make her a lesbian. It's just hair, but I'm afraid of a public uproar.

These responses indicate an internal level of fear of having to defend yourself or wanting to protect your child from the teasing they might encounter as a result of your natural choices. Thus, you are altering your parenting in order to attempt to accommodate the perception of mainstream culture.

When questioning if you are acting out of internal homophobia, it is often useful to replace the context with culture or religion. With GLBT families, we fear that although we are gay, maybe our children won't be. Therefore, our children shouldn't have to shoulder our burden. Although at first this seems to be logical thinking, on closer examination, it is clear that this form of thinking encourages passive parenting ruled by fear and shame.

If your family of origin is Jewish, for example, you may not identify as a Jewish adult, but, while you lived with your family, you lived in a Jewish household. Your parents probably did not try to protect you from your Jewishness. Despite the fact that being Jewish has led to persecution at various points in history, you were probably instilled with pride about being a Jew. Pride is a tool to counteract oppression. We must always remember to harness pride in the face of our fear.

Personal Exercise

Go back and insert a cultural identity or religion into the quotes above and see if you gain any clarity. Using the first example from the previous page, let's arbitrarily decide the men are Jewish. If they were concerned with religion instead of sexual orientation, their apprehension would be:

> We are trying so hard to raise our son to be "Christian." We don't know exactly what that means (laugh), but we don't want him to be called a Jew.

It becomes clear that in this statement the men would be trying to eradicate an important part of themselves from influencing their child. They would also be trying to raise their child as something other or foreign. Actions that stemmed from an intention to protect their child would likely end up in anger, confusion, and a lack of sense of belonging for the child. By trying to adhere to a perception of the status quo, they would be hurting their children—the direct opposite of their intentions.

When looked at in this light, it becomes clear that the parents are operating from internal messages of shame about who they are and their right to parent. What kind of inner messages do you hear when you think of your child doing something that is not traditionally "male" or "female"? Write these responses down. Do these responses stem from ways in which you, or someone you know, were treated as a child?

When you are clear about what your fears are and what the shameful dialogue you hold within yourself amounts to, then you can begin to discharge it. When left unexamined, however, this inner dialogue is often a mechanism of internalized homophobia.

Next, replace each quote above with a response of pride. What would you say if you did not hold inner messages of shame and/or fear? For example, a possible response from the mother who's daughter wants a crew cut could be:

> I am so proud that my daughter wants to defy what is expected of girls and cut her hair as short as the boys' hair in her class. Of course I did my motherly duty and discussed with her some possible responses people might have, and reminded her that hair takes a long time to grow. She is decided that she wants her hair short, and that's that. She has such confidence! She just doesn't seem to care what people think. She certainly has a proclivity to want to startle people with her autonomy. Go, girl!

There is a difference between concerns that stem from fear of being perceived negatively and fear that you will actually lose custody of your children. The next examples are quite different than the ones discussed previously.

Two fathers:

> We have to be very careful about who we hug, kiss, and cuddle our sons around. It is repulsive and infuriating, but many people think that gay men are pedophiles. Loving, nurturing behavior toward our children could be used against us as proof. For homophobes, loving our children is proof of perversion.
>
> This does not stop us from hugging, kissing, and cuddling at home, and we still walk with our arms around them in public. At least for now while they are young. But when we are in public, we try not to let them sit on our laps. Can you believe we do that? But we have to. We are terrified that someone will try to take them away from us.
>
> It is the same when our kids have friends come over. We are careful not to be too nurturing to our boys or to their friends. We are even concerned with casually touching other children lest their parents get the wrong idea. It would be much easier if we had girls. We wouldn't have to worry about this.
>
> That is the painful part. The good thing is that, so far at least, our boys are comfortable with themselves and comfortable with us. We are a very affectionate family. They ask for hugs, they cry, they dance. Hopefully these parts of them will always stay with them and not have to go underground.

Women raising girls have not expressed fear of losing custody of their girls for trying to raise them outside of the stereotypical gender expectations. Instead it has been more of a fear of feeling that people won't be able to see their daughters for who they are, but as something they, as lesbians, have shaped them into.

Two moms:

> I am afraid that she won't be allowed to play at other girls' houses. Their mothers will be afraid that my daughter's fearlessness will rub off on their girls. They think there is something immoral about having a strong and active four-year-old girl. They think it must be my "militant lesbianism" that I am forcing on to my daughter. They think her behavior is not natural. At the park, mothers actually pull their daughters away from my child. As a result she only plays with boys at the park.
>
> I did not know how deep all this gender stuff ran until I actually heard mothers telling their daughters not to climb too high and to stay close to mama while at the same time encouraging their sons to run off and play. It sure is an eye-opener!

I have tried to not let the reactions of the other mothers bother me. I am sure this phase will pass. My partner, on the other hand, is questioning what we are doing. She is afraid our daughter will become a social outcast. She does not want to forcibly contain our active daughter, but she does wonder if we overly encouraged this inner strength in her and if that was wrong.

Gay and Lesbian Type Casting

Interestingly, many lesbians and gays seem to give into gender stereotyping of their children right away. If I could tell you how many times I have heard a queer parent say to me, "I was hoping for a femme boy, but I got such a butch." This is said from the time that the baby is three months old. What can you truly know about a child at that point?

Butch/Femme Labeling

Resist the urge that many GLBT parents have to label our children either butch or femme. Allow and encourage your child to act both within the gender expectations as well as outside. All children need the fluidity of being both and so much more. Labeling and typecasting our children does them a disservice. It does not allow you to witness the unfolding of their magnitude. As well, it encourages a narrow, stereotypical lens through which your child views others.

Butch/femme labeling may have served the gay movement at one point in time. Such labeling may also be useful in your adult life; it is much too restrictive, however, to put on your view of a child.

Many lesbians initially have difficulty if their daughter exhibits stereotypically feminine qualities. Rather than permitting their daughters to explore and find out who she is and what she likes, lesbians often regard an interest in traditionally feminine behaviors negatively. They often express this as if it was a battle they lost. Then they say they just give in and give up. "What is there to do? You can't fight nature."

It is one thing to allow your child to develop into who they are, it is another to abdicate your responsibility to protect them from bias by labeling them as "feminine" and then fostering that limited perception of them. It is in no way more "natural" to embody feminine qualities that are culturally condoned than it is to exhibit any of the other qualities females embody. Is it not a contradiction to the experience of most dykes to continue limiting the female experience to accepted gender mores? By internally labeling your daughter, you are perpetuating sexism in the next generation. It's a bit ironic.

Gender Imprinting

The desire to be accepted often influences the way we raise our children. Gender development and sexism are huge topics; and it's not always as obvious as clothes and hugs. You'll find that you only do what feels right for you. This chapter will lead you through some specific suggestions of what you can do to resist automatic gender imprinting, and how you can adopt ways of looking at life that will encourage your child to have more freedom from gender.

In Utero

Gender imprinting begins in utero. Many of my pregnant clients have said: "I know I am having a boy because the baby is *so* active!" or "I must be having a girl, the baby is so accommodating to my needs—she is quiet when I need to sleep." With the common use of ultrasound to determine the sex of the baby in utero, this sentiment is increasingly compounded. Instead of nine months of gender free identity, parents can now start classifying their children into categories before they are even born. The nursery is decorated, clothes, blankets, even diapers are chosen based on whether or not a penis was visible on the ultrasound.

All of the baby's behaviors during pregnancy are then categorized within statements such as "It's so like a boy to never let me forget he's in there" or "Isn't it obvious I am having a girl because my pregnancy is so easy?"

It has been documented that people buying gifts for babies when they do not know the sex of the baby will buy gender neutral items. When they know the sex of the baby, gendered items are usually chosen (Pomerleau, Bolduc, and Cossette 1990).

I have been at the births of a number of babies where the sonogram was wrong. A baby of the unexpected gender is born and the parents are in shock. Had they not expected specific genitals, the baby would have been welcomed as it was. Their expectation of specific genitalia had radically altered their perception of their baby. After the initial shock, it is inevitable that the words "but what will we do with all those clothes?" finally escape. I always encourage families not to use the ultrasounds for sex determination, but to spend nine months simply loving "baby."

Babies

Boy babies and girl babies are socialized differently. Take note of what research has revealed about this (Crawford 1996). Studies have shown that one-day-old infants respond to speech patterns and rhythms. Both men and women have specific patterns and rhythms they use to differentiate when they are talking to a boy baby and when they are talking to a girl baby. If they do not know the sex of the baby, however, they use the "girl" patterns. If you notice, you will see that most of us continue to use different tones of voice and styles of speech when talking to boys and girls, and even men and women. We will discuss more about language later in this chapter.

Studies show that mothers emphasize language development in girl babies (Crawford 1996). They tend to imitate and repeat sounds made by girl babies more frequently than those made by boys. Likewise, physical development and coordination is emphasized in boy babies. Parents stimulate gross motor movements more in boy babies than girl babies. Also interesting in the gender socialization of babies and young children is that people tend to hold girls facing inwards, and boys facing outwards.

People we encounter on a day-to-day basis expect us to identify the gender of our babies as a necessary and important mark of distinction. I was at a party recently with my one-year-old. The party was full of people of various sexual orientations. I happened to be behind a lesbian who asked the woman next to her, in reference to my baby across the room, "Is that baby a boy or a girl? You can't tell from the clothes or the name." I spoke up from behind her and said, "It's a girl." The woman then said, first apologetically and then accusingly, "I hope I didn't offend you by asking, but *why* do you make us guess?!" I was taken aback by those two statements, and responded, "Gender isn't that important to me." Unfortunately there was not an opportunity for more of a discourse at that time. Nonetheless, the whole interaction made me realize how much gender rules are in place to make others feel comfortable.

The only way we are going to be able to change the unconscious expectations of gender manifestations is to intentionally be aware of what we ourselves do to foster gender difference. As you become aware of the tone of voice you use and the ways in which you interact with children, or all people for that matter, according to their gender, it becomes possible to change and equalize those patterns. It is with this awareness that you can then share your findings with others, both strangers and friends.

Large Scale Gender Indoctrination Methods

There are many images of gender stereotyping provided for children from a very young age. Long before children can talk they are bombarded with imagery that shapes their perceptions. These messages are constantly communicated to people throughout their lives. When you are aware of this form of mandatory, passive indoctrination, you can see how persistent it is. It is nonconsensual indoctrination. To get away from it, you have to consciously remove the sources. Yet some of the sources of communication of these gender expectations are not easily removable.

Billboards are a large and looming example of such communication. Likewise, television is one of the most obvious and insidious mediums. Although there are a few public television programs such as *Sesame Street*, which try to provide nonsexist imagery, these programs are few and far between.

Disney is one of the worst culprits in gender stereotyping. The female characters are always sexualized, even the young girls.

Exercise

Spend a day or even better, a week examining the gendered messages with which children are bombarded. Because this topic is so large, restrict yourself at this time to billboards, television, Disney, and whatever magazine covers are lying around your house. Take note of what you find. What are the most common qualities, characteristics, and behaviors of girls, boys, women, and men that you documented? How frequently did you find variance from these roles?

It is important to become familiar with the specifics of the gendered messages. It is only then that we can begin to resist this passive programming in our parenting. As LGBTs, we must actively resist and redefine this kind of programming to make room for ourselves.

We can use our queerness to our advantage here. We can drive down the street and see a billboard of an elegant woman drinking a beverage, and mention to our young child, "Oh, look at that drag queen" or comment about a billboard or magazine photo of a dirty coal worker turned away from the camera: "She sure looks like she works hard!" If your child says, "Oh, Mom, that's not a woman," it is easier to say, "But she looks just like my friend Maria—how do you know she's not a woman?"

What You Can Do to Challenge Sexism

Gender bias is so ingrained that even if you have been working on eliminating your biases for years there is still more to unlearn. Fortunately there are many, many actions you can take to challenge sexism.

Self-Reflection

As with overcoming any oppression, challenging and unlearning sexism must take place on many levels. Some of the most important work to do is within yourself. Take the time to self reflect on your experiences of gender rules, expectations, and limitations when you were growing up and throughout your life.

What, if anything, changed about your relationship to gender when you came out? Coming out is often quite freeing. This is often partially attributed to the gender freedom associated with being gay. Unfortunately, there are often large pockets of unexamined sexism and misogyny within the queer culture. It is important to identify the various messages you received about males and females from mainstream society as well as those from gay society.

Exercise

Take the time to journal about what is true to you about girls, boys, men, and women. What do you like about girls, boys, men, women? What don't you like about boys, girls, women, and men? Write quickly. Do not think about what you are writing, just let it flow. When that is complete, write quickly about what you think is different in parenting a girl and parenting a boy? When you have completed this exercise you will find a place from which to start exploring your own personal biases.

Limit Exposure to Mass Media

When your children are young it is important to limit their exposure to mass media. Passive imagery is powerful. It can perpetuate stereotypes in a very insidious fashion. Consider the following suggestions:

Magazines

- Don't thoughtlessly leave out magazines; the cover and advertising often epitomizes the worst of gender stereotypes.

- Only leave out imagery you feel to be empowering.

Television

- Choose your child's exposure to television carefully.

- Do not leave the television on in the background.

- Tape your child's television shows so you can watch them together and fast forward past commercials.

- Consider allowing your child to watch only public television.

Movies

- Prewatch movies you have not previously seen to screen for biases.
- Watch videos and movies together.
- Enter theaters after the previews have been screened.

It is often hard to believe that exposure to television and movies actually has an impact on our children. The following story exemplifies just how influential even passive exposure can be.

Mira's family became very disturbed that she was acting out domestic violence themes in her imaginative play. Her dads went to her preschool teachers who assured them this theme was not covered at school. Finally they approached the neighbors where she plays on Tuesday and Thursday afternoons. It turned out that the parents watch videos while the children play in the same room. A few weeks before they had watched a movie involving a very violent household.

After that, Mira's parents were very clear about the passive absorption of the media and clearly communicated to all caretakers that they did not want Mira exposed to television or videos without their permission. You, too, may want to consider instructing all caretakers of your children, including the parents of your child's friends, that your children are not allowed to watch television or videos while playing at their house. This eliminates, or at least reduces, unwanted exposure and encourages play.

With older children the media becomes a rich source of education and conversation as together you can deconstruct what you have seen. It is still important to limit exposure as best you can.

Analyze Books, Television, and Movies with Children

We can make sure that our children become aware of stereotypes through actively analyzing books, television, and movies. The depth to which this is possible dramatically increases as your child grows. Remember to make sure that you are communicating on an age-appropriate level. Do not introduce too many complex ideas at once. Take the time that your child needs to make sure that your child is grasping the concept and not internalizing the stereotypes instead.

Exercise

Explore together what stereotypical actions and behaviors are commonly depicted for males and females in the media you are viewing. After you have completed that, go a step further and breakdown the additional stereotypes of males and females when race, ethnicity, or religion is portrayed. From there you can explore together common themes of storylines that perpetuate sexist beliefs.

Make a list of what you come up with. Laminate it and attach it to your television. Whenever you watch a show or movie, consult the list afterwards to see which stereotypes were represented. This is a good use of commercial time as well. In the case of television shows, you then have the opportunity to write to the station to complain about what you viewed, and provide suggestions for what you would rather see.

Awareness of inequity is not enough. Taking action teaches children practical skills to counteract oppression. Taking action reduces the risk of internalizing the inequities as they are accurately viewed as being outside of oneself.

Challenge Consumerism

Marketing encourages, perpetuates, and capitalizes on the gender divide. Most people do not take the time to examine the not-so-subtle messages being communicated to us on a daily basis. We are usually aware of the push to make us want to buy and to encourage us to buy, but are you aware enough of the gender stereotypes that marketing intentionally aims at our children?

Exercise

Spend a Saturday morning watching children's television. Focus on the commercials. Notice how the toys are advertised. How many girls' toys are advertised? How many boys' toys? How many boys' toys are active toys? How many girls' toys are inactive toys? How many boys' toys are sports oriented? How many girl's toys are beauty oriented? Notice the colors, language, speed, and music differences in advertising aimed at girls and advertising aimed at boys. How many toys are co-ed? If there are boys or girls in the commercials aimed at the other gender, what are they doing? How about the food commercials? What are the boys doing? What are the girls doing? What is your assessment?

Most adults do not realize just how calculating the marketing industry is in training our children. It is eye-opening. You will witness the most obvious of gender training. The girls are usually sitting, staring dreamy eyed at the new doll or beauty product aimed at them. They have long hair and the imagery is filled with pink. The boys are shown in active, physical play often with rescue themes. Boys and girls are rarely in the same toy commercials. The co-ed commercials are usually food commercials. In these the boy is usually the main character, the girl a supporting actor. There are moms concerned about nutrition and housecleaning.

After viewing the commercials it gives a parent pause. It certainly helps you to appreciate public television without commercials. Many parents ban or strictly limit television in their house after doing this exercise.

Toy Stores

After doing the exercise above you will not be surprised to discover that in most toy stores there are boys and girls aisles. Talk with your children. Make sure they understand that toys are to play with—there are no girls' and boys' toys really. Girls and boys can play with the same toys. As they age, it becomes easier for children to recognize the ploys of marketing. There are steps that you can take to refuse to support this level of sexism within consumerism.

- Refuse to buy gendered packaging (good luck).

- Refuse to shop in stores that label the boys' and girls' sections.

- Talk to managers, in front of your children, about the offensive messages being communicated with such marketing. Request gender neutral packaging.

- Buy toys for your children, but remove the packaging before coming home.

- Write letters with your children to the toy companies demanding that they stop sexist marketing and packaging.

- Start a toycott at your school, to avoid biased toys.

- Write letters with your children to stores that you no longer frequent explaining why.

- Shop at used toy stores that do not have gender distinctions.

- Volunteer to help your independent toy store reduce its bias.

By modeling action in the face of bias, you not only teach your child to recognize bias, you also teach them that bias is not acceptable. To point something out, but not to take action, helps to perpetuate apathy. The consumer market is aimed at consumers, thus consumers are the ones who need to change it.

Take the example of Jerry. Jerry is a nine-year-old boy raised by a single, bisexual mom. He has always had a strong, innate sense of justice. His mother has helped him to develop this part of himself. Last year Jerry noticed that the toy store in his neighborhood was encouraging sexism by separating girl's and boy's toys. There were marked sections for each. He told the person who was working there that this bothered him. The person brushed him off.

This made Jerry angry. He wanted to do something about the unfairness of the sexism. He talked with his fourth-grade teacher, who suggested he speak to the whole class about it. After some group discussion the class decided to hold a protest. They made signs that said "All toys for all kids" and "Just say no to sexism" and "This store is sexist." They arranged to meet with their signs in front of the store on a Saturday morning. Five children showed up. The manager came out to talk to them and agreed to rearrange the store. Way to go!

Examine How, Where, and Why You Buy Clothes

Conscious and unconscious gender programming through clothes starts with babies. Most people adhere to very strict clothing rules when dressing their children. For example, boy babies are supposed to be dressed in bold colors and stripes. Girl babies are supposed to be dressed in pastels, flowers, and lace. Girls tend to be dressed up like dolls; boys are dressed for practicality. Starting as babies, clothing designed for boys has sports themes and phrases such as "Little Slugger," whereas girls clothes are made to look nice.

What do you want to communicate through clothing? Because you are the one who chooses the clothes your child will wear, you may want to examine why you choose the clothes that you do.

There are some basic differences to take note of regarding children's clothing:

- There are separate departments for boys and for girls.
- "Boys'" clothes are sturdy and made to last.
- "Boys'" clothes rarely go out of style.
- "Boys'" clothes are rarely made in bright colors or soft fabrics.
- "Girls'" clothes are poorer quality, yet often more expensive.
- "Girls'" clothes are often sexualized because they are smaller sizes of women's clothes.
- "Girls'" clothes follow fashion and are usually not made for rugged play.

Language and Clothes

Girls are taught to be concerned about their appearances from early on. Part of this has to do with our objectifying girls constantly. Refrain from commenting on how a child looks whenever possible. If you must comment on clothes, choose statements that children are less likely to internalize as subtle gender reinforcement, such as, " I bet those pants feel good when you run" or "That jacket sure looks like it keeps you warm" to a girl. Or statements like, "I bet that sweater will feel cozy when you snuggle next to me at reading time" to a boy.

Try not to make statements identifying clothing as male or female unless you are trying to make a specific point. Refrain from using gender distinctions for clothes. Place the distinction on the marketing. For example, comment on the poorly made socks sold in the girls' section rather than on poorly made "girls'" socks. Encourage your child to notice and resist the sexism.

Young Children and Clothes

It is important to train children from an early age to dress for comfort and mobility. It is quite useful to teach them to look for quality. When you enforce quality, comfort, and mobility guidelines for clothes, shopping becomes much easier. I have actually added another guideline with my girls that eliminates a lot of needless arguing—they only wear natural fibers. Quite frequently the greatest offenders are clothes made from synthetic fabrics.

There are some general tips you can use to reduce the sexism you will encounter when shopping. Try to shop from used clothing stores where there are not labeled girls' and boys' sections. Order clothes online or from catalogs. Or, if you can afford it, shop from children's stores that are not big enough to have sections.

Monitor the language you use about appearance at all times, but especially when buying clothes. "Oh, that color is so good on you" is training your child to dress for others. "What colors would you like to try on?" is a much more open way of approaching it. Try to leave your preferences out of the decision once the two of you have established shopping ground rules.

Boys do not often have the experience of feeling differently according to the style of clothes they wear. Try to extend the variety, styles, textures, and colors of clothes you buy for your son so that he can experience comfort and freedom in his clothes. Cotton turtlenecks are a good way to introduce turquoise, purple, or other bright colors to his wardrobe. Let him choose the style of clothes he wants to wear; try not to conform him to standard male attire. Allow your son to increase his self-expression in the way he dresses.

Dresses and Skirts

If your girl likes skirts and dresses for daily wear, then you may want to use the splits test. If she cannot do the splits in her clothes, they are too confining for active play. Such clothes will restrict her movement, and therefore, her clothes will dictate her behavior. Perhaps you can reserve such clothing for more formal occasions.

Providing boy children with an opportunity to wear dresses and skirts is not only equal opportunity thinking, it is also allowing boys to experience the sensation of such clothing. Encourage boys to sleep and lounge in nightshirts. These can simply be your T-shirts. The issue of boys and dresses tends to push a lot of emotional gender buttons for people. It is often a fruitful area to examine your internalized sexism. Even if it is too much for you to want to incorporate dresses and skirts into your son's wardrobe, you can still bring the concept into your home through photographs. Drag queens, fairies, hippies, and men from various ethnicities wear skirts and robes on a regular basis.

When Buying Shoes

Shoe departments are often divided by gender. Try to find a shoe store that does not emphasize this kind of distinction. Select the shoes you would like to try on yourself. Salespeople tend to steer your child toward gender-specific shoes. If the salesperson does comment on your choices for shoes with statements such as "Oh, no, sweetie, those shoes are for boys," you can respond with statements such as, "We dress for comfort in our family" or "All of these shoes are for children."

Girls:

- Emphasize comfort, durability, and practicality over appearance.

- Always have a pair of sturdy, well-fitting athletic shoes for her.

- Everyday shoes must pass the run test. Have your child run around the store in the shoes she likes. If the shoes comes off, or her ankle twists—as most "girl" shoes will do—refuse to buy them. Shoes are to use every day, not to look good in.

- No heels on prepubescent girls. It sexualizes them.

- No platform shoes. They are impractical for running and can lead to sprained ankles.

- Girls tend to have many more shoes than boys. Does she need another pair? (The answer is always "yes" if she has outgrown her sneakers.)

- Always have a good pair of rain/snow boots in her size.

Boys:

- Boys shoes tend to be higher quality and more readily available, thus there is less to say about choosing shoes for boys:

- No action heroes on shoes—they depict unrealistic expectations for males.

- Always have a pair of sandals in your son's size. If you feel this will push it too far, buy river sandals.

Self-Reflection: Monitor Your Actions as a Parent

As parents we must monitor ourselves to prevent us from unconsciously endorsing inequities. We must monitor our interactions and conversations with other adults as well, making sure that we point out sexism and do not perpetuate gender stereotyping. Examine what your child observes men and women doing in their world. Strive to teach by example and to have strong role models in our children's lives who represent qualities we don't represent ourselves. Try spending an entire day interacting with your child as if they were the other sex. The role reversal test is often revealing. If you can take the same situation and reverse the gender roles, does the meaning remain the same? Unless the situation has something to do with anatomy, there should be no difference—as long as you're being nonsexist. Nonetheless, most of us discover when doing this exercise that many of our interactions, behaviors, and choices of activities are qualitatively altered.

Examine ways in which you play with your child. Imagine you have a boy/girl—what would you do? How would you interact differently? Many people discover, to their own chagrin, that they are more active, physical, and tend to joke around more with boys. Whereas with girls they tend to touch more, move less, speak more quietly, calmly, and about feelings.

Even parents who feel they are raising nonsexist children continue to buy different toys for boys and girls, offer different activities, decorate rooms differently, buy different clothes, read different books, and see different movies.

Parents hold boys and girls to different standards, with different outcomes. Boys are more frequently physically punished. Adults give boys more detailed feedback than they give girls. Many boy children learn that they can demean girls. This sexism hurts our children by fostering gender differences.

Lesbian Moms

Many lesbians, particularly women who identify as butch, have a high level of internalized misogyny. They frequently voice demeaning opinions about stereotypically feminine qualities and behaviors. This not only perpetuates stereotypes, but also gives strong messages to children. For example, if a girl knows that her mother hates long hair and says that ballet dancing is something only "girly" girls would do, how can she feel comfortable exploring such experiences herself?

It is best that lesbians who have strong, negative feelings about men address and contain these feelings. It is important not to make derogatory statements around children, or at all for that matter. Try instead to point out character qualities that you don't like. But be careful not to perpetuate stereotypes.

Gay Dads

Likewise, gay fathers can tend to overfeminize their girls. Once again, allow your child the room to express themselves in the ways that feel natural for *them*. If your child knows that you think women who do not put time into their appearances should just get a makeover, then you are limiting the appearances your child perceives as acceptable.

The World of Books

The world of books is enriching, enchanting, informative, and fun. There have been many strides in recent decades to create more books with strong female characters and to publish more children's books depicting people of color in positive ways. Books can serve to positively expose your child to ideas and experiences different than your own. Unfortunately, the world of books also continues to be one of the most effective mechanisms for constructing bias. Carefully selecting picture books for young children is very important because there is a visual image to go along with the words. The images can portray stereotypes that were not even mentioned in the words or they can provide your child with a positive image to reinforce a strong character or situation. The adage "a picture is worth a thousand words" is especially true with children's books.

It is an important challenge to find books that do not represent sexism. As you compile your book library for your child, review all books for stereotypes and bias. Remember to reverse the sexes of the books' characters in your mind as you do this. When sexual stereotypes have been assumed, gender reversal easily illustrates this bias. Periodically throughout childhood, evaluate the whole collection of books your child has. Your whole collection should represent a balance of positive images of both girl characters and boy characters. Do you need to add more books to balance out your collection? Should some of the books be removed from your collection?

Are you aware that the majority of books written for children still:

- have predominantly white characters

- refer to animals as male

- have the most important character be male

- include more drawings of males

- tend to have pictures of quiet, docile, submissive girls

- tend to have pictures of active, dominating, exuberant boys

- depict females within stereotypes as: incompetent, always caretaking children or animals, emotional, not fun to be with, mean

- depict males within stereotypes as: competitive, aggressive, never tender, clever, able to perform unrealistic acts

Likewise, it unfortunately still goes without saying, most books represent heterosexual models of love and family. Because this is the case, be sure to buy every children's book written with gay characters. Request that your local bookstores and libraries carry these books as well. Consider donating these books to your local library if they do not currently carry them. A list of these books is available in the Resources section at the end this book. Consider adding to the small, but growing number of these books and write your own.

Pronoun Reversal

When you read out loud to children, play with reversing the pronouns. This reversal of the characters' sexes should not make a difference. Invariably, however, it does. Reversing pronouns takes practice, but it makes many old, and sexist, classics more fun to read. Try using nongendered pronouns or titles whenever possible. Also, try removing or replacing the stereotypically descriptive adjectives of the characters that you do keep within the gender provided.

As your child ages you can discuss this practice with them and explain why it is important. When my older daughter discovered I was changing pronouns she was at first upset. But then it became fun for her. When we read *Winnie the Pooh*, she would choose each night which characters were going to be female and which male.

I also change gender pronouns to make sure that all couples are not heterosexual. There are many books we read out loud that have memorable characters with gay parents. Of course the author did not think of this, but the children we read to have the opportunity of experiencing a variety of family structures as typical. Likewise your children will have an easier time projecting themselves into the book.

Once your child is a reader, be sure to continue screening books. I am not promoting censorship, but rather involvement and guidance in the literature choices your child makes. Try to always have a handful of quality chapter books available for your young reader to pick up. Make sure that there are strong and resourceful girls, and caring and respectful boys depicted in the titles you choose. There are helpful resources that can guide your selection of good books. One such book is *101 Books for Girls to Grow On* (Dodsar 1998), which provides an excellent source of books for girls and boys.

Creating a Nonsexist Home

Just as it is important to periodically evaluate your child's shelves for bias, so is it important to evaluate your home as well. Our homes often unintentionally demonstrate environmental bias.

Imagery

Look at the imagery you have around your home. What do you see? What is missing? Do you have pictures reflecting qualities you would like your child to embody? Do you have photos of men and women you know in less traditional garb or doing an action usually attributed to the opposite sex?

Toys

Make sure that you buy a variety of toys and games for your children. All children need dolls, stuffed animals, or puppets for developing nurturing skills; plastic or wooden blocks for developing spatial and math skills; and sports equipment for coordination. With *all* purchases ask yourself, "If my child were a boy/girl would I buy him/her this item? Why? Why not?"

Also ask yourself when examining your child's home world: What is missing from this environment? What else would I make sure to have if I were raising a child of the opposite sex? Make sure that you have a well-stocked dress-up box filled with many gender neutral and gender specific clothes. Each dress-up box should have fancy hats, bras, ties, men's and women's old shoes in it, to name but a few items.

Encourage Gender-Neutral Skills and Interests

As parents we can encourage our children to develop a variety of skills and interests that are gender neutral.

- Foster friendships between boys and girls.

- Encourage all children—especially boys—to express their feelings, including fear and pain.

- Encourage girls to figure out situations and come up with creative solutions on their own.

- Encourage boys to feel comfortable asking for help.

- Support children when they speak out against bias.

- Involve your child in same-sex activities that challenge gender stereotypes (singing classes for boys, science camp for girls).

- Foster math, science, and computer development for girls.

- Encourage emotional articulation in boys.

- Support and encourage boys to play games that are stereotypically considered "girls' games."

- Validate nurturing qualities in boys by encouraging them to help in caring for pets or elders.

- Encourage team sports for girls.

- Involve boys in the expressive arts—art, music, dance, etc.

- Read biographies of women to your children.

- Teach children there is nothing inherently wrong with them, only with how the world treats them.

Talking with Children

It is important to talk to your children and ask them questions, to help them to develop their thoughts, and to widen the lens through which they view the world. Beginning when they are young, start asking questions with your child; some questions are timeless and need to be asked again and again in different ways and at different times throughout childhood.

When it comes to understanding and debunking gender constructs, stereotypes, and normatives these questions are helpful:

- What is a boy?

- What is a girl?

- What is a man?

- What is a woman?

- How do you know if it's a man or woman?

- How can you tell?

If the moment is right and your child is old enough ask:

- How do you feel when you can't tell if someone is male or female?

- Should you ask?

- How do you feel when you address someone by the incorrect gender?

As children become older you can ask questions such as:

- What could you do to step outside of your gender?

- If you were a boy/girl, how would you be different?

If your child has a concrete idea(s) about how they'd differ as a member of the opposite sex, you could suggest that you and your family engage in this activity for a day. With this exercise, however, you must set the ground rules that there is to be no stereotyping, making fun of, or degrading behavior allowed.

When children participate in dramatic play or writes stories, there are multiple opportunities to enforce positive imagery. Point out stereotypical descriptions, roles, and themes that they may be unconsciously perpetuating; then brainstorm together to find meaningful alternatives.

Remember that as adult GLBTs, many of us challenge the socially accepted gender structures in our behaviors and appearances. Make use of this with children. When challenging stereotypes it often comes in handy. For example, looking at pictures or talking with friends who are drag queens or drag kings is a rich source of gay history and culture, gender stereotypes, and the stepping outside of gender normatives.

Teaching Moments

As a parent, you know that there are wonderful times in life that allow for you to share a "teaching moment" with your child. Those times are very special because your child and the moment are both ripe to hear a new idea that will expand their mind to include a whole new way of thought. As parents, it is our responsibility to harness those teaching moments. Do not let them escape you, especially when your children are young and ask so many questions and are so sensitive to injustice.

My daughter and I were driving downtown a few months ago. We stopped at a light, and on the street corner a man appeared to be threatening a woman. He appeared to be in relationship with her, yet was yelling at her and had aggressive body language. We were in a hurry and in the "left turn only" lane. As I looked over my shoulder, I noticed the horrified look on my daughter's face. I turned my car around, pulled up to the couple and asked the woman if she needed help. She did not answer. The man said to mind my own business. I stayed and asked her if she would like a ride somewhere. She again did not answer. I told her that I was concerned about the way that man was treating her and was not going to leave until she could answer me. I then addressed the man and told him in not so many words to stop bothering the woman. As I was talking to him, and he was becoming feisty toward me, the woman got on a bus. We pulled away.

Many people would think it was dangerous for me to try to interfere—risking perhaps our safety and the woman's safety. Although this may be true, I could not idly sit by, especially with my daughter watching. My daughter and I spent the next fifteen minutes processing feelings and discussing why men treat women that way and why women let them. We also talked about the fact that women also treat women that way, and men also treat men that way.

Another good example of a teaching moment—although this one was not fully taken advantage of—occurred when I was in a residential neighborhood of San Francisco. I walked by a three-year-old with an adult. As I passed them, I heard the child say, "That man is wearing women's shoes. A man can't wear women's shoes." He repeated this over and over until the adult thought I was far enough away not to hear and replied, "You can't assume someone is a man just because they have short hair" (good answer considering I was in all "men's" clothes that day). He replied, "Oh, well, it's OK if a woman wears those shoes" and walked on. This was a perfect situation, a teaching moment that could have been used more effectively by talking about gender with this child. The parent could have talked about hair, clothes, shoes, assumptions, you name it.

Sharing Gender Awareness with Others

Parenting styles are very personal. There are as many approaches to parenting as there are parents. Many child-rearing practices are unexamined, although many stem from intentional philosophical choices. How can you share your feelings about gender and children with other parents without offending them? Many parents choose to remain silent when they want to say something because they don't want to interfere or be perceived as proselytizing.

Following are some practical approaches you can take that can make a difference and provide a context to share your thoughts and practices on the subject of gender:

- When your children are babies or toddlers, start a parent's discussion group about gender issues and parenting.

- Coordinate for a speaker to come to your preschool and arrange for a group discussion to follow.

- Coordinate parent workshops through your child's school on promoting gender equity in the school. Follow up with a monthly caucus on the subject.

- Read books together, in a group or with a friend.

- Give family members and friends books as presents

- Create handouts, such as "20 Things You Can Do to Resist Sexism," and leave at your child's day care, school, or camp.

Many parents are open to learning about these subjects when you don't imply that they are doing something wrong. If an expert comes to speak on the subject, or if you share the enthusiasm for a book, you are more likely to find an opening.

There have been a number of books written recently on the subject of sexism in the schools and the far-reaching implications for both boys and girls (see Resources section).

For children to develop empathy and respect for others they must develop a variety of ways to respond to prejudice and discrimination they see toward others. As parents, it is our job to see that our children foster both a strong and positive self and group identity. Our children most likely belong to multiple groups for which they will need strong identities. We also must foster development of bias awareness, and we need to cultivate an ability in our children to stand up in the face of inequity. These skills are helpful throughout a lifetime.

6

Culturally Sensitive Child Care and Schools

The Ongoing Process

School and day care are the places where our children spend most of their time when they are away from their families. Thus, the nature of these environments has a direct impact on our children. Finding child care and choosing schools is a priority for all parents; however, as LGBT parents, we have additional considerations when selecting an appropriate setting for our children. It is usually not as easy as automatically sending our children off to the neighborhood public school.

This chapter will cover how to find good child care, preschool, and primary and secondary school environments for our children. It will also discuss, in detail, what to look for in a school, how to talk to teachers, how to have a positive influence on the school, and how to access resources for teachers.

What Kind of Child Care Is Right for Your Family?

To find the right child care for your family you must evaluate your needs and the options available in your area. Of course, your needs will vary according to how your family life is structured. Some LGBT families arrange their lives in such a way that their baby/child stays home with them, or with family members and friends, until their child is old enough for school. Other families find that from infancy forward, their child spends more time with outside child care providers than with their families. In these situations, your child care provider(s) become your child's primary care giver. It is, therefore, all the more important that you find someone sensitive to your child's specific needs.

Not only do we need to find a safe, warm, nurturing, and affordable situation that is compatible with our parenting philosophies—a challenge for any parent—but we also need situations that honor and respect our families. Be sure to leave ample time to find such a situation.

Although it is not necessary to find child care before you need it, many families start to research child care options prior to becoming parents. It is helpful to ask like-minded parents what they do, or have done, for child care. Gathering local references is always a good place to start. Deciding whether you would like to find a day care center, a small in-home day care, or a provider who comes to your home is the first decision that must be made. Many LGBT families choose to have a child care provider come to their home when their children are young, and then transition their child directly into preschool. Costs for an in-home provider can be defrayed by sharing the care with another family. Although some in-home providers are more costly than day care centers, this option can provide reassurance that you know and trust the person caring for your child. You are in control of the physical environment and there is no need to interface with other unknown parents and their responses to your family.

Selecting a Child Care Provider or Preschool

As LGBTs we have specific considerations to make before even interviewing a care provider or visiting a day care or preschool facility. When crossing this new threshold of parenting, it is important to once again self-reflect on the impact that internalized homophobia may be having on your approach to finding appropriate arrangements for your child.

Should I Come Out When I Am Just Looking?

Before you begin your search for the right environment for your child, you must first answer a very important question to yourself: Whose responsibility is it to come out? Is it yours? Will it be your child's? Is it the day care's or school's responsibility to try to guess? Deciding this ahead of time is very helpful. I believe it is your responsibility from the start to come out to the organization caring for your child. This way you will be able to accurately and effectively screen any given environment for their level of cultural sensitivity. If you are seriously considering sending your child into a particular environment, it's a very good idea to come out prior to enrolling your child.

Being out during your search allows you to ask valuable questions that you would not bring up otherwise. Coming out to care providers and/or school administrators can make you very nervous. Nonetheless, the more confidently you mention it, the more comfortably you will be received. Every child has the right to be safe in the place where they are being cared for and/or educated. If you do not come out, you cannot gain as accurate a feel for an organization's policy on queer families and what their approach to your child will be.

Both physical and emotional health and safety are required to learn. If your child does not feel safe, they will be directing their energy toward self-protection instead of toward learning. Therefore, the issue of how your family will be received and whether the staff will intervene on behalf of your child—and every child—should be paramount in your decision.

Needless to say, if there is absolutely no choice in locations and you feel that it would be in the unequivocal best interest of your child for you to not come out, then so be it. However, there are usually more choices than first appear. Make sure your fear is based on the actual circumstance and not exclusively on your fear.

Phone Screening

Regardless as to what kind of day care you are looking for, it is important to do some initial phone screening. Asking direct questions on the phone will save both you and the school valuable time and potential discomfort. In addition to the questions you find important to ask about philosophy, it is helpful to reveal your LGBT status on the phone. That way anyone who would not feel comfortable with your family can say so from the start.

Many queer families feel that coming out on the phone is going overboard. Other families feel that if the provider actually met them in person they would overcome any previous homophobia. This attitude is fine, but once you have your first interaction with someone recoiling in horror when they realize the nature of your family, you realize it saves time and emotional energy to come out on the phone. I have spoken with a number of families who neglected to come out initially, sometimes due to a language barrier, and then encountered serious homophobia when the connection was made.

Questions to Ask

In addition to coming out, you may want to ask the potential provider the following questions:

- Have you worked with children from LGBT households before?

- Do you have any LGBT family references I could contact?

- If not, do you have any LGBT people in your own life?

- Does your staff receive any diversity awareness training?

- Can you envision if it would be challenging for any of your staff to relate to our family?

- Do you feel this environment would be a good match for our family?

- Do you feel our child and our family would feel welcomed by the other families?

Asking these types of direct questions will help you establish a genuine feel for the comfort level this provider has with your family structure. After you make a number of these phone calls, you will see that there is a dramatic difference in how people respond to these questions. Once you have found a few who respond in a way that makes you feel comfortable, you can arrange to meet with them or to visit their day care or preschool.

When you meet with someone who will be providing day care in your home, then you're obviously not screening the physical environment in the same way you would an out-of-home care. Regardless, it is not only essential that an environment feel right to you, but that the person, or people, who will be spending time with your child answer your questions appropriately, and that you feel *good* about leaving your child in their care. *Never compromise on child care.*

The following section addresses what to consider when looking at both child care settings and preschools. Although the surroundings may differ according to the ages of the children served, there are shared and overlapping considerations for any early education environment. Often child care centers cover both infant and toddler care; therefore, it is important to consider what will become important to you as your child ages. Doing so, you can pick the best environment for both your short-term and your long-term needs.

What to Look for When Visiting a Day Care or Preschool Environment

There are a number of situations that you will be looking at when you visit a child care setting. You will be checking for philosophical resonance, kind staff members, and a clean, safe environment. Additionally, it is imperative to assess the providers' attitudes and approaches toward issues of equity and diversity. Although at first this may seem extreme, this awareness will ultimately have a significant influence on the experience your child has both at school and in the world. The messages, both direct and indirect, that your child receives during their formative years will impact your child's innate comfort level, self-esteem, and worldview.

Some settings have specific philosophies about issues of diversity, but most do not. Therefore, it is important to develop questions and ways of examining any environment that will expose the underlying assumptions being made. Always ask questions about the makeup of the families attending this center. Are all of the families from two parent homes? Are single parents, foster parent, or grandparents raising any of the children? When asking these questions, listen carefully to the answers to see if the provider has judgment about one "right" kind of family. Notice if the language used to talk about families is inclusive or comparative.

Likewise, although you will have looked around to notice any apparent diversity among the students, ask directly about the racial, religious, and ethnic makeup of the families. The use of language in response to these questions will be a big tip-off as to the open-mindedness of the center. The answer itself will give you insight. The more homogeneous the group, the more your family will stand out. It is also important to ask questions about the staff: What is the racial, ethnic, and religious diversity of your staff? Are you making attempts to change that in any way? Do you have any out LGBT staff members? If so, how have the families responded? If not, how do you think the parents would respond if you were to hire an openly gay staff member?

Asking these questions is an equally important means of revealing the school's values and unspoken philosophy as is asking questions about structure, playtime, and discipline. In a group care situation, it is important to have the other parents be open, respectful, and welcoming of not only your child, but your family as well. Finding a setting that feels safe to you is paramount.

Screening for Bias

One way of looking at issues of equity in action is to look around the room for indications of gender awareness and unexamined gender bias. Remember it is more often the fact that we, as LGBTs, have stepped out of cultural gender expectations that triggers homophobia than actual knowledge of our LGBT status. Thus, to change the essential indoctrination of gender limitations, and to provide a comfortable and safe preschool/child care for our children, it is best to find an environment that pays much attention to gender issues.

Whenever you are screening a day care center, preschool environment, or after-school program, it is important to have a good look around the room. If you think you like a place, spend the better half of the morning observing. Notice the images on the walls: What is present?

What is missing? Notice the books on the shelves, the layout of the room, the interactions between children, and the interactions the adults have with the children. Bring a pad of paper to document your findings so that you can review them later.

Imagery

- Are there the same number of girls as boys displayed on the walls?

- Do the pictures show girls in active play?

- Do the pictures show boys in contemplative or caring roles?

- Do the pictures depict equal numbers of girls as boys in leadership roles, helping others, making decisions?

- Do the pictures show equal numbers of boys as girls expressing their emotions?

- Are there images in each area of the room that display both sexes involved in that area's activity (i.e., science, dress up, cooking, blocks, art, etc.)?

Layout

- Look around and see if the room appears to be set up with gender equity in mind.

- Is the room designed in a way that has a "girls'" area and a "boys'" area?

- Are the blocks, dress up, and kitchen areas combined or separate from one another?

- Are there boys and girls playing together in each area?

- Do the activities appear to be gender segregated?

- How about outside play? Are the girls just as active as the boys?

Monitor the Interactions

- Do the teachers use the same tone of voice when speaking to boys as when speaking to girls?

- Do they use terms of endearment with the same frequency for both sexes?

- Do they touch boys and girls with the same frequency?

- Are the children allowed to play exclusion games?

- Is there a school policy around exclusion?

- If so, how do they explain it to the children?

- Are the children encouraged to work out solutions to their own problems with the help of adults, or do the adults tell them how to solve their difficulties?

- Is the approach to conflict resolution different for boys than for girls?

- In examining these interactions, pay special attention to emotional expression.

- Are boys allowed the same amount of time to cry as girls?

- Are girls allowed the same amount of time to talk about what happened as boys?

Questions to Ask the Staff

When you ask the teachers questions about sexism, you can weave in questions of bias as a whole. That way, even if they have not worked with children from LGBT families, you will have a direct sense as to how they approach issues of equity. Many teachers believe that they are not giving preferential treatment to one gender or the other. However, in 1992 the American Association of University of Women proved that even teachers who were aware of the tendency for teachers to let boys dominate classroom discussion, to call on boys first, to allow boys to call out answers, but not girls, and to let boys give longer answers than girls, etc., still were documented doing the very behaviors they were trying to avoid (Wellesley College Center for Research on Women 1992).

Ask the staff members the following questions and notice their responses. Their answers will help you to finalize your decision about whether this is the appropriate environment for your child.

- How do they address sexism in the classroom?

- How do they respond to sexist (and all biased) remarks made by children?

- What do they do to keep informed about sexism and early education?

- Are they open to learning more about this subject?

- Do the teachers and/or staff receive any training on issues of diversity?

- Are they open to parental feedback and suggestions regarding these issues?

You want to find an environment that will honor your needs and value the presence of your family as a part of their community. Teachers should be approachable and interested in learning about gay issues as they pertain to preschool and early education. If you sense that the teachers are uncomfortable with you or with your approach, then you must keep looking. We have a right to safe, quality child care for our children. Do not let internal or external homophobia confuse the issues for you.

Once You Choose a Facility or Provider

Selecting a day care or preschool environment can take a lot of time and consideration. Once you have made a choice that feels right to you, it is important to start asking yourself some very important self-reflective questions, such as:

- How do I want to interact with my child's education?

- What level of involvement do I want to have in my child's education?

- Is parent participation an important part of school for me?

- If yes, how will I arrange my work life to make that a possibility?

- Whose responsibility is it to "come out"?

- What role do I hope the school will have in relation to my family?

- What are my expectations of this preschool?

It is important to use the time when your child is in preschool as a small, safe, first step into the larger educational world. Practice different roles and different approaches of identifying and communicating your needs and your expectations as a queer family. Practice a variety of ways of communicating to children and parents about your family. These years serve as a wonderful opportunity to learn about yourself and your approach to education. Preschool serves as a time to clarify your values and what is important to you, and to gain experience interacting as a queer family in a straight context.

Educating Care Providers about Your Child's Needs

Once you have decided on an environment, you can educate the providers about your family and the particular subsequent needs of your child. Ideally you have selected an environment where parents are valued as a vital part of the community. If this is the case, then it will be easier for you to have an open and reciprocal relationship with the teachers. If you set a comfortable tone of open communication, then you are much more likely to be well received. Such a tone will let the staff know that it is OK to ask questions.

When educating teachers and staff, it is important to start with the basics. First let them know about your family: What kind of language do you use to talk about your family? What does your child call you, and any other parents they have? After discussing pertinent issues pertaining to your family, you can move into a greater discussion about families.

Show them how to use open language when talking about families. For example, you can encourage them to use the term "parent" instead of "mom" and "dad." You can request that they talk about family as people who love us, not necessarily people related by blood. By being this open, there is room to discuss children with more than one home, adopted children, children raised by foster parents, children raised by relatives, and children from queer households. Providing examples of how to open up family discourse can help the staff to support all children.

Look to see if the facility has any books that depict nonheterosexual families. You may want to provide them with book lists, books, and educational resources. For preschool, I recommend that all LGBT families own their own copy of *Both My Moms' Names Are Judy* (1994). You can arrange to show this brief film to all of the staff, or ask them to watch it on their own time. The resources listed at the end of this book will help the teachers to answer children's questions, as well as their own questions, about how to handle new situations as they arise. They also provide book recommendations and teaching materials.

If there are diversity trainers who work with teachers in your area, make a recommendation. Suggest a regular time for you and the staff to check in to ask questions and brainstorm about creating a safer environment. Remind the staff that in the absence of a two-gender, two-parent family, Mother's Day and Father's Day can be difficult. Point out that this is the same for children who are raised by grandparents and other family members, and for children with absentee parents. Many schools have been known to shift to a new "Family Day" holiday. If you would like to go one step further, ask to come into the classroom to talk about Pride Day.

If You or Your Child Encounters Homophobia

There is no reason why you should ever feel like you are required to be subjected to ongoing homophobia—especially when you are paying for preschool and day care out of your own pocket. This is essential to keep in mind because when you or your child experiences homophobia it can be hard to remember that you have options. Depending on the circumstance, you can decide what is the most appropriate response to such an incident. It truly depends on the particular situation and whether the homophobic action was intentional or unexamined. For example, if a parent says that her son cannot come over to your house because she does not want him exposed to "your kind of lifestyle," then it is blatant homophobia. If, on the other hand, the teacher is talking about a child and says, "He's such a little pansy," then you have someone who needs to be educated. Blatant and unintentional homophobia are both challenging.

Blatant Homophobia

Blatant homophobia is difficult because you are up against the belief that you and, by extension, your child, are bad. If there is a teacher who is blatantly homophobic, then you are probably in the wrong environment. However, if your child was already attending the preschool when they hired a new homophobic teacher, then it is important to address this. As soon as you become aware it, go to the director or the head teacher with your concern. Be very straightforward (no pun intended) about the kind of remarks you have heard, and about the absolute inappropriateness of hiring such a staff member. If they choose to continue with that teacher, then it may become warranted for you to leave. If the school is not dedicated to ensuring the safety of your child, then you are in the wrong environment. Remember emotional safety is as crucial to health as is physical safety.

Unintentional Homophobia

Working with unintentional homophobia is an easier burden. Sometimes you may feel comfortable addressing the offender directly; sometimes it is more appropriate to report your concern to a staff member and ask them to deal with it. When you are the first LGBT family in the school, then there is often a lot of basic education and unlearning for the staff to do. It is not your job to do this, but, in most instances, such education will fall on your shoulders. If you don't do it, who will?

Homophobic Parents

The most difficult form of homophobia to confront is when other parents respond negatively to your presence in the school. Or, for example, when one or more parents state they don't have a problem with your child in the class, as long as your family is not discussed. This is a tricky line for educators to walk: Which parent's opinion is more valuable? Which is right? If you have established open lines of communication with your child's teachers, and at the beginning of the year have provided them with resources about handling queer issues in the classroom, then these issues will be easier for them to deal with. Depending on the apparent allegiance of the school and on your available options, you may choose to work with the school as they navigate this kind of conflict or you may choose to search out another environment for your child.

Preschool should be a fun, enjoyable, learning environment for your child. Ideally you will find a situation that is compatible with your family values and none of the difficult issues will remain a problem for very long. It is always important to remember that there are choices. You are never trapped in a homophobic situation—you can always leave and find another option that works better for your family.

Primary and Secondary Schooling

As your child becomes school age, you reach another transition point as a queer parent. Entering into the institutional school system can feel like feeding your child to the wolves. It is the school years that most of us have looked toward with trepidation when we decided to become parents in the first place. Do not let your fears lead you to feel defeated before you have even engaged. Whether your child attends a public or private school, your hard earned money is paying for it, and your child, as with every child, deserves a safe learning environment. This is a fundamental right.

Let your vision of how things should be act as your guide for how you will navigate the school system. To do so, you must become clear about your own hopes and fears. Once you know what you want for your child, and you have clarified your preexisting assumptions and fears about what school is, then you can work to manifest your vision.

Exercise

Set aside some time to explore your feelings about school. Designate a full page of your journal and write at the top "The Ideal School." Then ask yourself: What are my wildest dreams about how school could be for my child? As the ideas come to you, write them down. Include as many details as possible.

In your mind, look around the school. What does it look like? What do the students look like? What kinds of activities are they doing? How about the teachers? What is the philosophy of the school? How is your child treated? How is your family treated? What is the relationship between your family and the school? How about the staff? What kind of a feeling do you have when you envision interacting with the staff? How do you feel at the school? How do you feel interacting with other parents? This is your highest vision. It is helpful to keep this paper accessible over the course of the school years. Add to it as your vision develops. This will be your internal guide.

Next, at the top of another sheet of paper write "My Worst Nightmare Regarding School." On this paper, write down what you imagine the worst-case scenario would be for your child at school. What are you most afraid of? Again, be specific.

On a third piece of paper write "What I Expect." Write down how you assume school will be for your child. Notice the feelings in your body as you write this. Write those feelings down, too. Are you hopeful? Do you feel discouraged? This paper is insightful because it will often reveal how your own experience in school has continued to affect your attitude about school now. When you become aware of any limited beliefs you hold, or if you realize that you are entering into the school years with a defeatist attitude, then you can take the time to change these beliefs. If you find this change is necessary, take the time to share with yourself, or another person about your school experiences. When you focus in a positive way, you can separate your past from your child's future.

An Illustrated Example

Frieda is a single dyke mom living in Texas with her five-year-old son, Jack. Her lists looked like this:

The Ideal School

- happy children

- everyone welcome

- nobody perceives Jack as different

- gay issues have no charge to them

- a few LGBT teachers

- great curriculum

- no teasing of any kind permitted

- collaborative feeling

- strong peace-building curriculum

- small class size

- enthusiastic teachers

- multi-cultural curriculum

- strong involved parent body

- other single parents

- other queer families

My Worst Nightmare Regarding School

- Jack will be teased every day because of me

- no one will like him

- no one will stand up for him

- he will learn to be afraid

- his teachers will not like me or him

- the principal will not want to discuss it

- he won't be invited to any birthday parties

- he won't make any friends

What I Expect

- there will be no gay teachers

- gay issues will not be discussed

- people will use "queer" and "fag" for name calling

- there will be no other children from gay families

- he will make friends

- the curriculum and all discussions will be about heterosexual life

- their ways are set; there is no room for change

- none of the parents will like me

- I will just have to accept things as they are

- there will be no queer parents

When Frieda looked at her lists she was able to clarify her vision for herself and to separate that from her fears and expectations. Having done so, she was able to approach each school that she visited and see how it compared to her ideal vision. She chose to lead with her hope rather than her fear or acceptance of what she assumed to be an unchangeable system.

Selecting a School

Most LGBT families do not have a blanket trust and reassurance that our neighborhood school will be the best place for our child. Perhaps you are fortunate and the neighborhood school is indeed the most liberal school in your area. However, you will not come to know that until you do some research.

Just like selecting a preschool, choosing an elementary school with care is perhaps the single most important influence we have regarding the quality of our child's experience. Granted, with all the care in the world, we are not able to guarantee an emotionally safe atmosphere, but we will gain an informed feel for the school environments available in our community. Many families actually choose to relocate to a different area or even to a different part of town to be closer to a more welcoming school environment.

Private School

A number of LGBT families choose to send their children to private schools. Although this is not a financial option for many families, most private schools do provide some financial aid. People who choose private school have often made that choice because they feel that the school environment is more open and receptive to their families than are public schools. By spending time in each school in your area, it becomes apparent which schools have the most liberal attitude. An open and liberal approach to education is often a political view. Therefore, it is helpful to focus on the political philosophies of each school.

With smaller class sizes, and usually fewer disciplinary concerns, the teachers in private schools are often more available (and willing) to try out new ideas and approaches. This kind of atmosphere is conducive to GLBT families and to accepting and integrating our feedback.

Parochial School

Most LGBT families tend to stay away from strict parochial schools as their direct indoctrination against gays and lesbians is so strong. As an experiment, I went through our phone book and called all of the parochial schools. There were more than thirty schools listed. I asked each one, "Do you have any children from gay or lesbian families attending your school?" All of the Catholic and all of the Jewish schools said that they had children from gay and lesbian families attending and that they were more than welcome. (A clear indication that I live in the Bay Area!) In the smaller Christian schools, people hung up on me, told me under no circumstances could such children attend, or they put me on hold after I asked the question and never came back on the line. Other schools did not have such an emotional response and spoke kindly to me saying that there were no students from gay or lesbian families and they felt that their school—being a Christian school—would not be the right place. When I asked if a child from a Christian gay or lesbian family could attend, they all said that because they instruct from the biblical model, children from "such families" would not feel comfortable. You can learn a lot on the phone!

Public School

Most families send their children to public school. As LGBT families, it is important to visit each of the schools in your district and to carefully select the most open and welcoming environment. It will be worth the daily drive to have your child attend a school that is more supportive of your family. If you do have activist tendencies, then a public school is often the arena where you can help to make the greatest change.

Home School

A growing number of our families are turning away from the formal educational system and choosing to home school their children instead. This seems to be a particularly appealing option for families who live in small, conservative areas where their child or their family has not been well received in the existing school. There is a growing home school movement across the country in response to the declining quality of education in public schools. There are many wonderful resources available on the Internet for perspective home schooling families.

Determining If the School Is a Good Match

As with finding a preschool, the best way to know if a specific school environment will be a good match for your child is to spend time at the school. You will want to not only go on the regular school tour, but you will want to spend time talking both with the principal and with the teachers. If you really like a school, then it is well worth the time taken to spend a morning in the classroom and on the playground. Remember a school is not one teacher or solely the principal; therefore, it is important to meet a number of the teachers, not just the one who will be teaching your child that year.

Ask Questions

Although they're not fully responsible for the school climate, administrators definitely help to establish the overall tenor of a school and do indeed have influence on the day-to-day life of the classroom. Therefore, it is helpful to ask the administrators directly what their philosophy is on diversity, with special attention to nontraditional families, such as your own. Listen clearly to the responses given. Do they use affirming language? Do they include LGBT families with other "problem" families? Can they say the words "gay," "lesbian," "bisexual," or "transgender"? Although teachers tend to be more liberal than the administrators, and they most certainly are the critical factor in the education experience, a conservative administrator will set the parameters for what is allowable/permissible for teachers to discuss.

Some schools will very clearly state that all children are welcome (they are required to by state law), but they will neither discuss nor defend homosexual choices. Other schools, whether or not they directly support our families, feel that each child is indeed entitled to a safe school experience and, thus, instruct their teachers to not allow gossip or teasing of any child. Still other schools create an environment that is welcoming to families and children of diverse backgrounds. There is a wide spectrum of responses that you will hear if you ask simple policy questions. Once again, a school can look quite nice and friendly, but until you come out and then ask pertinent questions you will not be able to accurately judge and predict the actual quality of your child's experience.

Observe Interactions for Openness and Equity

Observing interactions in the classroom and on the playground are good ways to gain a real life sense as to how issues of equity are addressed. By paying attention to the level of awareness with which gender interactions are monitored, you will have a very good way to track all issues of equity. Take a notebook to record your observations. If you do this in a number of schools and classrooms, you will see just how useful a tool it can be.

Observe how the teacher speaks to girls and speaks to boys. Is there a noticeable difference in the type or amount of instruction, criticism, or praise? Is this the same across the subjects? As mentioned earlier in this chapter, studies have shown that without attention paid to doing otherwise, teachers treat girls and boys differently (Wellesley College Center for Research on Women 1992).

Girls and gays are often perceived to be within a "harmless" category and, therefore, experience approved bigotry. That is, in situations where children would be stopped from speaking in a derogatory manner or treating someone in a discriminatory way regarding race, ethnicity, or religion, girls and gays are not afforded the same protection. Gay and gender-based references need to be off limits just as other bigoted references are.

Ask the teacher how they address sexism in the classroom. There have been many studies done on gender imbalances and the detrimental affects that this level of institutionalized sexism has on children; if

your teacher is unaware of these studies, you have a pretty good indication that their level of general awareness is equally ignorant. Ask what
they do to keep up-to-date about the research or sexism, and other
issues of bias. Ask how they respond to sexist (and all biased) remarks
made by children.

If the teacher is unfamiliar with the research on the subject of bias
in education, ask if they are open to learning more about the subject.
The answers to these questions will help you finalize your decision
about whether this is the appropriate environment for your child.

Communicating with Teachers
Once You Have Chosen a School

Once you have chosen a school for your child, the next step is to
arrange a meeting with your child's teacher. Ideally, in this meeting or
before, you can ascertain if the teacher will be receptive to your family.
Internalized homophobia often makes the first steps of communicating
with teachers more difficult than it needs to be. It doesn't matter how
out you are, there seems to be a universal parental nervousness about
coming out and discussing the particular needs of your family with your
child's teacher. This nervousness is exaggerated because you are aware
that it is not just you, but also your child who is at risk to receive a negative reaction. This is compounded by a desire to live an open life. This
nervousness is to be expected due to the very real and the feared internal and external issues that arise when advocating for and portraying
your family.

After coming out to your child's teacher, you will decide how
in-depth you would like the rest of the conversation to be. Remember,
you are setting the tone for this conversation, so try to be as comfortable and relaxed as possible. This communicates a message of openness
and approachability. At minimum, it is important to communicate your
expectations that your family structure should not be a problem in the
class. When there is more than one teacher per grade level, you may
want to ask the teacher directly which teacher would be more appropriate for your family; you would be happy to make the change. You can
also directly ask the teacher to call you if they become aware of any
teasing or ridicule directed toward your child, whether or not they feel it
was addressed or insignificant.

Then, if you would like, you can ask some additional questions.
You may want to ask if the teacher has worked with children from
LGBT families before. You may want to discuss how the concept of
families is presented in the classroom. You may want to discuss whether
the teacher is open to suggestions for how to become more aware of
bias. If this is too extreme for you, you may simply want to ask the

teacher if they have any questions. Let the teacher know that it is fine to ask you questions as they arise. Communicate that your goal is for everyone to feel safe and comfortable, and you understand that the teacher may need some education and assistance to accomplish this.

Being the First Queer Family in the School or Classroom

When you are the first queer family that your child's teacher has worked with, both the teacher and the rest of the school community will be on a sharp learning curve. Although more and more schools are beginning to move beyond tolerance into acceptance and antidiscrimination, it is a slow process. It is important to appropriately walk the line between letting other people take the necessary time they need to transform, and not allowing our children to be used as test cases. At this point in time, LGBT families must look out for our own rights.

It can be a difficult transition for educators and parents alike to embrace our families. There is generalized confusion about gay issues. Many people believe that by simply mentioning same gender households or the words "gay" and "lesbian" in the classroom that they are now discussing sex in school. Resentment can build as there is a feeling that we are infiltrating their once tame and protected world. People fear that merely having a child from a LGBT family in their child's class will expose them to lifestyles they deem inappropriate. It is such a fascinating concern, as it always seems to indicate that not only is being queer a choice, but it is an alluring choice that their own children might make.

Help Prepare Teachers

Most teachers are aware that young children cannot have their families rejected or discounted. A child's entire identity at a young age is inseparable from their family. A child's family is their source of identity and love; family cannot be denied. If teachers ignore the situation and hope that it will go away, they're mistaken. Children are inquisitive and they will ask very specific questions of the teacher. Many teachers are initially uncertain about how to answer these questions. For this reason, they need to have access to teachers' resources. Otherwise your family's presence can feel overwhelming simply because the teacher won't know how to answer the questions the children ask, or how to respond to parental concerns. To aid your child's teacher in learning how to incorporate your child into the classroom it is helpful to provide the teacher with resources. Make up a resource packet and keep extra copies on hand. Each year you can pass one out to your child's teacher, teaching assistant, music teacher, physical education teacher, etc. It isn't enough to do this once, you must keep providing resources every year.

The more clarity a teacher gains in understanding that discussing family life is not discussing sex or morals, the easier and more confident they will feel. When it becomes clear that discussing a child's parents and home life is not "condoning" it, then the teacher is more able to address the concerns of other parents. It becomes an issue of cultural acceptance—an awareness and acknowledgement of difference—not an issue of personal approval. When the teacher reaches this level of understanding then there is no longer a need for controversy.

Ideally you can help to establish a culturally sensitive environment in your child's classroom. Your role in this process can take any form as long as it feels consensual for you. It could be as simple as attending school events with your partner or it could mean leading a gay awareness discussion at a staff meeting. It is up to you. It is essential, however, that both you and your child's teacher are aware that expecting silence to be an appropriate response to children's questions places a large burden on your child. Without providing any support, you are asking your child to interact with peers who are most likely filled with misinformation. Silence is the voice of complicity and, thus, if no one answers questions or speaks up on behalf of your child, then you are asking your child to face a daily life filled with rejection and prejudice.

Many LGBT parents assume having a queer teacher would be ideal. Unfortunately that is not usually the case. If the teacher is gay, they may not feel comfortable with you. If they are out, it might make them feel that too much attention is being drawn to them or to feel afraid of being accused of pushing an agenda. Likewise, if they are not out, having you in their classroom can increase their fear of being outed.

What Level of a Engagement Do You Want to Have at School?

When you have chosen a school for your child to attend, then you must make some preliminary decisions about how you would like to interact with the school. There is a wide spectrum of possibilities regarding the kind of participation, influence, and interactions available. Each time your child moves to a new grade, and each time your child moves to a new school, these questions come up. When children are younger, many parents feel that it is easier to have a stronger presence and influence over the day-to-day life in the classroom. This is for a combination of reasons, not the least of which is that parent participation is more common in the younger years. Also, social studies revolve around the family and family life in the younger grades.

To distinguish the most common types of school involvement, I have categorized it into three separate levels. Your level of involvement may deepen or pull back according to the age of your child and the nature of the school. Each level builds on the one before it.

Level 1

Involvement at Level 1 means being a visible LGBT family in the school. This does not mean you need to overtly identify yourself as queer to everyone you meet, but that you reference your child's other family members in conversation just as heterosexual people do. Ideally you are an involved parent in the classroom. You volunteer your time, drive for field trips, and acquaint yourself with the other children in your child's class. This form of visibility allows the children and teacher to know a real live LGBT person.

Make an effort to attend all school functions. Bring your partner and/or coparents to back-to-school night, assemblies, school picnics, etc. This visibility as a family helps people normalize your family and, by extension, all queer families. Then, on all school forms that you fill out, cross out the inappropriate entries (such as "husband" or "wife") and write in "parent." Add extra pages to accommodate your family if there is not enough room on the existing form. Make sure to list all parents on school rosters as well.

This is silent activism. It is your visibility as a family in the school that will ultimately affect some of the greatest changes. There is a big ripple effect by simply being another family, doing all the same things that families do. Over time, the children, other parents, and staff will come to accept your family as just as valid as their own. The key here is visibility. You provide your child, and ultimately all of the people you come in contact with, a great gift when you are an out parent. Your presence becomes your power.

Level 2

Being involved at Level 2 moves beyond silent activism and brings in education of the educators. Many parents feel comfortable sharing time and resources with their child's teacher or with the entire staff to help them become more familiar with gay issues. This is more of an active stance to take.

A parent who is involved at this level makes time at the beginning of each year to select the appropriate teacher for their child, and then schedules a meeting to discuss both their family structure and curricular concerns and suggestions.

Level 2 includes:

- Taking the time to question the teacher of young students about how they will address gender and bias issues

- Brainstorming with the teacher about responses to the use of homophobic language and beliefs among the children

- Bringing up concerns around heterosexist curricula, such as family trees and activities around Mother's Day and Father's Day

- Discussing appropriate changes to school forms with the administrator

- Providing the teacher with a resource list or packet for them to review on their own time

- Watching together or lending to your teachers a copy of the short films *It's Elementary* (1996) and *Both My Moms' Names are Judy* (1994)

These kinds of interactions provide teachers with resources and information that they can integrate as they see fit.

Many parents feel comfortable with this level of involvement. Also, Level 2 parents make themselves available to teachers if they want to use them as a sounding board for new ideas and concerns as they arise. There is a line that most Level 2 parents feel is touchy to cross. They feel like they can provide information up to a point, but that it would be pushing too much of a personal agenda to bring books into the classroom. Likewise, it can feel too vulnerable to think of talking directly to the class about gay issues. (They do not want to have their own life put up for show.) If a classroom discussion was something the teacher was open to, then many Level 2 parents choose to have a third party, who is also queer, talk to the students.

Level 3

Level 3 parents incorporate the presence and education of Levels 1 and 2, and then take it a step further into helping the school to increase awareness and to institute change. People who work at Level 3 have a vision for what optimal educational conditions would be, while realizing the vast distinction between that vision and where most of the schools are today. If you would like to do some of the political work needed to secure such changes, then review the following suggestions and work to implement the ones that are within your means given your available time and energy and the political climate of your school.

In the Classroom

There are many different ways in which you can help children develop a broader view of families and relationships. As children age, you can educate them on the political context that permeates the lowered GLBT social status. It is appropriate for all age groups to bring a rainbow flag to the classroom for Gay Pride month in June. All children can hear a presentation on the significance of the rainbow. The six colors of the rainbow flag is used worldwide as a symbol of queer Pride. The rainbow reminds us that the GLBT community is a diverse community composed of many different people. When you volunteer in your child's classroom, you can bring in books to read out loud to the students. You can choose books with gay, anti-oppression, or "building relationships across differences" themes. After you have read the book you can talk about the themes in the book. You can donate queer friendly, age appropriate books to your child's classroom each year in honor of a gay celebratory day.

As children age, you can bring photos or a slide show about the Gay Pride Parade. For middle and older age children, you can arrange with the teacher as part of their history or social studies unit to talk to the students about the Gay Liberation Movement. You can also arrange for a speaker to come from Parents Family and Friends of Gays and Lesbians (PFLAG) to talk to the school. Some parents approach middle school and high school classes with talks about stereotypes around gays, and allow them to ask the questions they have always wanted to ask. You can also follow national and local politics about gay rights and talk about these issues with the children.

Progressive Curriculum Building

There are many elements involved in progressive curriculum building. Two of the necessary ingredients are willing educators and available resources and training. Progressive curriculum is the ultimate vision. Wouldn't it be wonderful if a teacher were presenting a math problem and said:

> Sarah's family had a loaf of bread. Sarah's mom ate three slices of toast. Her other mom ate two slices of toast. There was one piece of toast left. How many pieces of bread were in the loaf?

There are a number of different organizations across the country that are working to develop such curricular guidelines and gay-specific modules. To have a teacher be able to present such a curriculum, the first place to start is by helping the teachers recognize and unlearn heterosexist bias and assumption. There are diversity workshop leaders who help teachers become more sensitive to the issues of bias in education. Some of these trainers also incorporate LGBT issues. At the charter school that I helped to found, we required all teachers and parents to attend anti-oppression workshops that addressed issues of bias (race, class, sexual orientation, etc.). We also held teacher trainings specifically on developing a queer friendly curriculum. At this training the teachers were able to go home with resource guides. The workshop provided the teachers with a forum to ask their questions, to voice their concerns, and to come up with a school-wide approach for how to implement such a vision.

Parent Organizations

Whether your child's school has a PTA or parent committees, you can utilize your parent organization to effect positive change. You can join or form the diversity or antibias committee. The people who sit on this committee will not necessarily be LGBT themselves, but more than likely they will become your base of in-school allies.

As a committee you can work to organize parent workshops on issues of equity. You can sponsor an evening to show the short film *It's Elementary* (1996) to the parent community. You can arrange for the *Love Makes a Family* photo exhibit to come to your school (see Resources). This is a photo and text exhibit that depicts GLBT families in a beautiful, informative, and loving way.

As a committee member you can also work to ensure that each classroom has age appropriate books that depict gay and alternative families or have queer characters. As well, if the school has a library, you can work to make sure that it has copies of these books.

School Board

If you would like to go even one step further in your activism, then you can work to change the policies of the school board. Depending on whether you are working with a public or a private school, working to change such policies might actually result in changing the policies for all of the schools in your city or county. You will want to press the school board to adopt antidiscrimination clauses and hate crimes policies in their bylaws.

Antidiscriminatory public policy that includes sexual orientation is now being included in some schools around the country. Many school boards have an antidiscrimination policy that does not include LGBTs— this is unacceptable. You can work to add us to the protected list.

It is our job as parents to help create a safer world for our children. When we come out to our children's school and we make ourselves visible, we are creating change. The change must come in the minds of the adults influencing our children and in the approaches of these institutions. We must act not only on behalf of our children, but on behalf of all the children who will grow up to be gay, lesbian, bisexual, or transgendered. This is our responsibility.

PART III

Supporting Our Children

7

Our Children's Issues

There are thought to be millions of children in the United States with at least one gay or lesbian parent. That is a lot of children! Unfortunately, not all of these children know that their parents are gay, and not all of them are in contact with their gay parent. Nonetheless, you have to imagine that the majority of these children do have a relationship with their parents and, therefore, are impacted by the fact that one or both of their parents are queer. In the past decade there has been an ever-increasing number of children who are born into openly queer households. The number of openly queer families is growing exponentially both as it is becoming safer to be a queer parent in our society, and as the resources to do so are becoming more widely accessible and available.

Some parents do not come out until they are already parents. Other parents are queer, and know it, right from the start. How long you have been out, and how comfortable you are with who you are, brings with it differing experiences for your children. Regardless, the biggest influence on your child's relationship to coming from a queer household will be your attitude and self-esteem. The political climate of the community in which you live, and the real life experiences of your children, then mold your child's experience of their situation.

Children who come from gay families have a unique experience of life. In this chapter we will explore some of the most common issues our children face. We will also explore some strategies for helping yourself and your child through some of the most common situations. As your child ages you have less of an immediate influence over how they handle any given situation, as they will be navigating their own worlds. However, as they enter into the world more and more, they will be drawing on their past experiences and the foundations of self-esteem and communication skills that you help them to build.

Although our children are not necessarily GLBT themselves, they are part of the queer culture. So, just as we have learned to, our children learn to straddle multiple worlds. As they enter more fully into their autonomy, they try out new ways of sharing about their families until they find the approach that makes them feel most comfortable. Like ourselves, our children learn the nuances of coming out. As they become older, they find themselves making daily decisions about when, how, and if to come out.

Our Children's Issues Are Changing

When you begin to realize the large number of children from queer families already out there, and the growing number of out GLBTs that are creating family, you can surmise that very soon our children will not feel so alone. The number of GLBT families is changing dramatically. For example, even in the Bay Area, I know very few children my ten-year-old daughter's age who come from queer households; and, of those we know, most of their parents came out after they had children. When she was young, and a gay parent spotted another gay parent, we would go out of our way to introduce ourselves, exchange numbers, and become friends on the basis alone that we were both raising children in GLBT families.

Times sure have changed! For my younger daughter (age two), my family can be selective about our queer parenting friends because there are so many to choose from. We attended a GLBT family day event recently where there were more than three hundred queer families with toddlers. On Mother's Day 2000 we were invited to a lesbian moms' picnic, where there were to be more than forty moms. On the same day, another lesbian moms' picnic in the area boasted thirty moms. These were picnics of personal friends, not public events—which makes the numbers even more staggering. No matter where you live and how many, or how few, GLBT families there are now, you can be secure in the fact that the number will be radically growing in the near future.

Thus, at least some of the issues that we fear our children will face, and the issues that some of our older children have faced and continue to face, may become normalized by the time this next generation of children enters school. For example, many moms worry how their child will feel having been conceived with donor sperm or frozen sperm from a sperm bank; many dads wonder how their children will feel about having been birthed by a surrogate mom they may never know. However, when there are so many children being brought into the world through alternative means, these variances will cease to be perceived as peculiar, but rather as equivalent options.

LGBTs may choose to create family in a less conventional fashion than society currently dictates; however, that might be the only "alternative" circumstance about us and our children. Likewise, our children might be from an interracial or transracial family, they may be adopted, they may have special needs, and they may live in an alternative household—each of which may add to their "alternative" nature.

Depending on where you live and the community into which you bring your child, your sexual orientation will have varying degrees of impact on your child. The issues of our children grow and change as they do.

The Early Years: Zero to Three Years Old

Raising a baby through the toddler years provides us time to adjust to being a GLBT parent. When our children are this young, we are the ones who filter any negative reactions to our family. We are the ones who are rejected by our families of origin. We are the ones who are not admitted into playgroups. We have this time to learn how we want to respond to people's questions and reactions. In the early years, the experiences our children have being raised in a queer household are on the level of early imprinting more than anything else. Child development theory supports the notion that the early years of life are sensitive times of growth when children are deeply influenced by the nature of the environment and by the relationships that surround them. This is the same for children from parents of any sexual orientation. At this age, there is really no reason for the experiences of our children to be different from children in any other family.

Much of a child's sense of self and self-esteem are set during these early years, before they have even entered into a social network of their own. These are the years when you, their parent, can most easily shelter them. In these years, they are cared for either by you, by someone you know and trust already, such as a child care provider you hire, or a day care situation that you have screened and approved. Thus, the main people they come in contact with love them, and where they spend their daily lives is surrounded by people who love them for who they are. At this age, your sexual orientation should have no direct impact on your child's day-to-day life.

Children under four years old are too young to process the concept of homophobia. They are too young to understand closeting. They are trusting. They experience the world in terms of whether they feel safe and cared for, or if they feel afraid and unsafe. The reasons for their feeling unsafe may, at times, be a perception of homophobia, or it may be a reaction to a barking dog—the result is the same, fear from not feeling safe.

The best you can do for your child at any age, but especially during these precious formative years, is to raise them in a house full of love.

Choosing the Closet

Babies and young children have no ability to (consistently) censor themselves verbally. They are creatures of the moment, and once they learn to talk, they speak whatever is on their minds. Thus, if you want to stay closeted, you must be closeted around your young child. Being closeted in your own home is a tragic consequence of being closeted in the outside world, at least when your children are young. Because babies and young children are innately connected to their emotional senses, your child will pick up on your closetedness.

Unfortunately, because your child is too young to understand gay politics, your actions will not be interpreted as closeting behavior. Instead, your child will perceive an untruth—a secret—that results in a pervasive sense of tension in you and, therefore, throughout the home. Thus your home is permeated with the lie, the secret you are hiding from your child. When you are closeted at home, there is no place where you are safe to express yourself fully in front of others—not at home, not at work. Your child perceives your constant level of unease and can even internalize it. Self-esteem of young children is directly, almost empathically, reflected by the self-esteem of their primary caregivers. When there is no "home," no feeling of safety, within your own self, you may be unintentionally undermining your child's self-esteem.

Can you choose instead to live in a house without closets?

Babies and Toddlers Don't Perceive Homophobia

Although you certainly may experience an uncomfortable increase in the homophobic responses of strangers after you have a child, it takes a number of years before your children are able to process the nature of the attacks directed toward you, them, or their families. If your baby or toddler does have the unfortunate experience of having homophobia directed toward them, it is important to remember that your child does not understand homophobia. The homophobia is *your* understanding and *your* experience. At this age, your child is faced with another reality completely. Sometimes a comment or action will go right over their head, as it is truly directed at you.

Healthy Responses to Homophobic Occurrences

If your child is involved in a traumatic situation due to someone's homophobia, it is important to address it as you would any other trauma your child suffers. First, remove your child from the dangerous situation, then comfort your child emotionally and physically. Allow your child to express their feelings about the situation so that you can see what the trauma was for your child. If you can help it, do not over-lay your experience onto your child. Your child had a separate experi-ence that needs to be uncovered, soothed, and healed.

Jan, a single mom in Michigan, said that while she was at work one day, her baby sitter and her baby sitter's girlfriend took her six-month-old baby for a walk in the park. Shortly after arriving at the park, they were surrounded by a gang of young men taunting them with homophobic slurs, sexual gestures, and threats of violence. They felt paralyzed with fear; they had never imagined that anyone would act that way when a baby was involved. They were able to escape, but they were mugged and forced to hand over all of their personal belongings, including the stroller, before they were able to do so. The women understood the reasons for the attack and had to both report the attack to the police and recover from an emotionally traumatic hate crime. As caregivers, however, their job was to soothe the crying baby who had been in a loud and scary situation.

Although homophobia is very hard to accept and even harder to see directed toward our children, the early years provide us with a form of emotional shelter. By no means are you or your children immune to homophobia, but at this young age, your children are probably too young to process the content that caused the trauma. Thus, dealing with homophobia in your early parenting allows you a grace period where you do not need to address with your child why people are hateful. Instead you only have to address your child's emotional response to the trauma experienced. The primary response your child needs is to be comforted and soothed by you. Here's another example of this.

Brenda and Conrad—An Example

Brenda is a transgendered woman living in Southern California. She is also a lesbian. Although she "passes" most of the time, when she does not it can be very scary. The gender issues she triggers in others have led to violence on more than one occasion. This is something she was afraid of when she was considering having children with her part-ner. She did not want to put her children at any additional risk, and she did not want her children exposed to the occasional venom that is directed toward her. However, she and her partner, Wendy, really wanted children. They decided together that they would not let fear decide for them whether they would be parents.

One day Brenda was at the supermarket with their son, Conrad. Conrad was almost three years old. Conrad was in front of another little boy in line. They were making funny faces, and blowing "raspberries" at each other. The line was long and they had been playing for a while. Brenda turned around to make small talk with the child's mother. When the mother saw her she started to scream, "Oh my god, she's a freak! Get your filthy child away from mine! Heaven help me, my son is going to die—that child spit on him. Help get me out of here! Does anyone have disinfectant? This is an emergency!" Brenda did not wait to hear anymore, she scooped her panicked child up and quickly left the store.

On the way to the car, she tried to calm herself down. She kept telling Conrad, who was crying, that everything was OK, they just needed to leave the store. When they finally got in the car, Conrad was in the middle of a full-blown tantrum. Brenda held him in her arms. Conrad was really upset. When he finally got his words out, it became clear that he was so upset because they had not bought the bananas he wanted to eat. Brenda could not believe her ears. He was not questioning that crazy woman, he wanted the bananas! They drove to a nearby store, Brenda's heart still racing, and got bananas.

That night at dinner Conrad told Wendy, his other mom, that some lady had yelled really loud at Mommy in the store and he had to plug his ears, but it was OK because they got bananas at the other store. Conrad was able to talk about how red the lady's face got and how scared her yelling made him. It was about the intensity of the woman's rage, not the content that had scared him. He was not developmentally able to ingest the content. The experience had been traumatic, but it was over for Conrad. Brenda and Wendy had a lot of further processing to do, but they were able to recognize that for Conrad, buying him the bananas and encouraging him to talk about the incident was enough.

Preschool and Kindergarten

Preschool and kindergarten age children do not question the validity of their family—at this age, they accept it at face value. With careful screening of your child care providers, you can delay any uncomfortable feelings your child may develop later on from being "different." It is at this age that children begin to explore societal constructs and roles. Through this developmental awakening, your children will become aware that not all families are like theirs. Unless they are exposed to narrow minds, they will simply explore the differences that they see around them rather than judge difference as bad. Children are naturally inquisitive and will pose many questions to you and to others about the nature of family. How they are responded to at these times will directly shape their perception of the world. Therefore, it is our responsibility to think before we answer, to give the broadest view of life to our children.

Questions that children ask at this age are not usually emotionally based, but are more curious in nature. So when your two-year-old child first asks you where her mommy is, you do not need to panic and think "Here it is the moment I have been dreading . . ." In asking this question, she is not indicating that she feels incomplete, she is simply trying to reference herself. An answer as simple as "Oh, sweetie, you don't have a mommy, you have two daddies. There are lots of kinds of families and we don't have a mommy in our family" will often suffice.

Sometimes, however, what started off as curiosity is quickly followed by "but I want a mommy" and a tantrum. Once again, at this age it is unlikely that she is expressing an actual sense of loss, but instead a desire for something she has seen elsewhere. Often coming back with "Would you like to pretend that I (or the cat, your doll, etc.) am your mommy today?" is all that is needed. If that is not sufficient, then it is usually helpful to ask your child, "What is a mommy?" This will usually clarify what it is that your child is actually asking. Your young child can then say, "Well, mommies on television bake cookies and you don't bake cookies. I want cookies! I want a mommy!"

At this age, your child will be comparing their family to other families they know. Thus, it is helpful to make contact with other GLBT families, and other families who have different configurations than your own. This way your child can learn to recognize that there are many similar and different faces of family. Exposure to a variety of differing family structures at this age helps to imprint open minds for life. Take the time to discuss the many ways to have a family. Buy picture books that represent many different families and forms of family.

When Does Your Child Become Aware That Their Family Is Different?

There comes a time when your child gains awareness that you are GLBT. This first awareness is best if it is led by you. If they are comfortable with the words that you use to describe your family, then the words will not be so charged when they hear them from other people. Many children can tell you that they have two dads, or two moms and two dads. They know who is partnered with whom in their own family. However, it takes maturity to understand that that means that they are GLBT. And from there, it takes maturity to grasp the social implications of such relationships. The age at which this moves from an *awareness* that you are GLBT to a beginning *understanding* of the ensuing implications is different for each child. This is often a gradual awakening. When a child begins to experience the implications of their parents' sexual orientation, however, they begin to realize that it affects them.

This level of recognition, and the subsequent ability to put words to it, takes time. It develops as your child matures. For my own daughter who is raised in a very out household, and comes to work with me all the time in a queer family-oriented midwifery practice, it still took many years to fully grasp the queer concept. Through first grade she would still ask, "Now what is a lesbian again?" Now, however, in the fourth grade she is actively refining her "gaydar" and points out GLBTs on the street. This awareness continues to progress and eventually, over many years, gains a political contextual understanding.

When children have been brought up with a gay positive perspective, they expect to be accepted. When that is first questioned it can be devastating. The age at which your child experiences direct consequences from talking about their family is the beginning of this awareness. This eventually brings with it the understanding that discussing family structure can have personal ramifications. This leads to their initial understanding of "coming out." Personal experience and interviews reveal that many children don't develop this level of awareness, sensitivity, and a recognition of a desire to self-censor for protection until they are in elementary school. Up until that point they assume that they and, by extension, their family will be accepted. A beginning understanding of the implications of growing up in a queer household usually develops in relation to school family curriculum, or to comments or questions made by playmates or classmates. This understanding matures as your child matures.

Navigating the Straight World

If your child has the fortunate, and well-deserved experience of being openly and warmly accepted by classmates, teachers, camp counselors, neighbors, and parents alike, then they may never internalize homophobia. By the time they experience a negative reaction to GLBTs, they will be old enough and confident enough to openly stand up for all equity. From the dozens of parents and children I have spoken with, however, it seems our children are confronted with homophobia and a lack of appreciation for their family somewhere in their journey through early or middle childhood. At this age it is natural to personalize a homophobic response.

Before there is a direct negative reaction to one's own family, it is easy to start internalizing homophobia if your care providers are not trained to examine their heterosexist assumptions—and most are not. For example, if in preschool the teacher says or agrees with the children when they assert that only a man and a woman can be married, then your child is receiving heterosexist indoctrination. If your child speaks up and says, "But my dads are married," and the teacher responds with, "But that's not a *real* marriage," or "But boys are not *supposed* to marry each other," or "Well that's different," then your child is being taught that her family is "wrong."

Similarly, if two boys are hugging each other and an older kid yells, "That's gross, only fags hug each other," then your child is also receiving a clear heterosexist message. These kinds of dialogues are often pervasive. Yet they can be the very kind of interactions that our children never report to us. Without careful screening of your day care, camp, preschool, and school setting (see chapter 6, Culturally Sensitive Child Care and Schools: The Ongoing Process) it is safest to assume that this kind of dialogue will happen—without helpful adult interference—on a regular basis. Although it should not have to be our responsibility to educate others about appropriate use of language, it often becomes our job if we want to witness change.

It is beneficial to realize that gay slurs and heterosexist assumptions are indeed the norm in your child's life outside of your home. Television, books, and magazines all reflect heterosexual society. Thus, if you would like that to be counteracted with some gay friendly influences, it is up to you and your support circle to provide that. Helping your child learn to recognize prejudice and bias are an important part of raising and maintaining your child's self-esteem. This provides them with a context and a language to reference discriminatory behaviors. It helps them to depersonalize the experiences and to learn to identify why such comments make them feel bad.

The Ins and Outs of Coming Out for Children

Your child will have an ever-evolving relationship to whom they tell what about their family. Children start off trusting and, over time, develop caution as people have negative responses to their family structure. Depending on the safety and philosophy of the environment, your child may decide not to come out in certain situations. When your child (or for that matter an adult) chooses not to come out, your child feels that they have to protect themselves from feared negative reactions. They are having to lie, omit, or simply not talk about important family members and aspects of family life. Keeping secrets as a child creates internal pressure and stress.

As children age, they speak less and less about their families in school and during other activities. Thus, it becomes a question of when, if, and how to come out. If your child has been hanging out with someone at the recreation center and wants to have them over to play, then it becomes important to bring it up. Until that point the conditions of their relationship had nothing to do with *their parents'* sexual orientation. Thus, in some ways, coming out as a child from a queer household is even more complex than coming out as a GLBT. Some children have fears that we, as parents, will out them simply by entering the room.

Although they may be proud of us, at times they experience internal conflict by feeling like coming out is not their choice.

How Our Children Talk about Coming Out

When talking with older children about whom they tell about their LGBT families, they all respond in surprisingly similar ways. Some say that their whole world has always known so they don't have to deal with this issue. They have lived in the same neighborhood, gone to school with the same children, etc., all of their lives. Everyone knows and nobody cares. Most middle and older children say that when they are in a new environment they have to try to guess how each person will respond. They will only bring it up to people that they think will respond favorably. Because it is not that important to talk about their parents, it does not always come up that regularly. However, anyone considered a friend definitely knows.

Most middle and older age children do not experience a blanket trust that everyone will automatically accept them and their family. They become more self-conscious about coming out both to adults and other children because they are aware of the potential for homophobic reactions. Children in the older grades are afraid of losing social standing if the "wrong people" were to find out about their family structure. Other children are simply shy and do not want attention drawn to them or to have to answer people's questions or to explain their family structure. Likewise, some children are afraid that they would experience group harassment speared on by "bullies," "mean people," "snobs," or "socialite ring leaders." With adults, they become afraid of the negative and sometimes hostile reactions to hearing about their families. Needless to say, children tend to use caution in whom they come out to.

At some point in the older grades children begin to have a political awareness about injustice. If your child is confident and not too shy, it is common for them to stand up for issues of equity in their schools. When questioned, numerous older children spoke of having educated peers and teachers alike on heterosexist language and issues of gay rights. As they age, children say they feel less alone because gay issues are a national hot topic, and there are others their age who are interested in securing equal rights for GLBTs. Whether your child will move to this level of activism is completely dependent on the nature of your child and the receptivity of the environment.

As students leave middle school and enter into high school, it tends to become "cool" if you have something different about you. At that age, children don't really identify each other based on their parents, so there is actually less room for homophobic reactions. Of course, differences will more likely be overlooked if your child is popular, and more of a hurdle if your child is outside of the primary social circles. As children get older, with whom they can be friends is not influenced by their parents as much as when they were younger. This can help to reduce any potential homophobic reactions from other parents filtering their child's experiences.

Interestingly, children seem to be more trusting of either adults or children, but, often, not equally of both. When questioned more thoroughly, it seems to be contingent on who, in their upbringing, had negative responses to their family. When the negative responses have come from other children, then adults will be trusted to be more understanding and accepting. On the other hand, if the negative reaction to their family came from an adult, then children may find themselves doing less censoring in the presence of other children.

It does not matter how old your children are, it can be awkward and anxiety producing to feel different. As a minority they will most likely face many prejudices and stereotypes from people who find their family offensive. Teens have expressed internal struggles about having to question cultural and religious constructs from such a young age. Studies show that although our children do experience more stress, they are also better adjusted (Patterson 1992). Older children also can grapple with the desire to find support for the judgment that society puts on them because of who their parents are, while not wanting to betray their parents by seeking support.

Fortunately there is a wonderful organization, Children of Lesbian and Gays Everywhere (COLAGE) (See Resources), that provides both online support and support groups for our children in some of the major metropolitan areas. They also have a newsletter for our children.

AIDS, Breast Cancer, and Death

Because so many gay men have died of AIDS, if your child is raised by gay men it is important to talk to them about what you are doing to protect yourself. In the 1980s and 1990s many children lost their gay fathers to AIDS. Although information has reduced the epidemic in the gay population significantly, your children will want, and deserve to know, how you are keeping safe.

Likewise, breast cancer rates are particularly high among lesbians (Roberts, Dibble, Sanion, et al. 1998). If your child is raised by LGBT parents, they therefore have a greater likelihood of having a parent or close friend die of AIDS or breast cancer. Many of our children must process grief, loss, and queer medical politics from a tender age.

When the Adults Are Closeted

If you are closeted, but out to your children, then you are encouraging your child to closet as well. In closeted families your child usually has a limited number of select friends who know, but it is understood by everyone to be a secret. This can become an additional burden for your child as they can harbor confusion and increased fear that rides on your fear. From the sampling of children that I have spoken with directly, children from out households don't really think about hate violence or custody issues in relation to their parents' sexual orientation. However, for children whose parents are not out, and families where the parents don't even discuss their sexual orientation with their children, they have significantly more fear that something "bad" is going to happen to their family.

Extended Family

Children whose parents are not out to extended family members express stress around trying to remember how to talk to their relatives. One child expressed it well when he said that it was as if he were supposed to tell his grandmother that he had a sister instead of a brother. His attention would always be on focusing on the pronouns he was using and trying hard not to mess up and be questioned. He is always trying to maintain a story about his other mother who is not supposed to be anyone other than a roommate. As a result, he would rather not see his grandmother because he feels like the whole time he is with her he must monitor himself, acting and censoring his behavior when he would rather be honest and open.

Many children express anger and resentment at the artificial constructs that their parents make them uphold, as they should. Some children say that it has significantly limited the quality of relationship they can have with their relatives because it is all based on a lie. Children from closeted single queer parents do not seem to have this same stress. They can more easily understand that their parent does not want to discuss their dating relationships with their family. This is different, however, because it does not have as direct an impact on them. That is, it does not deny the child, parents, and other meaningful relationships; it is simply a choice about whether their parent wants to come out. Nonetheless, when we ask our children to lie for us, we are putting our fear and our shame onto them. We are asking them to take on our issues.

Teasing, Taunting and Potential Ostracism

What we, as parents, usually fear the most is the teasing, taunting, and potential ostracism that our children may face because of our sexual orientation. For most children it is not as bad as we fear it may be. Most likely for every new generation of children, the frequency and fear of such incidents will be declining. Most children, however, will at some point experience at least one painful episode of homophobia directed at them. For some children, it will be many more than one incident. Keep in mind, however, the same can be said for almost every child regarding something. Shorter children, larger children, developmentally delayed, developmentally advanced, you name it, children tease about it.

As with all oppressive and discriminatory behavior, however, antigay and gender policing behaviors should not be tolerated or permitted. When children are teased, ridiculed, or attacked, they learn to be fearful. When you experience this form of behavior you can feel like you have to hide, like you are all alone, and like no one understands you. As parents, we can encourage our children to develop inner Pride, and teach them skills for weathering difficult situations. We must, however, also listen to our children—there are times when they may be truly emotionally or physically unsafe and need parental protection and possible removal from the situation.

How Parents Can Help Their Children

As GLBT adults, we all know, or can remember, what it is like to enter into a completely new environment and have to figure out whom to become friends with, and to whom it may be safe to come out. The same is true for our children. Any time we can identify with their experiences, we can help to smooth their fear by taking small actions that make them feel much safer.

Establishing Allies

It helps to establish allies within any environment. It actually serves most to establish these contacts when first entering into a new situation, *prior* to any ridicule occurring. When your children are young you can help by prescreening an environment. You can come out on the phone and ask if they anticipate that having a child from a queer family might pose a problem. You can say that you want everyone to feel comfortable, so if this might not be the "right" place, you understand. You can provide an opening for them to suggest that it may not be a good match for your child, without them having to sound like they might be discriminating (and thus be open to a lawsuit). It is valuable to leave an opening for such a communication without at anytime sounding like you are apologizing for your family. (See chapter 6, Culturally Sensitive Child Care and Schools: The Ongoing Process).

When starting any new program you can ask the director if there are any other children from queer families, or if there have been in the past. If you receive an affirmative answer, you can share that with your child. Make a point of finding out and identifying any other queer families, and of meeting the children in those families. Likewise, scout out any queer staff members or especially understanding, progressive adults. Once these allies have been identified, you can ask them directly to support your child. If they agree, you can introduce everyone to one another. Then if trouble arises, your child knows that they can come to one of these people.

Just knowing that there are allies helps to eliminate the feeling of being all alone. By helping your child to identify supportive allies, you reduce the burden on your child of having to energetically determine who is "safe" and who is not. It provides some pre-established islands of safety.

Providing Children with Skills to Recognize and Cope with Inequity

It has been documented that children from gay families have more stress than children from straight families, but they also have more skills to deal with that stress. It is also said that their verbal capacity tends to be extraordinarily high (Patterson 1992). The fact is that our children often achieve a higher level of social sophistication and appear to be more open-minded than most children raised by heterosexuals (Harris and Turner 1986). This is primarily due to the need to navigate social relationships more consciously from a young age. They also tend to be sensitive to the issues of justice, and they become social activists themselves at a surprisingly young age. Brave, outgoing children from queer households have been known to approach a teacher for support and to talk to their class and to other classes about stereotypes and gay people. Some have been known to start a school-wide ban on hateful language (Both My mom's Names Are Judy 1994).

Our goal is to provide children with the skills to recognize inequity and to develop effective coping skills. When developing such awareness, it is less likely that children will internalize and personalize the inequity. With such skills, they have the capacity to develop an innate sensitivity and empathy toward all forms of discrimination and oppression.

Processing Homophobic Incidents Together

When your child is confronted with homophobia it is important to allow your child room to express their feelings about the incident. Remember, unless you were raised in a GLBT household, you have never been in the situation that they are in. Your goal should be to let your child know that it is safe to process difficult situations with you. Focus on your love for your child rather than on your anger at the homophobia or frustration at your child's response.

A nice form of support is to ask open-ended questions and really listen to the answers that your child shares with you. Good questions to ask include:

- How did it feel when they said that?

- How did you respond?

- Did you tell anyone when this happened?

- If so, how did they respond?

- Did anyone stand up for you?

Sympathize with your child. Take the approach of an ally, not a critic. Thus, if your child did not do what you would have wished, do not project that as a weakness onto your child. Remember, do not let your reaction to the situation dominate the experience. Try to put your feelings aside as you address your child's needs. (This can be quite difficult, as immediate reactions to hearing about homophobia directed at our children can be very strong anger, shame, or guilt.) Then, only after your child has completed their expression, you can take the time to share your feelings with your child if you feel like it would be appropriate and supportive.

Once all of the feelings have all been shared, it is important to go one step further. However, be sure to wait until the feelings are complete. This may mean waiting for another day to finish the conversation. When the time is right, take the time to brainstorm together. Explore questions together such as:

- If you had a chance to go through that again, can you think of other responses that you could have had?

- Is there anything that we should/could do now to help you feel better?

- Are there things that I can do to help prevent something like this from happening again?

- Is there anything that *you* can do to help prevent something like this from happening again?

Sometimes there are actions that you, as a parent, can do to help, or ways that you can support your child to create a safer environment. For example, you can meet with relevant staff to share about the incident. If appropriate, you can provide educational materials, or provide a resource list for the staff to access. (See Resources for suggestions.)

One Incident Can Scare Children into the Closet

Sometimes all it takes is one incident or one homophobic person in a child's life to scare them into the closet for a long time thereafter. My daughter had very intentionally been raised in open, diverse environments that appreciated and even celebrated difference and diversity. Some of these environments I had to create myself. She attended the charter school that I helped to start, which was based on an antibias curriculum. Nonetheless, in second grade, my daughter had a child in her class who was virulently homophobic. She took to whispering homophobic statements into my daughter's ears.

When she shared these incidences at home, we nurtured her and encouraged her to express her feelings. Let me tell you, it is not always easy to contain your own reactions to hearing that your child is experiencing homophobia. After helping her with her emotional processing, we sat down as a family and decided what to do. The day after she shared this with us, we talked with her teacher. Her teacher was very supportive and promptly addressed this issue with the other child's parents. Her class discussed homophobia at a class meeting, and established a formal ally system for supporting anyone who was being treated unjustly, not just with homophobia, but with sexism, racism, adultism, etc.

Even with this supportive response, my daughter got the message there was something about her family that was not safe to share with everyone. At age seven, she moved from awareness of difference to firsthand experience of homophobia. Other children have moved into this much earlier, some much later.

From that point on my daughter has carefully selected who she tells that she has two moms and when she tells them. Although her whole class at her new school now knows, she took half a year to tell them. As usual, we were out to all of the staff at her new school, had both of our names on the school roster, and attended school functions together. But for the first time, she did not want me to come into her class to talk about gay issues. This school is much more conservative than her last school. In the beginning, she was actually dodging questions about who I was. My partner, Colleen, would pick her up on most days, but when I would come to school the children asked, "Who's that?" and "Is that your aunt?" She would mumble and leave quickly.

It broke my heart to see her living in fear. We would talk about Pride endlessly at home. However, how she navigates her world is up to her. She was out in all of her other extracurricular life, just not at school. She said she needed to know everyone first before sharing with them about her family. This was a whole new game she was playing, once she had experienced homophobia firsthand. She was coming out.

In our family, we have a policy that we, as parents, will not closet ourselves, and we discussed that clearly with her. That meant that if anyone asked me directly who I was, I'd say I was her mom. One day a staff member at her new school revealed to the children she was gay. This information was well received. That was the open door for which my daughter had been waiting. They were standing in line at the time and she mumbled that her moms were gay too and the rest is history. No bad reactions, but my daughter experienced months of internalized homophobia fearing the possibility of another negative response.

When You Adopt an Older Child

People who choose to adopt older children are courageous, compassionate, loving people who are willing to forego the traditional parent/child bond for a unique and deep familial connection with a child who has already experienced life, and loss, and whose personality is already formed. When you consider adopting an older child, concerns regarding your sexual orientation are but one of the many things that you will take into consideration. Nonetheless, your sexual orientation will have an impact on your child.

Resist any temptation to closet yourself to your child. If you are not ready to be out to your child, it is probably best that you do not adopt an older child. Older children have usually suffered through so much change, disappointment, and loss that it is very important to create a safe environment built on truth and trust. If you are not out to them and at some later point they discover or you share your sexual orientation with them, they can feel betrayed again, and it can seriously undermine the trust you have worked so hard to establish. How your sexual orientation will affect your child and impact your family depends primarily on their past upbringing to this point. Coming out to children who have previously been raised in a straight environment can have a significant impact on them. Sometimes it can be a smooth transition, and other times it can be incredibly challenging for all involved.

For example, Lexa and Diana started fostering Charlene when she was eight years old. Charlene's mom was a distant associate of theirs who was having a drug problem. The understanding was that they would foster her until her mom got her life together. When Charlene was ten, and her mom was in jail again, Lexa and Diana, with the approval of Charlene and her mom, formally adopted her.

Until Charlene came to live with Lexa and Diana she had never before met any lesbians. At first they did not discuss it directly; she simply lived with them in their home. Over time, Charlene started to ask direct questions and they would answer them. It took the first year of living with them before she learned the word "lesbian." For Charlene it was a smooth transition. Lexa and Diana felt that they had a lot of very basic unlearning and relearning to do with Charlene. They had to unwind the heterosexual assumptions that she had been indoctrinated with, but there did not seem to be any homophobia to unlearn. They were lucky. Charlene, who just turned twelve, is now quite familiar with lesbian culture and lingo. However, for all three of them it was a cross-cultural experience for Charlene to reach that place.

Andre and Tom, on the other hand, did not have an easy go of it. Andre and Tom adopted Michael when he was nine. They were out to him from the start. Michael and Andre are African American Tom, on the other hand, is white. Michael had come from a very hard childhood and was very street wise when he came into their family. The transition was challenging. Michael did not like "fags" or "whiteys." Over time and through lots of love and patience Michael came to love and trust his new family.

It was a very trying time for Andre and Tom, because for the first time in their lives, they had to face homophobia on a daily basis—and it was within their own home. Michael was very verbally expressive about his thoughts about "homos." Michael is now fifteen and is confronting his own sexuality. Although he's straight, a number of his friends are bisexual. He recognizes that if he hadn't come to live with Andre and Tom, he never would have been able to stay friends with his friends if they told him they were bisexual. Now he says that it doesn't matter to him, as long as they don't start hitting on him! He no longer makes homophobic comments and has learned to remove racial remarks from his daily dialogue.

Coming Out When Your Child Is Older

When you come out as a parent, there is no rule of thumb as to how your children will accept your change in sexual orientation. A lot of it depends on how your child's other biological parent responds. If your child's other parent is not involved in their life, and you have been raising your children on your own, then the transition is often welcome as you are falling in love with a same-sex partner and there are good feelings in the house. If your child's other biological parent, however, does not handle your coming out well, then there is a good chance that your children will feel like they have to choose sides.

If you come out when you are in a straight marriage and your coming out effectively breaks the family up, then your children will usually have a much harder time with it. This is not necessarily from homophobia; rather it's because their world, as they know it, is falling apart. In the ideal world, you, your ex, and all relatives openly embrace your change and the children can ask questions and transition smoothly. In reality, change is rarely that smooth. Your children usually experience a combination of understanding, acceptance, and confusion.

In any event, depending on the age of your children, they may only partially accept the "new" you. A number of children that I have met in these situations have felt like it was fine, as long as all of their friends didn't have to know. They had internalized homophobia and felt like they did not want to suffer or to have to defend their parent because of this new change. It is definitely important to realize that acceptance of the new you will take time. It is an adjustment period that you all will go through as you each explore what kind of impact this will have on your lives.

Sometimes coming out as a parent is complicated by the potential threat of losing custody of your children. In these cases, you may find that you have to stay closeted to your child until the dust has settled— even though you would prefer not to do so. For some families the dust takes years to settle. In these instances, closeted parents who so dearly wish to be out to their children have found it very helpful to keep a journal to their child, to give to them when they finally are able to share this part of themselves openly. The journal can help the child to feel less betrayed by the acting done allegedly on their behalf.

When Your Child Wants You to Be Closeted

Sometimes your children will want you to be closeted. Some children reach an age where they decide to not come out to others. Often this happens around junior high school. As a part of individuation and separation from their parents, they do not want to have to be identified in relation to their parents. The choice to not come out to friends can put them into a tight spot. It is hard to bring friends home. Children at this age may actually ask you to closet. You may find that they have moved your books around and are beginning to hide any obviously queer belongings.

How you decide to handle this is up to you. I encourage you to support your child through this difficult developmental stage, yet refuse to closet. Explain to them sensitively and with compassion why you will closet for no one, especially in your own home. You can then, together, brainstorm how your child can feel more comfortable given the parameters of your family life. Although as parents we want to support our children the best we can, closeting per their request is one of the worst messages we could communicate to them.

Being queer is an inextricable part of who we are. To voluntarily hide that part of ourselves is to agree that we should be ashamed and sensitive to the fact that part of our essential nature is offensive to others. As parents we try to teach our children to be secure and proud of who they are in all settings. What does it say for us to succumb to mainstream "peer pressure"?

Conversations to Have with Older Children

As your children grow older, some of the best times that you have with them are engaging in thoughtful conversations. These types of conversations are ones where your child has the freedom and encouragement to develop their own ideas and opinions without you jumping in with your own. These times also allow you to stay connected with your child and to let your child know that you remain interested and want to be involved in their life, even as they become young adults themselves.

You can explore interesting personal philosophies together and come up with new ideas and thoughts from this sharing. As any parent of older children can attest to, you cannot plan one of these talks, you just have to seize the opportunities as they present themselves. It is best to be willing to drop everything if your child initiates an important conversation with you—children cannot be put on hold, they are creatures of the moment.

Remember, it is always helpful to share from your own experiences. Our children love to hear of our struggles and our triumphs. They love to hear about our weaknesses as well as our strengths. And most of us learn very well from anecdotes.

The Benefits of Communication: An Example

Paul wanted to find a way to address with his son, Sam, how he did not feel it was right for Sam to be closeted about his family. Paul felt very emphatically that Sam should not try to hide the fact that his parents were gay. Rather than sharing in lecture form with Sam how strongly he felt, Paul decided to share from his own experience. When he and Sam were hanging out together one summer night, Paul started talking about how hard it was for him growing up Jewish.

He had grown up in a town where there were not many Jews and where Jewish stereotypes ran rampant and unchecked. When Paul went to high school across town from his junior high he decided not to tell anyone that he was Jewish. He really didn't think it mattered, and no one could tell just from looking at him. He felt he could hide his ethnicity simply by not disclosing it. That year at school he discovered just how many Jewish jokes and derogatory comments were told. After feeling uncomfortable just trying to ignore the jokes, he would try to mention that making fun of other people wasn't nice. That didn't work either because then the guys would say, "What's the matter? You're not Jewish so who cares." Paul told Sam just how stuck he felt. It was hard for him to go along as if he weren't Jewish, but he did not know how he could ever tell any of them now that he had been hiding for so long.

One day Paul came home from school to dinner to find his whole family disturbed. It turned out that his sister had found out that Paul was denying that he was Jewish and had mentioned it to his parents. His parents were devastated. His father had been a concentration camp survivor. They could not believe that within their own home, their own child would deny their struggle, their truth. His parents were hurt, flabbergasted, and shocked. Paul saw how much he had unintentionally hurt his parents. He also saw how much he had suffered himself with the lie of not disclosing. He decided he would not hide such an intrinsic part of himself anymore. He chose to take on the challenge of changing people's attitudes rather than trying to hide an important part of himself. In this realization, he recognized that he was proud to be a Jew and could not imagine wanting to hide that again.

After sharing that story with Sam, they had a great talk. They were able to question together whether it is ever appropriate to hide an intrinsic part of your self. They questioned whether it was a luxury to be able to hide in the first place. They questioned what it would be like to have a quality that is discriminated against that cannot be hidden. They questioned whether there was a family obligation to be proud of who you are and where you come from. They talked for a long time without ever addressing directly the issue of sexual orientation, their family, and the fact that Sam was closeting. Whether Sam changed his ways did not mean as much to Paul as being able to have thoughtful introspective conversations with Sam about the underlying issues involved.

Questions That Inspire Conversation

The following questions are starting points, or suggestions for topics about which you can talk with your older child:

- Do you have an obligation to reveal your sexual orientation or that you come from a queer family?

- If something is not necessarily outwardly apparent, does it need to be shared?

- What if there were a threat of gay people or queer families being killed, would you come out or would you closet?

These kinds of conversations are obviously for older children, but they are some of the best moments of parenting, when together you can challenge one another to broaden your thinking. Because there are no right or wrong answers to philosophical and theoretical situations, you have a wonderful opportunity to get to know yourself and each other more deeply.

Other valuable and more personal questions to ask your child from an open place include:

- Do you try to blend in?

- Are you afraid of being perceived as different because of the nature of your family?

- Are children who are raised by GLBT parents different?

- Are you treated differently because of your family?

- How does that make you feel?

- Do people use "gay" and "fag" as ways of describing people or their behaviors?

- How does that kind of use of language make you feel?

- How are GLBT children treated?

- Do you feel any affinity toward other GLBT children because you come from a queer household?

- Are you assumed to be GLBT?

- How does that make you feel?

- Are you GLBT?

Reassure Your Child That It's OK to Be Straight

We must, as parents, be careful not to fall into heterophobic behaviors. It can be automatic for some of us to talk disparagingly about straight people or to make fun of straight people in moments of frustration. This, however, isn't any more acceptable than derogatory comments being made about GLBTs or about any group of people. Many people are careful to only express discriminatory sentiments in the privacy of their own homes, so as not to offend anyone. Wrong as this attitude may be, it is especially inappropriate if you are making statements about men, women, or straight people around your children.

Many of our children express jokingly that they don't know what their parents will do if they grow up to be straight. Our children express some level of concern that they might not be as well loved as their sibling if their sibling turns out to be queer and they turn out to be straight. They say they don't really think that this is true, but they cite the numerous comments that have been known to come out of their parents' mouths.

We want our children to feel loved and supported for who they are and whom they will become. Chances are much greater that our children will be heterosexual than GLBT (Patterson 1992). If you want your child to feel unconditionally loved, watch yourself closely for moments of indiscretion. Also, it is helpful to periodically reassure your child that they may be queer or straight when they grow up, it's all the same to you. Remind them that all you want is for them to be happy and to experience love.

Exploring Their Origins

At some point in time your child will want to explore how they came to be. Whether you adopted your child, gave birth to your child, or used a sperm donor or surrogate mother, your child will go through this phase. Each child does this differently and at different ages. Some feel fine and do not question their origins; others want to meet the other adults who contributed to their birth (i.e., biological parents, donors, etc.) and feel like it is not fair if they can't. If the children in your family came to you in different ways, then each child may experience a certain level of jealousy.

As our children turn into teenagers, these issues transform, often dramatically. As your child leaves childhood and enters the teenage years, they will be raising more thought-provoking discussions about the choices you have made in your parenting. For example, whereas it may have been a nonissue up to this point if your child has a different ethnic makeup than you, it may become a huge issue as your child begins to experience the intensity of racial segregation and racism. Another common feeling for teens and young adults who do not know their biological donors is that of feeling half adopted. At this age, your children may turn away from you as well as question your initial decision-making process about being a parent.

These conversations are not always easy. As you approach this time it is worthwhile to review what your original desires were in having children and how and why you decided to create family in the way that you did. Become comfortable again with your choices. If you are comfortable, you will not need to defend yourself, and arguments will be much less likely to happen around these subjects.

Being Culturally Queer

Most children do not identify with the queer aspect of their family until they are older. In the younger years you are simply your child's family. Young children do not necessarily notice the differences between their family and other families, except to notice genders and family structures. At a younger age, there is a natural curiosity and acceptance about all families. At some point, however, your child will begin to notice and be able to name the situations in your lives that are unique because you are queer.

Our children often are not aware of the fact that they are being raised within the queer culture. Children who are culturally queer have been raised in a gay positive community. Often times our children are completely comfortable around other queer people and are familiar with various incarnations of our community expression. They become familiar with our lingo, language, humor, and customs. They often have a very broad understanding of gender presentation, gender roles, and gender expectations, which comes from being exposed to numerous GLBTs.

Our children may have a queer political view as they grow up hearing about various conservative politicians who do not support equal rights for us, and about the strides being made to secure our rights. They may be very familiar with the ins and outs of alternative forms of creating family. In fact, many of our children know about the so-called "facts of life" at a very early age. You know a young child is culturally queer when they ask, "But where is his *other* mommy?" Or, as I heard the other day, when a straight family was discussing a surprise pregnancy, a young child from a lesbian household responded, "Didn't you know that if you inseminated you could get pregnant?"

Our children begin to personalize and take pride in their family, claiming queer culture as their own. They become smart, independent thinkers who often have a level of autonomy that comes from being raised within a politically marginalized culture that bucks the very foundations of the mainstream. But watch out, being raised in this fashion is sometimes a mixed blessing! When you talk to your child from a young age about meaningful subjects, and when you have helped your child to be emotionally intelligent, then you will inevitably encounter moments of amazement as your child outwits, outsmarts, and out-logics you. Children are extraordinary. They will keep you running just to keep up with them.

The path of parenting is continuous. As your child moves into their preteen and teenage years, many of the issues about being raised in a queer household will stay the same, many will change. The changes will depend on your particular situation, how supportive their experience has been, whether they have to change schools, etc. If you stay connected to your child, and keep the channels of communication, respect, and love open, your relationship and your child's self-esteem will soar. The issues they faced growing up will become the gifts of insight that they will offer to the world.

8

Religion, Spirituality, and Gay Family Celebrations

Regularly examining the roles that religion, spirituality, and queer celebrations hold in the lives of our children is an important way of supporting our families. When we are clear about what we want for our children in these areas, we are able to do our best to help them have the necessary opportunities to develop and strengthen their spiritual sense of belonging.

Parents of all sexual orientations find themselves confronting the role religion and spirituality will have in the lives of their children. "Do I want to raise my child within a formal religion?", "Do I want to instill my child with a sense of spiritual identity?", "How do I do that?" are all common questions that parents ask themselves. These questions do not hold simple answers for any parents; the issues surrounding religion and spirituality are complex. Due to widespread religious bigotry, when you are GLBT the issues can be compounded.

In this chapter we will cover ways to bring religion and spirituality into your family, should you so choose, as well as examine the issues on these topics that commonly arise in queer families. Also covered are suggestions about navigating yearly holidays, and developing our own queer family celebrations.

Deciding How to Bring Spirituality into Your Family

Becoming a parent can bring the question of religion and spirituality to the forefront of your family. Parents who want to instill in their children a sense of values and a sense of the divine must grapple with exactly how they are going to do that. The fact that many religious and spiritual organizations are not only heterocentric, but are also fervently homophobic further complicates the issue. This institutionalized homophobia has led many queer adults to feel driven away from religion out of self-respect. The thought of re-engaging with organized religion is met with trepidation.

Examine Your Own Spiritual Practice

Examining your own relationship to religion and spirituality is the first place to begin the exploration of what you would like for your children. Some adults are still practicing the faith in which they were raised. Other adults have distanced themselves from the traditions of their upbringings. For some this was a natural separation that came with personal individuation. Others left their religious organization due to the repetitive, ongoing degrading messages about homosexuals. Some adults have found new spiritual or religious traditions in their adult lives, while others have forsaken the idea of religion and/or spirituality altogether. Our own personal relationship to religion and spirituality is frequently both multilayered and enigmatic.

Single Parents

When it comes to making the decisions about the spiritual and/ or religious upbringing of your children, there are definite advantages to being a single parent. Although your family of origin may have opinions to voice on the matter, *you* are the person who makes the decisions. There are no additional people, with their own perspectives, with whom to share this often emotionally charged decision.

Shared Parenting

When you are sharing parenting with others, the complexity of feelings surrounding religion and spirituality can quickly become exponentially magnified. It is common to have parents with different religious upbringings within the same family. Even if you, your partner, and/or your coparents were raised within the same faith, there can be dramatic differences in the role religion played in your life and in your family. Also in the mix may be your personal blend of the tradition in which you were raised, and the tradition you practice as an adult. We bring all of this complexity to our decision making about how to raise our children. Combine your personal complexity with one or more other people's personal complexities and you have quite a mixture. Thus, sorting out the answers to what role religion and/or spirituality will play in your children's life and your life as a family can be tricky.

Because historically many wars have been held between people of different religious perspectives, there is often an unexplored tension that crops up when having ideological discussions. When you are aware that seemingly innocuous situations may hold the charge of centuries worth of tension, it is easier to approach conversations of religion and personal beliefs with care. It is also easy to see why religions have recommended marrying within the faith, as it bypasses many of these conversations altogether.

Deciding whether there is value for your family belonging to a formal organization is a very personal decision. Deciding how to instill a sense of belonging and other values in your children is a deeply personal choice. When you are approaching these decisions, it is important to clarify and to prioritize your goals.

Exercise

Before you actually reach a decision with yourself or with your partner and/or coparents about what role religion and/or spirituality will hold in your family life and how you would like to accomplish that, it is important to clarify your own internal goals. Put aside a period of time to personally explore what is important to you regarding this part of your children's upbringing.

Spend a few moments quieting your mind. Close your eyes and take some deep breaths. Allow yourself to feel connected and clear. Now ask yourself, "As a parent, what do I want to communicate to my child regarding spirituality and/or religion? How would I like my life/our lives to communicate this to my child?" Write down in your journal what comes up for you. Answering these questions helps to bring clarity to the situation.

For example, you may have approached the topic of religion when feeling that you wanted your children to go to Sunday school. When you explored internally what your actual goal was, however, you realized that what was most important to you was that there were certain values that you want to instill within your children (being kind, compassionate, loving, etc.). Before doing this self-exploration exercise you may never have realized that it was actually the values—and not the religious school itself—that are important to you. Or, you may discover that it is not only the values, but the actual belief in the Buddha and the specific rituals and approaches to enlightenment that are most important.

When you become clear about your goals, having a meaningful and respectful conversation with others who are involved becomes easier. When you know what is most important to you, you become able to assess where compromise is possible, and where there is little or no room for change. Reaching decisions becomes smoother and more natural.

Spirituality versus Religion

There is often a difference between the concepts of spirituality and religion. *Spirituality* is a personal, internal feeling. It involves your own personal relationship to the divine. Spirituality drives a person to ask the existential questions of purpose, meaning, and belonging. Questions such as: Who am I?, What is life?, What is the universe?, Is there a god/goddess/divine spirit?, are all part of the spiritual quest.

Religion, on the other hand, is usually more of a formal construct. Through a shared system of beliefs held to with faith and ardor, people subscribe to a specific approach to life. Religion involves enacted tradition. Although your relationship to the divine may be explored, the existence of the divine is usually not questioned. By aligning one's life experience with an unseen order, religion allows people to integrate diverse aspects of life while imbuing life with a sense of purpose and direction.

A person does not need to be associated with any formal organization to have a profound sense of the divine in their lives. For many, religion does not provide them with a strong sense of spiritual connection; for others it deeply does. Religion and spirituality can be both separate and inseparable, depending on your experience.

Many queer adults feel that their sexual orientation has spiritual and religious-like qualities to it. As parents they strive to put that feeling into form. For many lesbians, their sexual orientation is inseparable from their spiritual beliefs and their political views; their lesbianism is a worldview. Such lesbians feel that their status as a lesbian is a totally unique cultural construct. They feel that in being a lesbian they have departed entirely from the heterosexual world and established their own complete lesbian worldview.

Numerous lesbians and other GBTs who feel this way have more of a pagan or goddess form of worship. This can be developed as a solo practice or with a group of like-minded individuals. Other parents who feel that their sexual orientation holds spiritual and religious-like components also often participate in other forms of organized religion. Nothing is mutually exclusive. As GLBTs we often have a distinctly personal blend.

Many GLBT families who send their children to formalized religious schools also celebrate the lunar holidays and the other seasonal holidays of the pagan calendar. I know Christian, Catholic, Buddhist, and Jewish children who believe in the goddess. Families who hold elaborate summer solstice rituals also go to church on Easter. One young child, dear to my heart, got her words jumbled in trying to explain to her traditionally Jewish grandparents that she was Jewish and believed in the goddess. She said proudly, "I am a Jewish loving Goddess."

When One Parent's Faith Is Dominant

There are families in which one parent feels very strongly about the role religion should play in their children's life and the other parent(s) do(es) not feel so strongly. Often in these families the parents decide to raise their children in the ways that feel appropriate to the most concerned parent.

Culture As a Part of Religion

I have held more than one GLBT childbirth education class where every family had one or more parents who had been raised Christian or Catholic, and one parent who had been raised Jewish. Each of the non-Jewish parents was no longer practicing the faith in which they were raised. However, the Jewish parents each felt very strongly that their children needed to be raised with a strong sense of Jewish identity. Some of the Jewish parents considered themselves to be practicing Jews, others just felt that the culture, traditions, and ways of thinking were critical parts of their heritage that they did not want to die. For the nonpracticing Jews it came as a surprise how intensely they felt. It was only through having children that they came to realize that their Jewish-ness was an inextricable part of themselves, a part they wanted their children to share.

Likewise many of the African-American parents that I have worked with have very strong ties to their churches. Going to church has held a very significant role in their lives, making religion much more than just religion, but truly the fabric of their families and communities. In the majority of interracial families with which I have worked where one parent is African American, it becomes a given that the children will go to church.

In both of these examples there is a large cultural component to the religion in question that cannot be separated from the faith itself.

More challenging situations are those where one parent feels strongly about their religion or spiritual practice and the other feels adamantly that the children should not be raised with any specific belief system. In these situations it may be helpful to seek counseling.

Discussions between Parents

Deciding to raise your children within the dominant faith of the parents may be an easy decision. It has the advantage of providing your children with only one set of traditions and dogma. But the ongoing family dynamics around religion are not always that simple. There are numerous discussions that need to be held among the adults that will likely crop up over time. These discussions can easily and quickly break into arguments, as there are many unspoken assumptions that are made about religion.

Consider the following questions:

- Is the other parent(s) going to forsake their own religious connections?

- Will the other parent(s) participate in the functions, holidays, services of the dominant faith?

- Will the other parent convert?

- What if the other parent wants to continue practicing certain traditions that are not a part of the children's faith?

- What about conversations that involve analogies from a different ideology?

The list goes on. These are the discussions that crop up in day-to-day parenting as you each begin to see the ingrained aspects of your upbringing. Remember, as difficult as it may be at times, try to approach these conversations and the situations that arise with compassion.

For example, Diana and Robert are coparenting their daughter, Julia. Diana was raised as a secular Jew, Robert as a Catholic. Both have an active spiritual life not connected to formal religion. They decided that they would raise Julia as a Jew, but with much influence from both parents' current spiritual beliefs. That meant they wanted her to learn to meditate, practice tai chi, and celebrate Chanukah. This had been an easy decision, not requiring much conversation.

When Julia was four years old she came home one day after spending the weekend with Robert, talking all about Jesus, about having been to church, about her beautiful new Easter dress, and about the Easter egg hunt where she had found lots of chocolate. Julia was exhilarated! Diana was able to give Julia some positive attention for a moment before calling Robert into the other room. What ensued was a large argument. Diana thought they had been quite clear about raising Julia Jewish. Robert agreed and said that Easter was just a fun spring holiday and meant nothing to him religiously; he had just thought Julia would love to go to the church Easter egg hunt since it was such a huge event. Robert could not understand why in the world Diana was so enraged; going to an Easter celebration did not mean that Julia was not Jewish.

After this experience, they were able to have some very specific conversations about what it meant to Diana to be Jewish, what it felt like to be Jewish in a predominantly Christian culture, and what was important for her in Julia's upbringing. Robert was able to listen and understand. He still felt that he would really like Julia to be able to celebrate Easter and Christmas. Although it was a very big stretch for Diana, they decided that Julia could celebrate Easter and Christmas as long as she did not go to church. If the holidays were truly secularized, Diana would do her best to tolerate it twice a year.

Interfaith Families

There are families in which each parent may hold strongly to their personal religious or spiritual traditions and wants the children to be raised with the same. Often times, when there is not one clear path, but multiple paths, this results in a multifaith or interfaith family. A *multifaith family* is a family in which each member of the family practices their own faith. In a multifaith family the children usually participate in all of the faiths being practiced and are allowed to make a choice as they age about their own personal affinity. Some families do not allow their children to make a choice until they leave home. Until that time, however, they must practice all of the faiths within the family. Other families allow their children to participate as they are called to do so without forced participation in all religious activities.

An *interfaith family* is a family within which multiple faiths are practiced, shared, and appreciated by all, even though the adults may have a personal affinity toward one specific faith. For example, the whole family goes to church on Sunday, but also goes to ashram for the Hindu holidays.

Having exposure to multiple faiths has the inherent benefit of exposing your children to different traditions, practices, ideologies, and approaches toward the divine. It also has the drawbacks of conflicting ideologies, overlapping holidays, an increased time commitment to organized events, and often conflicting ideas of what is "holy." When you acknowledge the apparent conflicts between the faiths, and help your children to navigate these differences, there is an opportunity for your children to achieve a level of great acceptance and gain a wide perspective they would not have gained in a monofaith family. If you do not assist in this process, or if multifaith conflicts are present within your own home or family, your children can become confused and feel the need to prove loyalty to a specific parent by pledging allegiance to their beliefs and practices.

In addition to minimizing potential conflict within your nuclear family, there is also potential conflict from the respective in-laws. Telling them directly that your family is either multifaith or interfaith and that your children practice both religions is important. It is essential to let your in-laws know in no uncertain terms that religious stereotyping, slurs, or other forms of intolerance will not be accepted around the children.

Deciding on the faith in which your children will be raised, however, is only one of the decisions to be made about religion/spirituality. What exactly does your decision mean? If you are choosing to raise your children within an existing faith, how will you do that? It is important to examine these questions thoroughly, both by yourself and, if appropriate, with your partner and/or coparents.

When You Want Religion, but Religion Does Not Want You

There are many benefits to being a member of an organization that shares a common faith. Being a part of regular meetings enables you to develop a social network of like-minded individuals and families. The community support available in times of need can take the place of extended family when you are separated from your relatives. Shared values and common vision often create fun community service activities. It can feel wonderful to share in both worship and community.

Because religions are used to enforcing the spoken and unspoken laws of a society, religious and spiritual organizations are often homophobic. Although some organizations are not overtly condemning of our souls, the underlying attitude is present. As GLBTs, many of us have experienced open hostility from our religious organizations and from their members. The overt and covert antigay religious teachings can make being out in your congregation a very uncomfortable experience. The thought of willingly bringing your children into such an environment is chilling.

Prior to parenthood, many GLBT adults were connected with a congregation where they were not out. They had long ago learned to filter out the homophobia of their religion in exchange for the benefits they received from belonging to it. It may have worked in the past to be a closeted member, or to filter out the antigay messages, or to actively work for change within the organization. Having children, however, lowers our own ability to accept intolerance. You do not want your children exposed to and indoctrinated with religious bigotry that would morally condemn their families. Yet you may also want your children to be able to experience the positive aspects of a religious upbringing. You may not want to leave your congregation or find a new congregation, but you do not want your children to have to learn to filter through bigotry.

Interestingly, the relationships we have with religious organizations often parallel the relationships we have with our families of origin. Our ability to accept or ignore intolerance, or even direct attack, is no longer feasible once there are children in the picture. It is as if our own self-esteem strengthens as we have to look out for the self-esteem of our children. (What a wonderful side effect of being a parent!) Look for the parallels in your life between your faith, your relationship to a religious organization, and the relationship you have with your family of origin; it is often quite insightful.

Finding a Gay Friendly Congregation

It is important to notice if you are immersed in homophobic institutions. Often times it is so commonplace to be discriminated against that we forget there are other possibilities.

In progressive areas with a large GLBT population, usually large urban areas, there are often welcoming, gay friendly congregations of every faith. These congregations and communities not only appreciate our membership, but will also perform our weddings, and other significant rights of passage for our children. Most of these congregations have or are open to having GLBT leaders. Some GLBTs find that a longer drive to a welcoming, open, and accepting congregation is well worth the benefits they receive.

For example, in the Bay Area, where I am from, there are a number of gay Buddhist groups as well as lesbian Buddhist groups, there are two GLBT synagogues, there is one specifically gay church, as well as many affirming "reconciling" churches. On a national level, there are groups that are working for change. Renewal and reform Judaism recognize and perform our weddings.

Within most religious organizations there are subgroups specifically for gays and lesbians that may be sanctioned by the larger organization. Joining one of these groups is another possible way to remain a member of your preferred organization, while feeling safe and working for change. For Mormons there is a group called Affirmation. For Catholics there is a group called Dignity. For Episcopalians there is a group called Integrity. GLBT religious and spiritual organizations and subgroups commonly advertise in GLBT publications. If your community does not have a local queer paper, you can look in the paper nearest your hometown. Or, call the organizations listed above and ask for friendly religious groups in your area. The local Unitarian church may also have appropriate community resources.

Some people settle for a religious community that is not overtly condemning or openly hostile toward our families—a community that may not approve of the LGBT "lifestyle," but one that respects the dignity inherent within all of us. Make the time to actually visit each of the different congregations or groups available to you within the radius you are willing to travel. Each congregation, meeting, and service feels very different. Visiting and evaluating each opportunity may be the difference between feeling safe and comfortable, or feeling like everyone is doing their best to welcome you, but they don't have any idea what to say to you because you are LGBT.

Holidays and Extended Families

The holidays can be a particularly challenging time for queer families. Holidays are traditionally family celebrations. Prior to having children, many gay couples either continued to go home to their individual families of origin to celebrate, or are completely separated from their families of origin at these times of year. It is not uncommon for groups of chosen gay family to celebrate holidays, such as Thanksgiving, together on a day before or after the actual holiday. This enables GLBTs to celebrate the holiday together with their queer family and friends before celebrating the actual holiday separately with their respective families of origin. Although it can be hard in a relationship to not spend the actual holidays together, many GLBTs choose this form of compromise.

When children come into the picture, however, acquiescing to familial demands, homophobia, or the fear of homophobia, often becomes less of an option. Families with children usually want to spend the holidays together as a family. Often their families of origin want and/or expect them to spend the holidays with their extended families as well. This leaves GLBT families with many different decisions to make around the holidays. It becomes even more complicated when there are multiple parents in your family who may or may not be coupled. Questions, such as the following, often arise:

- With whose family should we spend the holidays?

- Should we spend the holidays all together or should our children rotate through the respective in-laws?

- Should we all stay home instead?

- If your family of origin does not accept your partner or coparent(s), will you choose to visit them anyway, and leave your loved ones behind?

- Are you willing to send that message to your children?

- What will you do if you are not out to your family of origin, but now that you have children it seems more important to spend the holidays with your nuclear family?

- What will you say to explain this to your family of origin without coming out?

- Will you choose to come out?

Navigating the families of origin can be compounded if you are an interracial and/or interfaith couple. It can be just as uncomfortable to deal with the racism or religious superiority of your in-laws as to deal with their homophobia. If there is more than one element of prejudice at play, it can be virtually unbearable for all concerned. This can weigh heavily on your decision-making process.

Many people, however, really enjoy spending holidays with their families of origin and, for some families, holidays are the only time in a year that extended family gathers. To choose not to spend the holidays with the family would mean choosing not to expose your children to their biological family.

When a Part of Your Family Is Not Welcome

What do you do if a part of your family is not welcome in the home of your family of origin? How you handle this situation is a personal decision; there is no right or wrong way. However, forethought as to the long-reaching consequences of your decision on your family is important. It is also important to remember that you can change your mind over time and choose to do it differently.

One way that GLBT families work this situation is to visit the homophobic part of the family anyway. Perhaps you go for an extended visit, or perhaps you bring the children to visit for only one day, just long enough to see family members. Other families bring their partner and stay in a hotel. That way, you can visit the extended family and all be together for the nights and at least part of the time each day. If you are out, then any nonhomophobic relatives can visit at the hotel with all of you as a family.

Your Decisions Communicate Certain Messages

Any time you decide to leave your partner at home when you visit homophobic relatives, you are choosing to acquiesce to homophobia.

To the Children

What are you saying to your children? That your intolerant family of origin is more important to you than your partner and/or coparents?

That the holidays should be spent with *your* family, but not as a family? That when your children encounter or fear other people's homophobia they should lie or alter who they are to please others?

To Your Partner

It is also important to examine what message your decision is giving to your partner. Are you saying that your family is more important than they are? Are you telling them that they are an *optional* part of the family? Can you bring the children to your family for visits or holidays while they can not bring them to theirs? Does your partner's family not even recognize that your partner is a parent? Are you, in essence, able to claim the children as your own when the situation suits you? What does that say to the children, to your partner, to you? Is this the message you are willing to live with?

To Yourself

Of course, it is essential to examine what message you are sending yourself. When you acquiesce to feared or expressed homophobia, who are you serving? Are you just trying to avoid confrontation? Is this the healthiest choice for you to make?

Taking a Stand

Other GLBT families choose not to visit their families of origin unless they are all welcome. This can be handled in a number of ways.

When you are out to your family of origin, you can take a stand. You can tell them that you are only willing to visit them once *all* of your family is recognized and welcome. It is not unusual for members of your family of origin to come around over time when they realize that you are serious and that they will not see you or their grandchildren unless they do. There is always the distinct possibility, however, that by providing such an ultimatum, you will lose your ability to see your family and that your children will not have the opportunity to know them. How you explain this to your children is up to you. Some parents simply say that they don't really see or talk to their family and leave it at that. Others discuss with their children the homophobia and their need to take a stand. If you do choose to explain the situation more thoroughly to your children, be sure to present it in a way that does not leave your children questioning what is inherently wrong with them.

Some people are not out to their families of origin. In these cases, excuses are usually made as to why you are not coming during the holidays. If your family knows that you have children, but not that you are gay, you can arrange a visit without your partner for a less important time of year.

When Your Family Has Rejected You or Your Family

Being rejected by our parents or other extended family members is very hard to live with. Over time most of us find a way to come to terms with their limited views and learn to move on. During holiday times, however, the painful feelings of rejection are frequently heightened. Having children can make your loss of extended family easier because you are developing fun and meaningful traditions for your own children and family. On the other hand, when you have children the painful loss of extended family can be more poignant. If your family has recently rejected you, the pain around the holidays can be great.

It is important to be sensitive to the undercurrent of rejection and loss during holiday times when one side of the family is open and accepting and the other is not. It is easy to become so involved with your own issues that you neglect the impact the situation may have on your partner.

Maintaining Healthy Communication

Approaching holidays can be, at times, fraught with tension as families negotiate yearly who is in their family. It is essential for the health of your relationship and the health of your children that you monitor the nature of your arguments during holiday times. Holidays are traditionally stressful and, unless your families are unconditionally welcoming of you, there are added tensions of family rejection. This does not give you free reign, however, to blame your partner for someone else's homophobia.

Multiple Celebrations

To honor each part of the family, unless everyone lives locally and gets along well, it is often necessary to have multiple celebrations. This can be the case even when your extended family is welcoming and accepting of your nuclear family.

For example, Rick and David live in New York with their daughter, Carrie. Rick's family of origin is not that comfortable with his sexual orientation. Although they are theoretically accepting of Rick and David's relationship, when they all are together it feels quite tense and awkward. David's family loves Rick and Carrie and they all are able to relax and enjoy each other. Rick and David consider their gay friends, however, to be their immediate family. So, for Winter Solstice each year they host a huge gay bash at their house. They light candles for Chanukah in their own home as a family. Rick and Carrie visit Rick's family alone for Christmas dinner. (Knowing that he could come along makes it easier for David to stay home.) David prefers not to celebrate Christmas so it works well for everyone. At Passover they all fly to California and spend a few days with David's family. They feel very comfortable with their choices. They only expect tension when Carrie has her Bat Mitzvah, as they are not sure how Rick's family—being Christian—will handle an alternative gay Jewish religious rite of passage.

The Importance of Creating Queer Holidays and Celebrations

Ritual celebrations can serve as an important way of instilling Pride in yourself and in your children. These are not necessarily spiritual or religious rituals, but specific, yearly times of honoring our GLBT families. Creating yearly celebrations or activities that are specifically queer provides our children with opportunities to recognize and to celebrate our uniqueness. They also provide an invaluable sense of feeling connected to a queer culture. Thus, whether or not you know many other GLBT families, your family can celebrate all of those who have come before us, and all of those who are out there with us right now.

Creating yearly celebrations is a very important way to bring Pride into our lives. Pride is developed, it is not a given. And, in the face of the societal bigotry that inevitably filters into the experience of your children, Pride is a healing balm that helps to affirm our worth. There are many ways and natural times to do this. You can develop personal activities or celebrations around Gay Pride Day, Gay Pride Month, National Coming Out Day, and Gay History Month. These are times in the yearly cycle that can be used to encourage Pride, self-love, and social education in a positive and fun way. Likewise, maybe your family does something particularly special around Mother's Day or Father's Day, or you create and celebrate your own Coparent's Day. Some families take a yearly trip with other gay families, or go to one of the queer family camps, queer church get-togethers, or Family Week in Provincetown, Massachusetts, in August.

There are many options. You can choose to create a holiday or a yearly activity or both. Following are some examples of what families around the country have done. Remember one of the best ways to memorialize an experience for a child is to document it with photos. Then every year you can be sure to pull out the photos from years past that document your family's celebrations.

Gay Pride Day/Month

Many families use Gay Pride Day as a starting ground. Taking the time to recognize and celebrate Pride Day together is important. To build significance in the day, talk about it and plan for it in the weeks preceding the actual event. Building anticipation and creating decorations are a culture's primary ways of acknowledging a holiday. Simply encouraging children to make paper rainbow ring streamers out of construction paper, or to see how many pink triangles they can fit on one page of paper that you then hang on the wall, are some decorating suggestions. Some families collect various rainbow items and bring them out around Pride.

Perhaps you will choose to travel yearly to the closest Gay Pride Parade. Most Pride Parades are in June. For some families this involves a big trip; for others it is near where they live. Going to your Pride Parade of choice and the celebrations afterwards are an excellent way for your children to be exposed to many different faces of our community. It is also a wonderful place of belonging and Pride. In the San Francisco Pride Parade there is a very large family contingency that marches every year.

For families who do not hang a rainbow flag at other times of the year, hanging one on Pride Day or through the month of June is a way of standing out. It is an opportunity for others to ask questions and for you to take trips around the neighborhood looking for flags. Many families have a Pride Day party. Whether or not they are attending a parade, it is wonderful to have a potluck and invite every GLBT person you know.

Many families exchange gifts on Pride Day; it becomes "Queer Family Day." That, of course, has the added element of anticipation for the children involved as they make presents for each of their family members. Parents often use this month as a time to order or pick up Pride materials/presents for their children and themselves, such as rainbow ring necklaces, rainbow shoelaces, stickers, postcards, etc.

Some families choose to celebrate Pride Day as "Rainbow Day" and decorate themselves and their home with as many forms of the rainbow as they can. It's a very fun, whimsical way to honor your family.

National Coming Out Day

National Coming Out Day, October 11, provides an excellent opportunity for you to educate both your children and perhaps their schoolmates about queer issues. In your own family, you can use the day to discuss what it means to be out and to come out. You can talk about courage and bravery. You can talk about oppression. Some families choose to spend the day coming out. Every member of the family tells every person that they come in contact with for the day that they are GLBT or that their parents are GLBT. Then together at the end of the day you can all discuss what it was like and what other people's reactions were.

National Coming Out Day is also a wonderful time to honor any public figures who came out that year. As a family you can collect photos and articles about people who have come out during the year. Then as you discuss each person on National Coming Out Day you can do something special to honor them. One family I know creates a collage on poster board of the out celebrities, sports stars, politicians, etc. Each National Coming Out Day they pull out the posters from the years past and hang them in their home. They are able to see how many more people come out each year. It becomes a form of living history. If you choose to do such an activity, then it is a wonderful activity to share with your children's school.

GLBT History Month

The month of October, otherwise known as Gay, Lesbian, Bisexual, and Transgender History Month, provides us with another excellent opportunity to educate ourselves and our children. When children are able to draw the connections between their own lives and gay and lesbian history, a natural sense of Pride develops. Providing our children with the information they need to feel that their experience is not in a vacuum requires some research, however. Unfortunately, American schools do not routinely inform students about famous GLBT people in history. Children, therefore, do not have their personal experiences reflected in their learning. Of course, GLBTs are not alone in this experience, as girls and people of color do not have their experiences reflected either.

Creating a list of famous GLBTs throughout history and in our family histories is a good place to start. From there, your family can select a person to study each year. You can start with a list as small as: James Baldwin, Willa Cather, Errol Flynn, Michelangelo, Eleanor Roosevelt, Bessie Smith, Cole Porter, Sylvester, Martina Navratilova, Alice Walker, and Elton John. Once again, collecting this information in a binder or through other forms of documentation creates a history book for your family. It also creates a family record that is wonderful to look back on.

Bringing a sense of meaning, purpose, and belonging to our lives and to the lives of our children is a goal most parents share. As LGBT families, in order to do this we have the additional creative task of inspiring Pride in our children and our families. It can seem daunting to create our own family celebrations and traditions, but being able to develop and establish tradition is part of the fun of being a queer parent at this point in history. Take the time to create celebrations that are meaningful for your family and instructive to your children. Your children will thank you later.

PART IV

Evolving Models of Family

9

Single Parenting

People come to single parenting from a number of different paths. Some are single parents by choice, some become single parents because of unpredicted family restructuring, and some never consciously plan to have a baby in the first place. GLBT single parents, whether longterm or shortterm, face unique issues.

Single Parents by Choice

When you consciously choose to be a single parent you claim an amazing amount of autonomy. By making the decision to be a parent, you are stating to yourself and to the world that you alone have the right and the ability to parent. Unfortunately, single parents are often faced with mixed or negative reactions from friends and family, which can be very difficult because these are the very people from whom you would have hoped to have support.

Common negative responses to the news that you are planning to be a single parent can include many of the following:

- You are selfish.

- You are burdening the child by being a queer parent and a single parent.

- You won't have enough time to be with your child

- You're being unfair to the child.

- If you are a woman, everyone will consider the child a bastard.

- If you are man—especially a gay man—you are not supposed to raise children.

Even if your friends and family members change their minds and eventually support your decision to be a single parent, it may be hard to trust them again after receiving such negative reactions initially. In addition, you may feel restrained about asking them for help when you need it. Not asking for help is common for all parents; but for single parents by choice, there can be an extra element of hesitation. There is often a fear that in asking for help, with child care or for a financial loan in times of need, that you are opening yourself up for others to comment on or to criticize your choice to become a parent in the first place. This can contribute to feeling much more vulnerable when asking for help or to feeling as though you are not allowed to ask for help. Given the fact that you made the choice to be a single parent, you may believe that you should be able to handle it on your own. This is a nasty trap into which you should not allow yourself to fall. All parents need help raising their children. You are just as deserving of assistance as any two-parent family, if not more.

If you find yourself feeling that asking for help would be akin to admitting failure, then it is a good idea to re-evaluate your stance on what it means to have others help you. A good place to start is by asking yourself the following questions:

- What kinds of help do I need?

- What feelings come up for me when I imagine asking for that help?

- What is the worst thing that could happen if I took the risk and asked for help?

- What is the best thing that could happen if I asked for the help I need?

The answers to these questions often reveal old messages that were instilled in us as children. Being able to feel those feelings and separate outdated influences from the present day allows you to gain clarity. Answering these questions often gives you the lucidity to recognize that asking for what you need is a fine thing to do. People will then help you in the ways that they are able—or they won't—but at least you have asked.

Single Parents by Circumstance

There are additional issues for single parents who were not consciously planning on being a single parent.

Unpredicted Family Restructuring

When you begin parenting with a partner and then, due to unpredicted family restructuring, you become a single parent, it can be a very difficult transition. This transition is hard for everyone involved; it is usually a time of stress for the entire family. Obviously, this is exponentially compounded if you become a single parent following the death of your partner and/or your child's other parent.

It is easy to be overwhelmed in the initial transition stages of single parenthood. You may feel helpless and resentful that you now have to do everything by yourself. Additionally, you may be grieving the personal loss of a partner relationship. Although these feelings are quite common, it is important to keep them in control.

For your emotional health, for your child's emotional health, and for the emotional health of your family, try not to wallow in the difficult parts of the change. Actively try to shift the focus of your attention to the positive aspects of your new life when you find yourself dwelling on the negative. The situation won't change, but, with practice, your perspective on it will. Chapter 10 suggests ways you can reframe your family situation so that you can more comfortably adjust to your new family structure.

I was a single parent for the first five years of my motherhood. Although I had planned to coparent my baby with her father and his best friend, this did not work out. After a painful but fast adjustment of my expectations, I embraced being a single mom. I found that I absolutely loved it! It was comfortable, peaceful, and thoroughly delightful. I felt fortunate when I listened to the stories of the struggles my partnered parent friends endured regularly. Our home life together had no inside stresses, as there was no primary adult relationship to navigate and no one to negotiate decisions with. I made all of the decisions. I loved having this power. My daughter and I forged a very deep bond together; we developed a natural rhythm of alone time and together time within our home. At times I felt overwhelmed, but no more overwhelmed than I feel now as a partnered parent—just for different reasons.

Unexpected Pregnancies

Some queer women and female-to-male transgendered (FTMs) people do end up with surprise pregnancies. This can be a tremendous amount to process all at once, as most queer parents spend years thinking about if, how, and when to become parents. Once you become a queer parent in this unexpected fashion you can feel resentment about feeling railroaded into parenthood. Some lesbians or FTMs find themselves questioning their entire sexual and gender identity when they become pregnant after having sex with a man. The important piece of emotional work is to process these feelings and to not let self-doubt, resentment, or shame shadow your parenthood.

Creating and Fostering Community

One of the greatest tools a single parent has is their community. As a single parent it becomes essential to know on whom you can count and for what. When you are sick, you have to be able to call on someone to help you with your child. When something comes up at work and you won't be able to reach the day care until after closing time, you need to know who you can call in a pinch to help out. The need for community in situations such as these is obvious. However, feeling a part of a community not only helps us through life with support, but it also fulfills a greater spiritual need of feeling like we belong, of feeling the interconnectedness of life.

Your community may be made up of chosen or biological family members and/or it may be made up of neighbors, close friends, other parents, and child care providers. When some parents have babies they are already a member of a social network that includes children. This is wonderful because it provides a built-in network of people you can use as resources and support.

Many GLBT parents do not know other parents when they have children. You have to start from scratch trying to develop new friendships with other parents.

Be Aware of the Tendency to Isolate

One of the most common concerns for single parents is isolation. It can be so easy to become consumed by your day-to-day life of supporting and maintaining your family that you feel like you have no life outside of working, basic parenting, and staying on top of the dishes. At times, exhaustion replaces any energy that would otherwise be used to socialize. All parents, most especially new parents, suffer from exhaustion. When there is no one there to relieve you, exhaustion can readily become much deeper. Times like these can quickly lead to self-isolation.

The key to maintaining your sanity is to learn to recognize self-isolating behavior and to intervene when you become aware of it. Isolation can easily lead to inertia and depression. There are many subtle things we do that actually increase a feeling of isolation. For example, if someone you know invites you and your child over for dinner, don't let shyness, exhaustion, and the never-ending backup of housework let you decline. Say "yes" and take the night off.

As you take your child for a walk in the neighborhood or to the local playground, resist the urge to just nod or say "hi" to others around you. Instead, make the effort to strike up a conversation. Not only is this a way to make possible friendships, it becomes a means of feeling a part of a greater community.

In the American culture, it has become customary for parents to become isolated into small family units. Many people are raised with the ethic that it is weak to ever ask for help. Additionally, many GLBT parents are estranged from the built-in family and community support available to their straight siblings and do not know how to recreate such a support network outside of blood relations. In order to have an ongoing emotional sense of well-being, all parents need to break free of isolation. When you are not sharing parenting with someone in your home, it often becomes apparent more quickly how essential community is. As a single parent, if you do not have built-in community, you must learn to create community. The African proverb—"It takes a village to raise a child"—is true. As a single parent, community is survival. Thus, you learn quickly how to ask for help.

Learning to Ask for What You Need

Because creating community often takes concerted effort, look at your personality to see what kind of community would be best for you to foster. The issue of creating and fostering family is personal. It is quite common to have a network of people in your life who would love to help and support you in your parenting, but they do not know how and have not been asked directly. Thus it becomes your challenge to surmount inner isolation and create the community you want. Often the only component missing is you asking directly and specifically for what you need.

Exercise

To ask for help, you must first identify your needs. Use your journal to complete this three-part exercise. On the top of one page write "My Challenges/Frustrations." Then write down all of your current life challenges. You can do this in list form or by flow of consciousness. Do not limit yourself to parenting frustrations, but be sure to include them. On the top of another page write "My Needs/What Could Support Me." Once again, do not censor or judge what you write, just let it flow. This list is for you. After you have created these lists, examine them carefully. Make a note next to each of the items you listed regarding who in your life you could ask for help.

For example, Sally chose to adopt a child on her own when she was thirty-nine. Sally had never wanted to be a single mom per se, but she really wanted to parent and had not yet found the right partner. She adopted Allison, an eighteen-month-old girl.

She found new parenthood to be a combination of distress and excitement. She also found herself feeling disappointed with her friends. She felt like no one was helping her out. She assumed that if they loved her, they would be helping her at this time when she could really use a hand. When Sally was talking about this to her neighbor one day, her neighbor asked what kind of help it was that Sally wanted her friends to be giving. Sally realized she didn't know.

Sally found it insightful that she resented her friends for not stepping in to help her when she did not, herself, know what she needed. This inspired her to self-reflect on what was hard for her in this time of parenting. She then came up with concrete activities she would appreciate her friends doing. Her list looked like this:

Hardships/Frustrations

- sleep deprivation
- no time alone
- no time with friends
- no sex
- no partner
- no new clothes
- overwhelmed with parenting decisions
- questioning whether I am a good parent
- wondering if I am doing right by my child
- no time to exercise
- feel that no one cares how I am really doing
- wish I had someone to share the joys of Allison

What My Friends Can Do

- take me out to have fun
- take care of Allison on a regular basis
- hang out with me and Allison at home
- ask me how I am doing when they have time to listen
- validate my parenting
- help me meet women to date

Doing this exercise helped Sally to clarify her needs. It also allowed her to forgive her friends for not having helped out before. She decided to ask each person in her life for the support that she needed and see what came of it. Although it was difficult initially for Sally to ask for help, each of her friends came through, and Sally feels much less alone in her parenting.

Make the time to foster, strengthen, and develop your friendships. Invite your friends who don't have children to accompany you on outings. Invite a new friend with children to go to the park for a picnic with you. Have your friends over after your child is asleep to watch a movie with you. Invite your friends into your life; you do not have to arrange for child-free space in order to maintain your friendships.

Options of Community

There are a number of options for queer single parents to create a community of support during the parenting years. Some single parents develop a "council" or a circle of friends with whom they consult on a regular basis about important parenting decisions. This provides differing viewpoints so that the parent in question becomes more confident that they have examined the issue thoroughly. This model works especially well for parents who would rather not be a single parent, as it lends a collaborative element to decision making. Sometimes your circle will also provide child care. In this case, your "council" can discuss schedules, day-to-day issues, and philosophies of child rearing as well.

Some queer single parents prefer to live with housemates or in a communal living situation. This can greatly reduce both the isolation and the stress of being a single parent. Single parents who would not otherwise have thought of sharing living space, find this option appealing because there is someone there to stay with your child while you run out to the store, cook dinner, etc. Communal living does not necessarily mean living with others who take on the role of primary caretaker for your child, but it usually means living with people who know your child and can help out.

Many single parents find that making friends with other single parents is one of the most helpful and supportive options. There can be a level of mutual understanding with other single parents that is not available with anyone else. It is often a safe and reciprocal relationship. For instance, if you call up another single parent and ask for help because you are "losing it," they will usually drop everything to help you. You may or may not consider these other single parents to be in your intimate friend network, yet you know you would unconditionally help each other out whenever asked.

Developing Community

Meeting and developing community can take concerted effort. Searching out playgroups, parenting groups, family social events, and other neighborhood parents are all starting places. Often local religious organizations have family gatherings. Of course, being GLBT can add an extra element of difficulty in finding a parenting community, but do not let the fear of homophobia encourage you to self-isolate. Some parents put an ad in the local paper looking for parents with similar parenting philosophies or politics, or put up a flyer at the local parks and schools.

Some people have the luxury of buying community. They create community through hiring child care providers and attending the pay-and-play centers for toddlers. They can also afford to hire therapists to be their emotional confidants and to help them gain clarity on their parenting. These are effective ways of creating instant community while you take the time to develop additional support in your life.

Even if you do not have extra income to explore these options you can start your own play group or baby-sitting co-op as a way of meeting other parents. Sponsor a monthly family/community potluck for your neighborhood. As your children age, there are more opportunities to meet others: you can become active at your child's preschool or elementary school; you can join committees and attend PTA meetings, and all social events at your child's school; and you can become connected with your local community center or other established community groups.

When You Are the Sole Parent

When you have care and responsibility for your child twenty-four hours a day, seven days a week, your issues are definitely different than if you share parenting part of the time. One of the issues that becomes essential when you are the one and only parent of your child is to know when you need a break and to be able to take one. We all have moments, days, or phases of parenting when we are completely and utterly overwhelmed by being the one and only for our child.

Self-care involves engaging in regular activities in your life that are just for you. For example, for some parents exercise is the key to happiness and emotional stability. Some parents address this need by buying a running stroller or finding a gym that has child care. Others want to separate their exercise completely from their children so they arrange to exercise during a time when they can have regular child care prearranged.

Finding the balance between having enough time for yourself and enough time for your child is one of the biggest challenges a single parent faces. This struggle is often compounded by the overall stress of not quite having enough money or resources, or having enough money but a job that requires all of your time and energy. Because of the concentration of responsibility on you, there is a greater tendency toward isolation. Keep an eye on this, and actively seek out social and emotional contact when it becomes an issue.

When You Are a Coparent or Share Custody

There are unique challenges to sharing parenting with someone who lives outside of your home. There are also unique benefits. The most significant benefit is the sharing of responsibility, built-in breaks, and often a shared financial burden. Each family situation is different and brings with it its own set of issues. Clearly the person or people with whom you are sharing the rearing of your child are very important to your child. However, there may be tension between the adults. This can make finding common ground from which to discuss parenting issues difficult.

Depending on the nature of your relationship with your child's other parent(s) you may or may not be able to have conversations concerning parenting philosophies, or differing approaches to children and parenting. Such differences can be challenging to all involved. Likewise, you may not be involved or even consulted regarding significant decisions in your child's life.

Sometimes you may be sharing parenting with an ex from a straight marriage. This provides the discomfort of possible homophobia from your children's other parent. This can be especially hard if you are a parent who has no legal standing; but it is challenging even if you are a legal parent.

What Can You Do?

If you are a single parent but not the child's primary parent, you can often feel like your parenting is at the mercy of another person's desires. This can be quite frustrating. Refrain from criticizing or complaining about your child's other parents in front of your child. Remember, direct communication is always the most effective. Some single parents who coparent with others set up a regular time to meet and - discuss the day-to-day issues, and the greater decisions that need to be made. Some families choose to have a third party there if the meetings are tense. The third party is often a non-biased person who can act as a facilitator and someone whose job it is to hold the interests of the child central to all conversations. Sometimes the third party is a hired therapist.

There are, however, great advantages to sharing custody or parenting responsibilities of a child. Whether you live with your child for half of each week, every other month, only on the weekends, or for half of the year, you have designated times when you are responsible for their day-to-day care and time when you are responsible only for your own day-to-day care. Shared parenting can provide you with built-in alone time and time to develop your own personal interests. Many single parents who are sharing parenting are able to date more freely during the time their child is at the other parent(s) home. Some parents choose to work only during the time that their child is not with them and to dedicate all of their time to their child when their child is at their place. There are many creative possibilities.

There can be drawbacks to dividing your time between when your child is with you and time when they are not with you. This kind of compartmentalizing can start to feel like you are two different people— the "parent" and the "adult." This compartmentalizing can increase your sense of isolation. If you have two separate lives, then often the people in one whole part of your life may never realize that you are a parent and may never have met your child. This can feel like you are not sharing your full self. Likewise, the time when you are doing the day-to-day parenting can feel more overwhelming because of the time-intensive parenting that you do. It can also seem less important to develop parenting community or can feel hard to upkeep the needs of two separate communities.

Maintaining a Queer Identity as a Single Parent

As is the case for all GLBT parents, maintaining a queer identity as a single parent is not always as easy as it was prior to parenting. Parents are automatically assumed to be straight by both queer and straight folks alike. Maintaining a queer sense of self is important not only in terms of attracting potential people to date, but simply in terms of self-esteem.

Unfortunately, unless your queer friends are already parents, it is quite common to lose your friend base when you become a parent, because your interests and available time differ so dramatically. Likewise, many GLBT communities still remain unwelcoming to parents. Little by little this is changing, but it is very painful and disorienting to lose your queer community when you become a parent.

It is important to not feel like you have to give up your gay identity and/or queer visibility to become a parent. Many GLBT parents have a complete turnaround in their social lives, forming many more straight friendships. As your orientation of your life turns more toward child rearing, your day-to-day activities and conversations turn toward children. Your friendship circle and the people you end up spending the most time with are often people with shared parenting values. Parenting values usually take the precedence otherwise accorded sexual orientation when making friends, thus you may find yourself in many more social situations with straight parents and their children than with your queer friend group.

If you spend your social time at the park or in play groups with heterosexual parents, and your work environment is straight, and you are not dating someone, then it can be hard to feel like you are queer. To feel good about yourself and to foster healthy self-esteem, it is important to explore for yourself what makes you feel queer. For most people, it is not only queer visibility and recognition that are important, but a way of feeling queer when you are doing something considered to be straight, in a straight world. When you lose touch with feeling queer you can get depressed and your self-esteem can erode.

Determine What Makes You Feel Gay

It can feel very awkward to figure out what kinds of situations help you *feel* gay, when being gay is an intrinsic part of who you are. But it is important to do just that. "Feeling gay" is different for everyone. Being queer may also mean:

- Having a hip, or identifiably queer haircut

- Wearing clothes that are identifiably queer

- Sporting gay bumper stickers

- Going out to a gay bar once a month

- Hanging out at the women's bookstore

- Chatting online with other GLBT parents

- Reading gay literature and erotica on a regular basis

- Coming out regularly

Feeling queer usually involves feeling connected to other GLBTs, feeling a part of a collective identity. What helps you to feel connected to GLBTs everywhere? For most, it means having and maintaining queer friendships and/or being a part of queer organizations. This may mean making child care a priority in order to join the gay bowling league or the local softball team, or making a point of meeting other gay parents in your area or your state.

When, How, and Why to Come Out As a Single Parent

For many GLBT single parents, coming out seems optional. Because it can be more comfortable or easier to not come out, some parents find themselves staying closeted. Why does anyone need to know what your sexual orientation is when you are not even partnered? It can also feel more artificial to slip your queerness into conversations. It seems less of a potential conversation stopper to introduce or reference your partner than to simply identify as queer. However, the discussion of when, how, and why to come out is the same whether you are partnered or not. The issues of parenting and being out are thoroughly discussed in chapter 4, "Coming Out Every Day." By reviewing this chapter and its suggestions, your life and your child's emotional stability and physical safety will benefit tremendously.

Although it can often seem easier to not come out when you are a single parent, being closeted can lead to devastating circumstances in the future. Joan from Montana learned this lesson the hard way. Joan had separated from her husband when she came out. Joan was not yet comfortable letting people know that she was a lesbian; it still seemed too intimate and personal to have to tell people. She did not consider herself closeted, she just didn't think people needed to know her personal business. Besides, she only went out when her daughter was at her dad's house.

Joan found a lovely care giver who would pick up her daughter from school and care for her until Joan returned home from work. This arrangement worked very nicely. One day, however, when she came home from work she was met by a very disturbing scene. There, in the care giver's apartment, was the minister and a prayer circle of people. They were loudly praying, asking God to save the soul of her daughter who was being defiled by her mother's abominations. When she realized what was going on, she had to force her way through the crowd to her very scared daughter. From that point on, Joan has always come out to everyone, on the phone, when looking for care providers, camps, doctors, etc.

Coming Out to Your Child

Coming out to your child can also appear to be more optional as a single parent. If you are not dating and your child has no contextual memory of you being romantically involved with another adult, coming out to your child can feel strange. Our society has made us internalize so much shame regarding sexual orientation that simply coming out to your child as a single parent can feel sexually inappropriate.

It is never sexually inappropriate to come out to your child. Children start being faced with heterosexism from the time they engage with society. Certainly by the time they are playing with other children, by the time they are three years old, most children "know" that boys only marry girls and girls only marry boys. Thus, if you do not come out to your child when they are young, they will have automatically assumed that you are straight.

As with any other coming out, the longer you put it off the harder it becomes. And in the case with children, the longer you put it off, the more insidious the cultural indoctrination. As a single parent it takes intention and regular, age-appropriate references, to ensure that your child knows that you are GLBT.

You do not have to make any sexual references to come out to your children. Really, you do not need to make sexual references when you come out to anyone. Coming out to your young child is as simple as reading a picture book together that has a two-parent family. While reading to your youngster, you could say, "Look, that girl and her daddy live with the woman that her daddy loves. One day I might find a man or a woman that I love and we may all live together." Or saying to your young child, "Mommy loves women. One day I hope I will find the woman I want to marry." These kinds of statements worked into conversation on a semi-regular basis can help your child to know more about you.

As your children become a little older you can use the terms "lesbian," "gay," "bisexual," and/or "transgender." These are big words, and big concepts, and it often takes a while for children to fully grasp their meaning. But when they hear these words from you first, and they are used in a kind, loving, and descriptive way, then when they hear them used as slurs in the future they will recognize that as wrong.

As children age they will try to put you into their understanding of the world. Single gay father Gerald from Iowa wrote to me that he thought his seven-year-old son understood what it meant that his dad was gay until one memorable day. His son came racing in from school so excited to tell him that the art teacher was a lesbian so now they could get married!

Dating

Dating as a single parent is a complex issue. Some people are very eager to date, but are not looking for a partner. Others have no desire to date unless it looks promising because what they want is a long-term partner. Still other single parents are content being single and are not thinking about dating at all. Finding someone to date, and then navigating dating and parenting can seem like more work than it's worth sometimes. Commonly, however, once you are finally out with another adult on a date, you enjoy yourself so much, you wonder why you don't do it more often.

How Do I Meet People?

One of the biggest concerns for single parents is how they are going to meet someone. Most feel that they are not going to spend what little time they have going out cruising the singles scene. Single parents whose children do not live with them full-time certainly have more of an opportunity to engage in activities where they could meet other single queer adults. However, even full-time single parents can meet people to date.

The single parents and the previously single parents I have spoken with, all said they had met people to date while they were doing daily life activities. Two people said they had met someone at the gas station. One person reported meeting her long-term partner while her three-year-old was having a tantrum in the supermarket and she was at her wit's end. Four people met their future partners while getting their haircut, while many people reported meeting future partners through their child care providers. A surprisingly large number of parents said that they met people at the gym. All of these people were not out "cruising," they were just living their lives.

When Should the People I Date Meet My Children?

The question of whether your child should meet the people that you date is a very personal decision. Some parents feel quite strongly that their children should not meet the person they are dating, let alone spend time with that person, unless they feel it has developed into a relationship that will be long term or permanent. These parents often feel that their personal life is separate from their family life and should remain that way as a means of emotionally protecting the children. Once the relationship is on a committed level, then the children can enter the picture.

There are advantages and drawbacks to this kind of thinking. If this will only be a dating relationship, then you are able to have an adult good time without having to worry about how your children like this person, whether your date likes children, and how hard it will be on your children to bond with someone who will only temporarily be in your lives. However, if it turns out to be a long-term relationship, knowing these things becomes important. It can be heartbreaking to discover that you love someone who does not like children or who has a radically different and incompatible approach to raising children.

If the relationship is moving ahead and your lover has not met your children, it is very hard to judge how your lover will interact with them. This sets up the dynamic that there is a separation between your relationship with your lover and your parenting. Likewise, although it allows you to spend undivided time with your lovers, it also limits the time you can spend with either your children or your lover. If you do try to become one family, it can be very awkward as neither your lover nor your children are used to having to share you and your attention. In addition, your children may not like this person you introduce to them as a permanent person in your and their lives.

On the other hand, if you are someone who likes your children to be involved in your personal life, or you don't really have a choice because child care is so limited, then there are other considerations. What if your child really bonds with someone who you are not as interested in? What if your lover does not like children, but you really like your lover? What if you do not like the way that your lover interacts with your child, yet you have such a new relationship it feels hard to start addressing issues of child rearing? What will happen emotionally to your child if they witness and are involved in all of your dating relationships?

Your child is more likely to be accepting of your deepening relationship with your new partner if they feel involved in your life and feel like they are liked and appreciated by the people that you date. If you take the time to listen to your child's feelings throughout your dating relationship, then it won't feel like a new parent is suddenly sprung upon them.

There is no right answer. In my own dating as a single parent, I tried a number of different approaches. Although, when I dated anyone more than a few times, she was always worked into our lives. It would not work for me to have separate lives; it was too hard to imagine finding time and child care for formal dates all of the time. When I met Colleen I knew it was different from the start. It was like the *three* of us were falling in love with each other. That was definitely a first. The magic was with all of us. Whenever anyone asks how Colleen and I met, we tell our story and then my daughter always jumps in and lovingly tells the story of when she first met Colleen. Her story is short and is about the alligator sponge that came poking out of Colleen's shirt when she came to pick me up for our first date. But by meeting Colleen at the door, she felt like Colleen came into *our* life that fateful night. She always remembers that alligator!

The Rewards of Single Parenting

Being a single parent is a wonderful opportunity to have a deep and meaningful relationship with your children. Rise to the challenges of being solo and focus on the amazing opportunity you have to connect with your children. Although it is certainly more time intensive to parent on your own, you have the ability to know and love your children in ways that are much different than coupled parents.

Single parents often have a much greater sense of trust in the universe. Perhaps they start off that way or perhaps it comes as a badge of single parenting. The autonomy and self-confidence that single parenting gives you is a definite turn-on. Wear your badge of queer single parent with Pride.

10

Breaking Up and New Family Structures

Relationships need to be nurtured. It takes time and attention to nourish a healthy, satisfying, and long-lasting relationship. Often parents become estranged from one another due, in great part, to a lack of quality time spent together. Once children are in the picture, many parents let their relationship with each other slide. With work schedules and attending to your child's needs, there is often little time in a day for meaningful adult connection. It is all too common for parents to not prioritize each other in their day-to-day lives. When they do indeed have time together, it is often spent watching television or a video rather than connecting with one another.

If you do not make the time to talk to each other and intentionally keep the spark alive, over time it becomes difficult to remember why you married/partnered with this person. Oftentimes, no matter how big the problems in your relationship seem, they are strictly circumstantial. Love can usually be rekindled with enough dedication. It is not necessarily divorce that is needed, but rather a good therapist, a vacation together without children, regular dates together, and rekindling a little bedroom action. Even when a relationship feels completely hopeless, these four things usually bring the life back to any relationship.

It may be hard to imagine prioritizing your partner when you cannot even stand to be around them because they annoy you so much. When you have children, however, it is essential to know that you really have given it your all before you decide to breakup your family unit.

For many parents on the verge of splitting up, the extra incentive of the child provides them the determination to try again.

It Can Be Healthy to Separate

Whether or not you have nurtured your relationship, breakups happen. Sometimes it is healthier for a family to separate than to continue living together. When you have come to the clear decision that it would be best for the adults in your family to separate, it is important to try to approach the separation with as much calmness and consideration to all involved as possible. Granted there are situations where it simply may not be possible to have a peaceful separation (domestic abuse, drugs, or other out-of-control circumstances), but, in the majority of all breakups, it *is* possible to have it be respectful.

When a family with children separates, the adults no longer have the luxury of looking out only for themselves during a breakup. The stability of your child's whole world is at stake, and you must always try to remember to treat it with care. Most children would not choose for their families to divorce; they *would* choose for the fighting to stop, but they would not choose to have their family break apart. Breakups are almost always led by parents. Therefore, in times of separation it is vitally important to continue to practice responsible parenting. Although you cannot control your partner's behavior, you can take responsibility for your own. If you are keeping your children in the forefront of your mind, it will be more difficult for both you and your soon-to-be-ex to act out of turn.

Amicable Separations

An amicable breakup is a situation where two adults are able to act in a respectful, if not loving, way throughout their separation. They talk together or with the help of an objective third party, such as an impartial friend, mediator, therapist, or even a lawyer, to work out the details of their future relationships and obligations to one another and to their children. In an amicable separation all involved can feel like it is a family reconfiguration rather than a "breaking up." The language we use, especially with young children, can influence how the experience is processed.

Granted, amicable breakups are often difficult to achieve, but this form of separation is always best for the children. In an amicable separation you are able to hold the best interests of the children close at heart and to make decisions that honor the wishes of all involved. Amicable breakups are often best carried out when each parent involved is seeking personal counseling and often when the separating couple is also in counseling together.

Family Separation Ceremonies

Some families choose to honor the reconfiguring of their family in a similar way to the joining of the family. Some people have a reconfiguring ceremony. This can either be strictly with the family members involved, or you could ask close friends and family to join you for support. During this self-created ceremony you can choose to change your family structure in the name of love.

One family I know went into the woods. The parents and the children stood together crying. They were surrounded by six of their closest people. They hugged each other and cried. They spoke words to one another of how much they loved each other. The adults shared out loud the gifts they had received from their partner during their life together. They made verbal commitments to one another about their ongoing dedication to being excellent parents to their children. They committed to staying friends even as they found new partners.

Next, they each faced their children and told them how wonderful they are and that their separation had nothing to do with anything anyone had done wrong. They all held each other and laughed and cried. They then asked their support people to witness their separation and requested that their friends hold them to their intentions with integrity over the years should they want to stray. Needless to say, there was not a dry eye in the forest that day.

Creating Parenting Contracts at the Time of Separation

Amicable separations are often facilitated by preexisting parenting contracts that you may have drawn up together. These contracts can serve as a reference point if you come to a disagreement about intentions, roles, and responsibilities of each parent. These preexisting contracts should be amended at the time of breaking up to include any current intentions that were not included in the original agreement or that need to be altered to fit the current situation.

For the countless families who never drew up any papers, legal or otherwise, about their parenting relationship, the separation can actually serve as a good time to do so. Parenting contracts can be very useful, although not legally binding, in times of separation. Such a document will help you to clearly state your intentions and can be used as a very helpful guiding vision for current and future discussions. With the help of a third party, or on your own, you can decide together on issues usually decided upon with divorce attorneys. When you have answered each of these questions and other pertinent questions for your situation, you can write them into a formal agreement that you are both willing to sign.

Questions you need to answer include:

- How will you divide your belongings?

- How will you divide your money? If there is a large financial discrepancy either in current assets or in earning potential due to the fact that one parent was doing more child rearing and the other more wage earning, how will you account for that in your division of money? Will you have a temporary "alimony" arrangement?

- What are each of your financial obligations to your child? For how long?

- What kind of parenting rights are you willing to guarantee for the nonlegal parent (if there is one)?

- How will you divide custody?

- If one of you moves far away, how will custody be decided or altered?

- Is one of you going to be more of a primary parent than the other? How does this get decided? What exactly does that mean?

- How will decisions such as schooling, medical care, camps, etc., be made?

- How often will you reexamine your parenting contract?

- What will you do in the case of future difficulties with one another?

- Will any of this change if one or both of you partners with someone new in the future?

Clean Breakups Are Not Always Possible

No matter how much we might wish to the contrary, clean breakups are not always possible. Regardless of how hard we try, our emotions toward our partners in times of breaking up can taint our parenting. In GLBT families, all parents are not usually considered equal by the law. Legal rights, biological connections, and socially accepted roles all take precedence over the less conventional parent(s). Because there are no legal obligations to one another and no socially accepted ethical obligations required of us, too many LGBT families in times of breaking up are absolutely ruthless toward the nonprimary, nonbirth, nonlegal parent. Please be conscious of your choices and do not continue the all too true stereotype in our community for messy divorces when children are involved.

Deciding on Custody Arrangements

There is truly only one rule needed when deciding on custody arrangements and with whom your child or children should live. This rule is to love your children more than you hate your partner. When you are able to focus on the love for your child, you can let it guide you. When the focus is love rather than hate, you will be able to make decisions with which you all can live.

Always use love of your children as a meditation when you are making initial arrangements and future arrangements with your ex-partner. First, place your focus on the love you hold for your child. Then, let that love be bigger than all else. Next, if you can let yourself, know that your ex-partner has those same feelings of love for those very same children. No matter what the differences in the adults, the common ground in most situations is that you both love your children fiercely and you both only want what is best for them.

Take Matt and Carl. They realized that their rocky relationship was too much for either of them to want to try to continue. They had been in and out of relationship for fourteen years. When they finally decided their breakup was to be final, they were able to separate households with ease. All through their parenting of their ten-year-old daughter and four-year-old son, even when they were not committed to one another, they were committed to parenting. Never would either of them consider not allowing the other to continue their relationship with the children. Carl was the one who had legally adopted them, but that did not make him feel like he "owned" them.

All through their past breakups, and this final one, they kept their parenting relationship separate from their romantic relationship. This time they moved into new apartments. The children spend Monday, Wednesday, and the weekend with Matt, and the remaining days with Carl. It works fine for the children. They spend most holidays all together. They work out current parenting issues together, although if they cannot agree they have a therapist with whom they schedule an appointment for guidance. It is a very amicable situation.

Honor Your Children's Relationships

When you are not feeling close to your ex, it is sometimes a great challenge to remember the importace of their relationship to your child or children. It is easy to not want to share custody as a way of asserting yourself against your partner. If you have the legal and/or biological connection to the child(ren), it is often tempting to want to assume full custody. There may be many motivations driving that desire.

It takes great personal integrity to be equitable in times of strong feelings. It is vitally important to the health of your children, however, that you honor each of their parents equally. It can help you to do so by adhering to any contracts you may have made in the past with your partner. It is essential to stay in the present when deciding on custody. If *originally* one of you wanted the child more so than the other, it does not mean that both of you are not equal parents *now*. In these situations it is untruthful to hold yourselves solely to the original intentions; you must look at the actual development of connection.

I have witnessed many a messy divorce in our community and it deeply saddens me. Not being held to a legal standard of behavior when separating does not condone abhorrent behavior. Do not allow yourself to claim full custody just to "get back" at your partner. Take Carolyn and Maria. They had been friends for as long as they could remember. Finally they became lovers, too. There was not a lot of sexual charge between them, and they soon became accustomed to a life filled with deep love for each other, but very infrequent sex. This was fine for them at the time, they were in love with life and wanted to have babies together. They had agreed that maybe they would be nonmonogamous in the future.

It was decided that Carolyn was going to have the first child because she was older, and then Maria would have the next baby soon after. When Carolyn was pregnant, Maria went to a party and had a one-night stand with another woman. When she came home in the morning she realized that Carolyn would not take this well, especially because she was pregnant. However, they were committed to telling each other everything, so she told her about the affair. Carolyn was very hurt and angry. She also felt scared that Maria would leave her. Maria assured her that she had no plans to leave and would not have another affair. She honored her word.

After Carolyn gave birth she felt quite attached to their baby, Riley. Their bond was very strong. It was so strong that Carolyn could not imagine going back to work as planned. Maria volunteered to work more hours so that Carolyn and Riley could have more time together. Maria knew that she was going to start inseminating when Riley was seven months old, and soon the tables would be turned.

Maria and Carolyn decided to delay inseminating for a few months while they more thoroughly adjusted to parenting. They were not getting along very well and since Maria was out of the house so much working two jobs to make ends meet for the family, they rarely saw each other anymore. When Riley was almost one, Carolyn announced that she wanted to break up. Maria was shocked and asked her why. Carolyn said she could not trust Maria *ever* since the affair and so she no longer wanted to be with her. She would rather parent on her own.

Then came the real shock. Carolyn and Riley moved to New Mexico within a month of her announcement. Carolyn would not let Maria see Riley. She claimed Maria was not a parent because she had been working while Carolyn was doing all of the baby care. Carolyn claimed that made her the only parent. Riley is now five years old and Maria has not seen him since the day they left when he was eleven months old. Because they were unable to perform a second parent adoption, Maria has no legal rights. She has a son she will probably never see again.

Integrity

If Carolyn and Maria's story were an exception to the norm, we could say "isn't that too bad?" Unfortunately, it is not. It is all too common for queer people to breakup and not be allowed to see their children ever again. It is all too common to have partnered with someone who was already a parent, be a stepparent for years to your child, and then be completely cut off from your child.

This not only breaks the heart of the estranged parent, but the hearts of the children as well. The children are abandoned by one parent at the whim of the other. This can be devastating to a child, and it can have serious long-term repercussions on their ability to form lasting relationships.

In many families parents divide up the labor so that one parent spends more time parenting and the other more time earning money. Supporting the family does not mean that you are any less of a parent. It simply means you are spending less time with the child. This is a crucial distinction. In the heterosexual world, fathers are not routinely penalized by losing all contact with their children for financially supporting the family. Nor are they considered not to be a parent.

It is completely unacceptable behavior to determine at will what a parent is and is not to suit your current needs. When *we* utilize homophobic behavior we essentially condone others to discount our families. If we do not honor our families as valid who will? By being so self-serving, we are setting all LGBT families behind.

If You Think the Children Belong with Only You

If you feel that your children should only be with you, it is good to ask yourself why. There can be many reasons. Sometimes you can question your child's safety. If your ex has a history of violent or irresponsible behavior with the children, then this is a valid concern. Even if violence has been threatened, but not acted on, you have a valid concern. Strong emotions, however, can make it difficult sometimes to differentiate between an unsafe parent and someone who has hurt your heart but is still a safe parent. It can be easy for you to confuse your emotional pain with your ex-partner's ability to parent. Nonetheless, it is your responsibility to separate these two.

Some people want to maintain sole custody of their children because they believe that the genetic relationship they have to their children is much more significant than any other connection between family members. This is a particularly painful argument if you have created your children together right from the start. It uses traditional thinking to validate a nontraditional situation. This argument is often masking stronger feelings.

Examine Your Feelings

The feelings that usually underlie a desire to gain full custody of your child, whether you have the power to do so or not, is the fear of changing or diluting your relationship with your child. It is a very scary feeling to imagine not seeing your child every day. It can make you feel entirely out of control, scared, and lost just to imagine it. It is a combination of feelings and concerns about how not living together every day will affect you and how it will affect your child. Often a parent's identity is wrapped up in being a parent. The idea of having part-time custody becomes mixed up with being a part-time parent. Commonly intermixed with these feelings is the fear of no longer being able to control your child's upbringing. The biggest fear, therefore, is a fear of loss. Feelings of loss can be so uncomfortable that we will do anything to prevent them. By protecting yourself from the loss, however, you are forcing loss on your child who will not be able to spend time with their other beloved parent.

You need to address these core feelings inside of yourself so that they do not end up hurting your child. You do not want your anger and hurt to cause you to make decisions that will in turn negatively affect your child. Your child loves each of their parents. Listen in your heart to the needs and wishes of your child. When you are discussing custody, you should be letting your child's needs govern your decisions. Remember that love, honesty, respect, and communication are your most powerful tools.

What Happens to Siblings in a Breakup?

It is vitally important to the well-being of your children to try to keep siblings, whether biologically related or not, together even as the parents separate. It is all too common for the biological or legal parent of each respective child to lay claim to "their" child as the family reconfigures. Thus you are arbitrarily deciding that your relationship with the child is more important not only than their relationship with their other parent but also than their relationship with each other. You are taking away the best resource of built-in support and understanding that your children have—someone else who is going through the same experience as they are.

When you, your partner, or both of you brought children to the relationship, it is easy to think that you should take them with you when you split up with your partner. This perspective treats your children as commodities that come with you through your life. Indeed it may be appropriate for each of you to separate households again. However, this does not necessarily mean that the children, who have bonded with one another and consider themselves siblings or stepsiblings, should be cut off from one another. By keeping your children in the forefront of your decisions about their lives, you can discover many creative solutions.

Perhaps all of the children spend four days at your home a month and four days at your ex-partner's house a month. Or maybe you all have a weekly dinner together. If you had an amicable breakup and are still comfortable being in the same room as your ex, then you can all eat together. Otherwise one parent or the other can host the weekly event. If possible, do not hold it exclusively at one home. The children will need to feel comfortable in both homes to still feel like family.

Resist Having the Children Choose Sides

It is not appropriate to subtly or overtly put your child in the middle of the adult struggle. It has already been much documented that children feel responsible for their parent's divorces as it is. To require them to pledge allegiance to one or the other of you only further undermines their trust in their world. How can they pledge to one of you, when their love was never divided up this way in their heart. Allow your child to love all of their parents. Try, try, try to be scrupulous and to not criticize your ex to your children. The person may not have lived up to your ideals as a partner, but that same person is still their parent, even if you cut off contact with them.

Creating a space for your child to voice their feelings is very important. Allowing your child to independently express their preferences about custody is perfectly all right. Attempting to illicit preferences when they do not independently exist is not. If your child does express preferences in the separation process, it is important to listen. Do not always take what is said at face value, try to understand where your child is coming from. There might be something underneath what they are saying that is the real issue. For example, your child might say that they want to live with one parent only. But when all is said and done, it is just that that parent is staying in the same house. The child reasons that if they stayed with that parent, their house, their school, and their friends would stay the same. Your child simply did not want to lose everything familiar in their life in one fell swoop. Listening to your child often includes trying to help them identify what they are feeling.

When You Are No Longer Allowed to See Your Own Child

There is little pain that is so great as not being allowed to see your own child or someone you have come to love as a son or daughter. It is a sorrow so deep that it can be debilitating. You can feel like you are going to die, like you are going crazy, and like there is no point in living. It is common for anger at the situation to be delayed as you become completely depressed. It is also common to become unfamiliar to yourself as you desperately try to pursue your children.

If you have not secured a second-parent adoption, this is a situation where societal discrimination against our families can wound us deeply. Unlike for heterosexual families, there is little or no legal recourse for us. Often family and friends do not understand the depth of our loss because they never fully understood that we were parents. Many supportive family members and friends look at us as helpers to the "real" parent or as subordinate parents to the legal, biological, or otherwise "real" parent. This lack of understanding can be heartbreaking and isolating. If you were not out about your family structure or your parenting, the isolation of silence compounds the pain even more.

Take Action

Try to engage a mutual friend to act on your behalf with your ex. If you are the one who initiated the split, or if you are the one who had the affair, it is easy to feel guilty and to feel like somehow, because you were not the best partner, maybe your ex is justified in having sole custody. You have a right to have access to your own children. It is often our own internalized homophobia that brings us to question that right. If your ex-partner, society, family, and friends do not see what the big deal is, it is easy to think that maybe they are right. This inner homophobia can be debilitating.

If you can engage a friend or hire a mediator to work on your behalf, then hopefully they will convince your ex to agree to go to counseling or mediation with you. Sometimes you can enlist your ex-partner's family members to help act on your behalf. Remember that acting on your behalf is truly acting on behalf of your children, they are suffering from your separation as much as you are. Often with a third party, you can work out a mutually satisfying situation. If you hope to use this route, be sure to do your homework and find a few therapists or mediators to choose from who understand alternative families and will not cater to the position of your ex.

If violence or drugs was a part of your relationship, there is an excellent chance that no one will support you to gain access to your children. However, even in these situations, depending on the actual circumstances, you may be able to fight for supervised visitations. In

California, for example, there are centers where you can have a supervised visitation in a warm and comfortable play environment where you never have to come in contact with your ex. Explore whether there is a center like this near you. In any event, be sure to monitor your depression. If it is too distressing, seek counseling.

Using the Legal System to Gain Custody

Until our rights as queer parents are recognized in the legal system, and until our marital unions are recognized as legal, it is very hard for us to use the legal system to our benefit. If you are in a state where you have been able to adopt your child, then you have legal standing that should be able to assist you to maintain custody rights for your child. Because we are still living in a homophobic society, it continues to be more effective to use formal mediation than legal intervention whenever possible.

Some lesbian and gay parents have tried to use the legal system to regain access to their children. Unfortunately, there has been little success in the courts for nonlegal parents regaining access to their children. There is another undesirable side effect of using the legal system in a homophobic society—we don't want limiting homophobic precedents set about what constitutes a family. In addition, some queer parents are more socially disenfranchised than others. For these parents, using the legal system might result in additional unfair discrimination. Conceivably, legal action for these families might end up jeopardizing the child. For example, if you are transgendered, live in a polyamorous group family, are clearly members of the S/M community, or are in other ways deemed more queer than queer, your family may be at greater risk within the legal system due to mainstream prejudice.

Queer Stepparents, Coparents, and Other Marginalized Parents

When you are in more of a marginalized role, that of a queer stepparent or a partner of a coparent for example, it can be harder for you to maintain a parenting role in your child's life after a breakup. This is because the child's other parents are usually still involved. It is not that the children do not regard you as one of their parents, but rather that the parents don't see any need for you. This can be a difficult position to be in.

It is hard to be in a long-term relationship with someone and have no parental rights. If you speak with your ex about the situation, perhaps they will be understanding and allow you to see the children on a regular basis. However, they might just want you out of their life altogether, and, thus, out of the children's life by default. If the children have additional parents other than your ex, you may want to approach them for help.

Danny and Don broke up after six years. When Danny got together with Don, Don's son, Peter, was just one month old. Don was sharing parenting of Peter with Annette and Lori. Parenting Peter had always been a central part of Danny and Don's relationship. After they broke up, Don told Danny he could not see Peter. He said it would be "too confusing" to Peter. Danny was astounded and hurt. He and Don had been parenting Peter with Annette and Lori for six years. After trying numerous times to get through to Don, he finally approached the moms for help. Although they did not want to set up a formal custody arrangement, they felt wonderful having Danny take Peter for evenings and weekends when he wanted to. They knew how important Danny was to Peter and did not want to intrude on their relationship. Obviously, Don and the moms had some talking to do after that, but it worked out well for everyone. Don and Danny did not have to see each other, but Danny and Peter could still continue their relationship. Danny had been and still is "Uncle Danny" to Peter.

If you still want to spend time with your ex's children after your breakup, then it is crucial to assert yourself. Perhaps you could volunteer to do child care, or to have the children come over for one weekend a month. There are certainly ways that you can suggest to be involved in their lives, whether or not you are still given a "parenting" role. You could invite them on trips to the beach, or the local amusement park, or for a picnic. If you are not allowed such contact, then send them letters, cards, packages, and e-mails. These are ways that you can let the children know that you think about them, care about them, and love them when spending time with them is not possible. With this kind of contact they will eventually ask their parents to see you. After they ask enough times, they may eventually be allowed to do so.

Helping Children to Deal with Change

When your child's family breaks up, it is essential to recognize that they will be undergoing tremendous changes both inside of themselves and in their outer worlds. The more that *you* can do to keep stable and consistent, the easier the other changes will be for your child. Although it is healthy for your child to see you have emotions, try to have your larger personal breakdowns at times when your child is unaware or otherwise occupied. Monitor your phone calls so that your child does not have to listen to you "rag" on their parent indirectly. Remember you are not the only person affected by the changes; this experience is not just about you.

To help your child manage their feelings, you need to process your own grief and loss. It is a very good time to seek personal counseling. It is also a very good time to seek counseling for your child. Seeking counseling is not a way of admitting failure; it is a way of gaining support to help you move through transformational situations or crises more smoothly. The perspective that you gain in counseling will help you to have the skills and boundaries that can assist your child in processing their own grief and loss.

Consistency

During the time surrounding a change in family structure, a child needs continuity, consistency, balance, play, joy, and a sense of home in order to thrive. Their basic sense of trust and security has been shattered no matter what their age is. If there has been tension and fighting in the house prior to the breakup, then the children are also recovering from the trauma of that experience. Children are always significantly impacted by breakups. Their sense of loss can be overwhelming. This is challenging for children to process, but especially so if they are preverbal.

It is helpful to remember that children mirror the spoken and unspoken emotions of their parents. Thus, although perhaps initially relieved, adults and children alike will go on to feel: anger, sadness, self blame, and depression in the face of family reconfigurations. In the midst of these internal feelings, the outside world is often changing at a pace too fast to integrate. There are usually child care changes, housing changes, job changes, and many of the daily routines changing as well. Although these changes may feel cathartic to you and are keeping you busy, remember that consistency, familiarity, and continuity are what make a child feel most safe.

Honor the Past

Do not remove all traces of your life before the breakup from your child's home environment. Include in your home photos of all of you as a family, and photos of your ex with your child. Maybe you could make a photo album together, just for your child. This could be a joint time of remembering good times you all have had together. This is important, as often the months leading up to and following family breakups are overly focused on the negative aspects of one another. This will send a message to your child of continuity and safety.

As it is common for your child to go to extremes to prove their loyalty to you during and after a breakup (so that you will not break up with them next), do not encourage your child to disengage from the other parent when they are with you. To do so will only continue to support internal secret lives. It is best if your child can feel free to love each of their parents without feeling like doing so will disappoint you. Their love for their other parent will not disappear, they will simply stop sharing it with you.

Lastly, it is very important to realize that your child may be very isolated in their experience during your family breakup. There can be a tremendous sense of isolation for all children whose parents divorce; however, for our children, this isolation is often compounded by homophobia. Your child can receive very little external support during this time due to other people's homophobia and their subsequent lack of understanding of the impact the separation may be having on your children. Likewise, to protect themselves from others' homophobia, or the fear of people not understanding—that is, your child's internalized homophobia—your child may be less likely to reach out for support and to tell people what is happening. Please do not underestimate the burden of homophobia on your child during a time of family reconfiguration. This is a very important time for your child to receive support and to not feel alone. A friendly counselor may be your best choice.

New Family Structures

The face of family is always changing. Your family structure may metamorphose many times while your children are growing. If you started off single, you may find a partner. Perhaps you were living in a communal situation with other children and parents and then you and your child moved out on your own. Maybe you break up with your partner and enter the dating scene again. Maybe you have just come out of a straight marriage and your child lives part-time with you and your new lover, and part-time with your ex. Perhaps your family had two couples which broke up and repartnered, and now your child has four parents, four stepparents, and four homes. The face of the modern day family can transform over and over again.

Honor the Transformations

Because the face of family can have many permutations, the goal is to create healthy models of coming together and growing apart. This benefits us as adults and it benefits our children greatly. To create healthy models requires attentive parenting and a dedication to conscious relationships. Our queerness can be of assistance in this process because it is inherently more natural for us to recognize a variety of family structures. The key is to celebrate and honor each transition through which the family moves. This creates a positive recognition of change, rather than an emphasis on what has been lost or a fear of the future.

When we teach ourselves and our children to recognize, honor, and celebrate change, we are teaching ourselves and our children to recognize, honor, and celebrate difference. We are influencing ourselves and our immediate communities. Through living our home lives with awareness, we are acting to change the world.

Single Parenting for Newcomers

When you become a single parent after having been partnered, it is a big change. You may experience the change as a welcome relief, especially if you have become accustomed to living with a lot of tension or fighting in your home. There is no doubt, however, that there will be many adjustments for you to make. In general, your free time is reduced dramatically as you become solely responsible for your child when they are with you. If you have shared custody, you learn to take care of the errands and your personal needs during the time your ex has the children. If, on the other hand, you become the only parent to your child, then you quickly learn how to ask for help from others. Regardless, you will probably initially experience tremendous levels of overwhelming stress as you learn to do alone what you had shared with someone else in the past.

Family Ceremony

When you have settled in after the initial shock of being a solo parent, then it is time to do something fun with your children to acknowledge and celebrate this shift in your family. Creating a ceremony does not mean that you have to feel great about your new situation, it simply recognizes the changes and helps all of you to move into the new phase. If you are already feeling good about your new family structure, then it is a way of saluting your new selves.

In your ceremony you can create an event where you invite others, or it can be a private sharing between you and your children. One parent I knew decided to spend a special day with her four-year-old daughter. They said it was their "New Life Together Day." They decided together what to do. Each of them picked three things that they would like to do together on that day to honor that it was just the two of them in their new apartment. The day would also honor that now they would spend half of every week apart from one another. In the morning they played ponies. After that they made colorful nametags for their rooms. Next they made a special picnic lunch together of each of their favorite foods. After lunch they went to their favorite stores and they each bought something very special to honor this new change for themselves. Then they went for a walk around the lake and told each other what they were going to miss about being one family in one house and what they were looking forward to about being two families in two houses. They memorialized the day by taking and framing a photo of them together.

To create such a ceremony takes emotional courage. It can be very difficult to imagine planning and carrying out such a ceremony, yet the benefits that both you and your child will reap from ritual acknowledgement of your new changes will positively permeate your new lives together. The ceremony will always be remembered by your children.

Family Members Who Leave Your Life

When a family member leaves your life and you do not see them anymore, there is a natural grieving process. Your child also goes through this grieving. If you have had partners, children, parents, close extended family members, or siblings relocate or leave your family during a breakup, it can be very hard to trust new people to not leave you too. This can be especially true for children. Fear of abandonment can delay or seriously affect bonding.

It is sometimes common for a parent to have gone through serial live-in partners with whom they discontinue contact after they split up. For their children, this means that they have experienced serial stepparents and possible stepsiblings with whom they have no contact. This pattern is especially common for parents when they are in a less healthy phase of life. If this dynamic is something that your child has experienced, they will have to go through a healing process to begin to trust again.

If you move into a more healthy way of life, through entering counseling or a twelve step program, for example, your relationships will probably become stronger and more long lasting. If this shift has taken place, it will probably help ease your child's internal stress load to do something markedly different, such as having a ceremony (see section below, "Family Blending Ceremonies"). Know that it will still take time for your child to trust and bond, but that you are doing something definite to break the familiar cycle.

New Family Members

Each child will respond differently to the idea of new people entering their family. This depends a lot on the age of the child, their history, their relationship with you, how much they like the new person, and what your relationship to the new person is like.

New family members include new partners of yours, a new partner of your coparent, a new sibling, a stepparent who brings a child or children into your family, and any extended family members who come along with them.

It is important to remember that just as parents instigate family separations, so too do parents introduce new family members. It is valuable to listen to the feelings of your child and to try not to move too fast. If you allow your child room to express their feelings freely about the changes, they will be more accepting. It is also critical to allow your child and the new member their own time to bond together.

Bonding does not happen overnight. Some children are really open to new people joining their family and others are more wary. Respect your child's own time line for accepting the new person, even if it takes longer than you would have hoped. You must always reassure your child that you are not looking for a replacement for your old partner (if you had one), or a replacement for your children. Explain repeatedly that this is a different relationship and that your heart is big enough to share your love. You will also want to reassure your child that it is OK for them to love new people too; it will not mean that they love you or your ex any less. There is always enough room for more love in our hearts. Simultaneously, allow your child to be scared, shy, resentful, unloving, or whatever they feel.

Stepparent Concerns

Becoming a stepparent is never easy. There are existing family dynamics that were created long before you came into the picture. The situation may be compounded if you do not like the way your partner parents, if you do not like your new stepchild, or if you bring your own children to the relationship. Children are forever. It is very important to realize from the start that you are entering a relationship with an adult *and* their children.

As a new stepparent it is easy to feel left out of the parenting. It is important to openly discuss the parenting roles that each of you have and to express your fears and desires about becoming family together. To be done well, this is a transition that requires a lot of attention. Definitely peruse the bookstore for good books on stepparenting (see Resources). You might also see if there is a GLBT friendly family therapist in your area who could help you through the transition to family. You may be up against the numerous cultural icons that personify stepparents as evil. It is helpful to reach out for support before you need it.

Family Blending Ceremonies

Family blending ceremonies are special times when you blend new members into your family. It can serve the function of a wedding between adults and an adoption of new children and parents, and a solidifying of stepsibling relationships between children. If your adult structure has stayed the same but you are adding new siblings into the family through adoption or birth, then you could hold a family blending ceremony as well.

We held a blending ceremony for our family. When the three of us, Colleen, my daughter Gi, and I were ready to commit to being family together instead of just having Colleen as my girlfriend, we planned our ceremony. We sent out formal invitations to family and friends. It was our commitment ceremony to one another. Colleen and I were formalizing our union; Gi and Colleen were adopting one another, and together we were broadening our circle of family. After the ceremony we had a reception at our home. Because I already had a child, we needed a ceremony that reflected our commitment to each and every one of us—not just between adults. We have photos of the ceremony around our house. The ceremony allowed us all to make the shift from temporary to permanent. We blended our love into family.

Two bisexual and polyamorous families in Vermont decided to blend their families together. Each existing family unit had one child. There were five adults marrying one another. In their ceremony the children served only as ring bearers. The adults invited their families and friends. There was a reverend to officiate the ceremony. It was very important to them that their community understand and accept that there were three moms and two dads in the family. They wanted no confusion amongst the people they cared about, because they knew there would be a lot of confusion and discrimination from the outside world. The ceremony concluded with a beautiful hand-painted marriage contract that was signed by all five adults and the two children alike.

Family Continuity

When you honor your family transformations you create a sense of continuity for your family. Making the time together to acknowledge verbally and emotionally the changes in your family constellation is a very practical way of acknowledging change. It is wonderful to remember the past as you enter into the present. Having photos around from the past helps to link previous family structures to current structures. It is easy for adults and children alike to appreciate cycles and change when change is seen as something safe. Structure provides that safety. It may be both challenging and painful to find a way to honor your family reconfiguration, but finding the courage to redefine your family with love and intention is well worth the effort. Such dedication to accepting and recognizing change will create safety and emotional security for your children. Be brave.

11

Protecting Your Family

Legal Issues, Contracts, Documents, and Other Concerns

The times we live in are groundbreaking for queer families. GLBT families are gaining more attention from the public than ever before. This is creating greater legal opportunities to secure the rights of our families than have been previously available. It is exciting to see politicians actually lobbying for issues of equity that include queer issues. At the time of this writing, the first state ever, Vermont, has just awarded gay and lesbian families the same state rights of marriage afforded to heterosexual couples. This includes all parenting rights secured by the state of Vermont.

As exciting a time as this is, with an increasing number of states granting second-parent adoptions, and more states granting adoptions for openly queer parents, there is also a tremendous backlash. The Religious Right has taken on the queer family agenda with a vengeance. Because they feel that we pose a direct threat to "family values," there is an open, national battle going on about queer families in virtually every state in the nation. Queer rights *is* the civil rights issue of our time.

While some states are moving ahead and are making headway for our families, other states are introducing and passing measures that ban gay marriage and gay adoptions. These are proactive measures aimed at opposing any headway we are making for our rights. The movement toward securing injustice is spreading like wildfire. What had been a fairly silent legislative issue for the past two decades has become a primary focus of energy for those religiously opposed to our families. The Religious Right has a lot of money and is well organized. It is a daunting force with which to be reckoning.

There have been great strides for our families. In most places in our country it is no longer protocol to lose custody of your children simply based on sexual orientation. Nevertheless, there are still whole parts of our country that, in the words of Kate Kendell (2000), director of the National Center for Lesbian Rights (NCLR), "are uniformly intransigent when it comes to issues of equity and fairness for lesbian and gay families." In such areas, like the South, legal issues for bisexual and transgender families have not been brought to public attention yet.

In this chapter we will cover ways in which we can protect our families and ways in which we can help further the movement for securing our rights.

Balancing Denial, Fear, and Awareness

The truth of the matter is that queer families are at great risk. Our families are not protected in the same ways that heterosexual families are protected. Not only are we not granted the same basic rights of parenting, but unfortunately, at this point in time, there is the added element of our families actually being under siege. It is often more compelling and desirable to live in denial about the danger our families are in than to focus on this reality. This level of denial is dangerous.

Yet, how could we live our lives and raise our families if we were constantly focusing on what could happen to our family just because we are queer? People who do feel this fear, whether on a regular basis or following a specific incident, find that it leads to feeling selfish for having wanted children in the first place, feeling extremely intense fear in simple interactions with society, and feeling quarantined in your community. This fear can cause you and your family to live in contraction.

At times, each of us receives a wake-up call and more acutely feels the risk of being a queer parent; and, at times, each of us pleasantly slips into our lives and forgets that we do not actually have the same security as our neighbors. We must be aware of the inequity afforded to our families (and work toward changing that), while at the same time not allowing fear to dominate our lives. This is a fine balance to establish and maintain.

The goal is to feel good about ourselves and safe in our world without being in denial about the delicacy of that safety. Yes, it may be true that within your community or your family structure you have nothing to worry about, but can you say the same if you got a job transfer to a more conservative state? It is sometimes too easy to become complacent if you live in a tolerant community or too fearful if you live in a hostile environment. Finding the balance is the key.

Dealing with Outside Threats

The most common risks to losing custody of your children are breakups; extended family members; death; anyone filing a Child Protective Services case against you; and right-wing political organizations. Anytime custody of your children is threatened it is terrifying. It can be completely overwhelming. Because of all the emotions involved in not having access to your own child, it can be very difficult to think rationally about what your options are. Do not fight any threat to your custody alone. Reach out for help. Contact local queer organizations, national organizations, lawyers, friends, and family members. Resist the urge to fall into the isolation of depression, you will need all the help you can to win this battle.

Securing Legal Documents

Families where the relationships are not socially defined and accepted through the legal mechanisms of biology, adoption, or marriage are at risk in times of crisis. There is no recognized means for protecting our vital, yet unacknowledged, relationships. However, there are practical actions that we can take to protect ourselves and to increase our personal comfort level with the existing risks. It is often difficult to embrace the idea that we actually need to protect our families in these ways. Many of the GLBT parents I have spoken with, myself included, have delayed securing any of these documents for ourselves because we consider ourselves to be trusting people. We cannot imagine that we will actually experience unjust behavior from society, our relatives, or our partners. I strongly encourage you, however, to look at the situation from the perspective of your children. In creating these documents we are not only protecting ourselves from each other, we are attempting to provide security for our children in the event of unwanted tragedies. When we choose to trust instead of taking appropriate measures, we are not doing our job as parents. As parents we must trust, and provide as much safety, security, and continuity for our children as possible. Because our children are not afforded the same protection as the children of heterosexual parents, we are responsible for creating as much of a safety net as we can.

Overcome the fear, denial, and inertia that often prevent us from securing these documents and do it! Take the time, energy, and money needed. If it is at all financially feasible, seek the counsel of a lawyer who is familiar with our families. A lawyer can help you determine which legal options are available and most suitable to your situation and in your state. If seeking legal counsel is not within your financial means, do not let that stop you. There are great "do-it-yourself" resources available (see Resources section).

Second-Parent Adoption

Second-parent adoptions are by far the best way of securing your rights as a legal parent of your children. It is a way for any two parents to have a legally recognized relationship to their children. With a second-parent adoption, the natural, legal, or custodial parent is able to retain legal parenting rights, and the adopting parent gains the status of being a recognized parent as well. Short of having a second-parent adoption decree, there is no way to secure a definitively legally binding relationship with your children. This is the only mechanism that is legally acknowledged. Adoption decrees must be honored in any state whether or not that state itself grants such adoptions. Thus, if it is available to you, do it. Unfortunately, this option is not usually available for securing the rights of families with more than two parents.

There are many advantages to completing a second-parent adoption and having a legally recognized relationship with your child. Once you have completed a second-parent adoption you can insure your child as a dependent on your health insurance policy. In the event of a breakup, you can use the courts, if necessary, to establish child support and visitation protocols. If the other parent dies, your custody of the child will not be challenged. If your child needs medical attention, you are empowered to make decisions regarding their care. You have access to your child's school records. There are many other issues that simply do not come into question when you are your child's legal parent.

What Is Involved?

When you have decided to pursue a second-parent adoption, you will need to hire an attorney. Ideally you will hire a lawyer who understands and supports your family structure and who has before successfully petitioned for this kind of adoption. If you are having a difficult time finding a queer-friendly, experienced lawyer through your local queer organizations, contact the NCLR for referrals (see Resources section).

It is very important to ask your lawyer enough questions to ensure that they actually do support your family structure and will be wholeheartedly working on your behalf. Do not expect the attorney to volunteer disturbing information; ask direct questions, including:

- Have you ever before represented someone in the GLBT community?

- Do you have an opinion on what kind of family is best for a child to live in?

- Do you support the idea of second-parent adoptions and legal rights for queer families?

- What do you think about gay marriage?

Once you are clear that the lawyer will be working for you, it is equally important to feel that the lawyer will be able to successfully help you. In each county that grants second-parent adoptions there are judges who pass our adoptions and those who deny them. Your lawyer needs to have the experience or the effective contacts to ensure a working knowledge of the system. If your lawyer is not experienced but you wish to use their services, make sure that they are willing to accept suggestions and guidance from second-parent adoption experts such as the NCLR. You do not want to lose your adoption by choosing the wrong lawyer.

After meeting with an attorney, the existing legal parent will have two mandatory counseling sessions. If there is a biological parent already on the birth certificate, the process of their surrendering sole legal rights happens at this time. Then, after filing for adoption, the prospective adoptive parent will have a very personal interview with someone from the department of social services. This is followed by a home visit from a social worker, fingerprinting, and tuberculosis (TB) tests. This process can vary slightly from state to state.

Many parents feel that the counseling, interviews, home visit, and fingerprinting are demoralizing experiences. The questions that are asked are often very personal and probing. It certainly can bring up your own internalized homophobia, and, at times, the sometimes thinly masked homophobia of the social worker. If you can emotionally prepare for this aspect of the process it will be easier to endure.

After all of those steps have been completed, a hearing is held. If the adoption is successful, the birth certificate for each child in question is changed to reflect both parents. Then you can celebrate!

Costs

The costs involved in second-parent adoption vary from state to state. It is safe to assume that you will be spending between $2,000 and $5,000. This effectively makes second-parent adoption cost prohibitive for many families. Nonetheless, it is highly recommended that you pursue a second-parent adoption in states and counties where it is possible. Explore ways to reduce the costs, and start saving as soon as you can.

People have thrown adoption parties to raise the funds, and/or taken loans from friends, family, or credit cards. In some areas, there are lawyers who will provide a sliding scale for low-income families.

Legal Climate for Second-Parent Adoptions

To date, courts in more than twenty-one states have granted second-parent adoptions for queer families, and only Florida and Utah have laws explicitly prohibiting second-parent adoptions for gays and lesbians. Although no one is officially tracking how many queer families are using this option, the NCLR estimates that there are tens of thousands of families who have successfully completed second-parent adoptions (Kendell 2000).

As queer families continue to attract attention, some states are passing or trying to pass legislation aimed at prohibiting gays and lesbians from adopting or foster parenting children. In some of these states, the legislation also effectively prohibits second-parent adoptions. However, once you have secured a second-parent adoption, it must be recognized on constitutional grounds in all states.

An interesting case was decided in Vermont recently: A nonbiological mother entered into the court system to try to regain access to her child whom she had been raising with her ex-partner. The courts denied her formal custody rights on the basis that second-parent adoption is available in Vermont and the couple had not chosen to adopt. Although this was one situation in one state, it causes you to take pause. If you do not secure a second-parent adoption in a state or county where it is available, this choice could be used against you.

Personal Issues

An interesting dynamic occurs in many families as they decide to pursue second-parent adoptions. Because second-parent adoption is the only definitively binding legal recognition our families have, deciding to pursue one can bring up a lot of emotions. Similar to the experience heterosexual people report around being married, we can experience "cold feet." This is the closest equivalent queers have to marriage. After you adopt, you have a legally binding relationship not only to your child but, effectively, to your partner and/or coparent. You are liable to follow custody and child support mandates in the event of a breakup. Effectively, any escape hatch you may have subconsciously held open closes when you adopt.

From this perspective, you become more accountable to your partner and children, and the unexpected stress of this can bring up tension in your relationship. Have compassion for yourself and for your partner at this time. As with all transformational times, you may question the foundations of your life. Make an agreement in your relationship that you will not bring up whether you should complete the adoption once you both have definitively decided to pursue one. The adoption should never be held as a threat over one parent's head. This is an unfair and unnecessary power play.

Uniform Parentage Act

The Uniform Parentage Act (UPA) is a relatively new available option that is currently being used instead of second-parent adoption as a way to legally secure parenting rights for queer families. To date, the UPA has been used by a small number of families in three states and is quite rare outside of California. This parenting decree is based on the belief that the intent to parent, not biology, is what makes a parent. Granting our parenting rights through the Uniform Parentage Act has amazing, far-reaching possibilities. It is a great way to affirm the nature of our families. Be aware, however, that although the UPA does grant us full parenting rights, the same as secured with a second-parent adoption, it is so new that there have not been enough people using it to see if it will standup in all states. At this point in time eighteen states have enacted their own model law for UPAs that has been codified in the state rules, but only three states have used the UPA for LGBT families (Hwang 2000).

Advantages of the UPA

The UPA does appear to be a very ingenious way to secure parenting rights in climates that are generally hostile toward queer families. There are a number of pleasant advantages that are causing some people to choose this route instead of second-parent adoptions where both are available. First off, the decree is based on the premise that you are a parent simply if you say you are. Thus, UPAs support our families. This is quite different from a second-parent adoption, where the legal parent is counseled about giving the child up for adoption, even though, in reality, you are sharing parenting and no child is being given up at all.

With a UPA, there are no home visits and no counseling sessions. The department of social services is not involved in your life. The UPA is usually somewhat less expensive than second-parent adoption. Also significant is that the paper work can be completed during pregnancy or adoption proceedings. This enables the UPA to be granted much sooner than a second-parent adoption—often within the first month of parenting.

Drawbacks of the UPA

Because there is simply not much practical experience with using the UPA, it is difficult to accurately assess the risk factor involved with it. In the state of California by 2000, only a few dozen UPAs had been granted. Regardless, in a state or county where second-parent adoptions are not decreed, UPAs may be worth attempting.

There is a relative risk of a third-party challenge when using the UPA. In Colorado, where there is a statute against second-parent adoption, a family is currently in the process of having their use of the UPA challenged. The department of vital statistics, which does not want to change the child's birth certificate to reflect two parents of the same gender, is challenging it.

It is generally not advised that you use the UPA if you have a known donor or if your child has more than two parents. This is so because there is more room for interpretation of your intention when you were creating your family, as it does not mimic the traditional two-parent family. In fact, there has been at least one case where a lesbian family trying to use the UPA was denied on the sole grounds of using a known donor.

In addition to the possibility of a UPA not ultimately holding up legally, another drawback is that it may not be uniformly accepted in every state. If that is the case, you may end up having to second-parent adopt as well in order to secure your parenting roles. You may not, however, be able to have both a second-parent adoption and a UPA. Be sure to seek the advise of a competant attorney.

Important Alternative Documents

If a second-parent adoption is not an option and the Uniform Parentage Act won't work in your circumstance, then, unless you are legally married to your partner, or you are single, your family is at risk. Even when there is no secure legal route to ensuring the parenting rights of the nonbiological/noncustodial parent there are some actions that you can take to provide documentation of your role as parent in your children's life. Although these are not as legally strong as full parenting rights, they do clearly state your intentions. Despite the fact that these things take time to do, please make the time to do them. When our relationships are going well we often do not think we need to document our intentions on paper. When our relationships are breaking up, jeopardized, or otherwise in crisis, however, it is often too late.

Although it is difficult to find the time as a parent to draw up these documents, do not let that stop you. These are the documents that will help to protect our children. The following suggested documents help to clearly delineate the shared commitment to, and responsibility for, the children in your family. Without this documentation, your partner, the courts, or a homophobic relative could argue that the nonlegal parent is nothing short of an unpaid baby-sitter. Unfortunately, many parents and children have been split apart in situations where documentation may have served to protect and honor their bond. There is no guarantee that such documents will be honored, but without them there is no opportunity to find out. Do not wait until it is too late. Create these documents today.

Parenting Contracts

It is strongly recommended that every GLBT family draw up a parenting agreement or contract. It is best to create this document prior to the birth or adoption of your child. If you are entering into a relationship with or as an existing parent, create such a document as soon as the relationship has moved to the level of shared parenting. Your document can then be revisited and updated periodically to reflect any changes.

The primary purpose of such a contract is to establish—without a doubt—the nonlegal parent's role and status in the child's life. It confers the title and responsibility of parent and unquestionably defines the nature of the adult/child relationship. This signed written agreement clearly states that, in the event of a dispute, the nonbiological/noncustodial parent(s) have a right to a continuing relationship with the child, the same as any other legal parent in a similar situation. A parenting contract will probably not be enforceable by a court of law, but it will certainly be helpful when seeking mediation or arbitration.

A parenting contract that commits each parent to using binding arbitration or mediation in the event of a dispute creates an enforceable contractual relationship between nonlegally married parents. A parenting contract demonstrates the mutual intent of the parenting relationships and plainly states that the adult/child relationship is not contingent on the adult/adult relationship. In the event of a dispute, it is up to each of you, and outside agents, to uphold the contract.

It is recommended that you include the following provisions in your document:

- Define the financial obligations you hold to one another and to your children, both within your existing relationship and in the event that you split up. It should state that each adult acknowledges and agrees that "Though (name of parent) is not the biological or adoptive parent of the child, they are a 'de facto parent' who has formed a 'psychological parenting relationship' with the child."

230   *The Queer Parent's Primer*

- Clearly state that both of you acknowledge and agree that this relationship should be protected and promoted just as any "legal" parent's relationship would be.

- State, in detail, each parent's current and ongoing commitment to the children, i.e., food, shelter, clothing, medical, etc.

- Include a procedure for establishing custody arrangements and financial obligations in the event of a family restructuring. This procedure should clearly delineate the parents' arrangement regarding day-to-day caregiving and decision making.

- Make a written agreement to seek second-parent adoption if it becomes or is available in your state.

- Include in your parenting contract a clause that states that if the legal parent is no longer able to care for the child because of death or legal disability it would be in the best interest of the child to remain with the "de facto" parent.

- Reference all other documents that pertain to the welfare of your child.

- Name each child being included in this agreement so that there are no grounds for interpretation at a later date.

- Secure separate lawyers for each adult involved.

- Most importantly, delineate a plan for future dispute resolution that commits to using binding arbitration or mediation.

The benefits of a parenting contract are that it creates and documents the status of the nonlegal parent/s. It also establishes criteria for determining custody and support arrangements.

Supporting Documentation and Other Important Life Planning Documents

In addition to your second-parent adoption, UPA, and parenting contracts, it is very important to create supporting documentation. The greater the paper trail, the harder it will be for anyone to challenge your relationship to your child. Draw up wills; revocable trusts; nomination of guardianship papers; medical authorizations for each other and the children; durable and medical powers of attorney; authorizations for travel, access to school records, bank accounts and other assets; and life insurance that nominates your children as the recipient(s). Having a joint bank account from which you pay for your child's daily expenses helps to document financial support. If you do not have a shared account with your children's other parent(s), be sure to save a record of transactions that provides some level of evidence that you provide on a daily basis for your children financially.

Staying Out of Court

Going to court should be an absolute last resort for queer families. On a practical level, litigation is emotionally draining, traumatizing, and expensive. Generally the outcome of litigation is undesirable for both parties, and you can end up feeling like a lot more has been lost than has actually been gained.

In many states you do not have the authority to bring a lawsuit to court unless you are a legal parent. If you are a nonbiological/nonadoptive parent trying to regain visitation or custody rights, your case may not even be heard. Courts often will not pay any credence to what may indeed be in the best interest of the child, when the person in question has no established parenting relationship to the child through marriage, birth, or adoption.

Thus, if you are the legal parent and you choose to utilize the legal system which ignores—by defining them as inconsequential—the relationships of our children to their parents, you are choosing to use homophobia as a means to suit your own ends. When we use homophobic systems of thinking to make decisions about our families, we are damaging both our collective interests and the interests of our own children.

Binding arbitration and mediation are personalized, respectful, and less expensive ways of reaching resolution in times of dispute. In a mediated settlement, both parties have their voices heard. When they reach agreement, it is through empowerment rather than through an impersonal legal decree.

Special Considerations for Various Parents

Queer parents have so many variations of family configurations that there is not a blanket set of recommendations that can be used for all LGBT families. This diversity can make securing parental status even more challenging as our families are often far different than the traditional two-parent heterosexual family configuration.

Transgendered Parents

Regardless as to your legal relationship with your partner (if you have one) and your children, it is essential to draw up a parenting contract. In addition to all of the other elements of the contract, it is important to include that you are transgendered and that your partner has full awareness of this. If you do not clearly state this fact, then your partner or other parties may act in the future as if they did not know that you were transgendered, and they may use it as grounds to secure full parenting rights for themselves.

The issues of transgendered people and parents are beginning to be heard by the courts. Fortunately, the major national queer legal organizations are devoted to the cause of serving and representing transgendered people, whether they identify as lesbian, gay, bisexual, heterosexual, or another sexual orientation. Unfortunately, both within the courts and without, transgendered people not only face sexual orientation bias, but are also confronted with significant misunderstandings, judgment, and fear regarding gender nonconformity.

It is the recommendation of the NCLR that, as with gays and lesbians, if you are transgendered and you are denied custody and visitation rights of your children, and you have tried everything else, by all means go to court (Kendell 2000). The legal issues of transgendered parents are often complicated and unenviable. Many transgendered parents, however, have the advantage of being legally married to their partner. Likewise, many transgendered parents are biologically related to their children. This, barring biases, grants them full parenting rights. Unfortunately, generalized fear—or perhaps *terror* is more accurate—regarding this level of gender self-definition can complicate legal matters. Be sure to find a lawyer who understands and respects the intricacies of your situation.

Single Parents

As a single parent, it is very important to draw up legal documents prior to parenting. If something should happen to you that would prohibit you from parenting your children on a temporary or permanent basis, custody would automatically be granted to your parents first, and your siblings second. If this is not desired by you, your wishes are much more likely to be honored if you have already drawn up a will, durable power of attorney, and guardianship papers clearly nominating who you would like to have custody and why.

Families with More Than Two Parents

There have been a small number of third-parent adoptions granted in the Bay Area for families with three parents. However, this is by no means the norm, as they have not been granted elsewhere in the country. Therefore, families with more than two parents must act in accordance with what would most accurately reflect their family. If the children are biologically related to two of their parents, then you need to decide if one of the biological parents will relinquish their legal rights and responsibilities to the children so that the other parents can adopt.

Often two lesbian parents will choose to parent with two gay men. In families where mothers are the primary parents and the dads are coparents, and they all live in an area where second-parent adoptions are granted, it is common for the nonbiological mom to second-parent adopt and for the biological father to relinquish his legal parental status. In all families with more than two parents it is important to document! What you write down on paper often will be the only documentation you have that reflects the true nature of your family.

Be sure that all the parents clearly spell out the nature of each adult's relationship to the child. When you have drawn up the document, be sure that each parent signs it. Be as clear as possible so that, in the event of a future dispute, you can reference a document that truly reflects the nature of your family, and the nature of the bonds the child has with each parent.

We Are Our Own Greatest Threat

The tragedy about queer parenting is that there is a tendency to fall into the trap of oppression. We are perhaps our own greatest source of pain. As a GLBT community, we do not hold ourselves to a community ethic. It is not the courts who are to blame when we break up and do not let our ex-partners continue to parent our children. It is not the Religious Right who changes the rules midstream and no longer recognizes our existing relationships as valid.

We are the ones who separate our children from their parents. We are the ones who define, and redefine, family to meet our needs. We use heterosexism to justify our choices when it works to our advantage. We use homophobic laws to try to prevent our ex-partners from seeing our/their children. We are the ones who are hurting our children, ourselves, our loved ones, and all other queer parents and parents-to-be.

By continuing to drag our children through messy divorces that utilize antigay logic, we are doing serious damage to our families, to the queer family movement, and to the attempts to gain legal equity and protection. If we continue to convey that our families are disposable, with no need for long-lasting ties, we only harm our best interests.

Creating a Community Ethic

As GLBTs, we must create and uphold an affirming and consistent community value for the restructuring of our families. If we wish to raise emotionally secure children with a strong sense of family, they need to see a community that holds parents to a standard even in times of trouble. We must protect our children. Decisions about the care and custody of our children should always be based on the relationship the child has with each adult, not on the relationship the parents have with one another, or on the legal claim one parent may hold. When we no longer feel love between the adults, we must still treat our child's family with dignity, compassion, and respect.

In an attempt to create a set of standards, the leading legal and community advocate groups for queer families established some very specific guidelines. To obtain a copy of the thirteen-page document, please contact the Lambda Legal Defense and Education Fund directly (see Resources).

The overarching aim of the standards, which are listed below, is to help families maintain the status quo for their children to the greatest extent possible at times of crisis or a breakup.

1. Be honest about existing relationships regardless of legal labels.

2. Consider the dispute from the perspective of the child or children.

3. Try to reach a voluntary resolution.

4. Try to maintain continuity for the child.

5. Remember that breaking up is hard to do.

6. Seriously investigate allegations of abuse in determining what is best for the child.

7. Honor your agreements.

8. The absence of legal documents is not determinative of the issues.

9. Treat litigation as a last resort.

10. Treat homophobic laws and sentiments as off limits.

(Lambda Legal Defense and Education Fund)

In order for community guidelines to become a community standard or ethic, the guidelines must reach and be accepted by that community. Consider adopting a pledge to use these standards, if needed, in your own family. Include these guidelines with your other documents, and attach a copy to your parenting contract. Make a copy of these standards and distribute them at local queer parenting meetings or events. Encourage your local queer press to publish these standards as well. Do your part in creating an equitable and just approach to honoring our children and our families.

Organizations That Are Fighting for Queer Rights

If you or your family is at risk, it is important to know that there are a number of organizations out there who are fighting very hard for our rights (see Resources section). Contact them right away if you feel that you are under siege and ask for their advice. Because these situations are on the increase, these organizations cannot take on every case. They must take on cases that will be precedent setting and/or have as few "holes" in them as possible. They will, however, help you to find resources that will support you in your struggle. If at first someone puts you off in one of these organizations, keep trying until you receive some solid advice.

These organizations are our hope; they are our torchbearers. Without these organizations leading the way, we would not have come as far as we have and we would be moving forward at a much slower pace toward securing equal rights for our families. Remember to donate your time and energy regularly to these and to your local organizations: National Center for Lesbian Rights (NCLR), Lambda Legal Defense Fund and Education Fund, American Civil Liberties Union (ACLU), and the Gay and Lesbian Advocates and Defenders (GLAD).

There are a number of actions that we can take to increase the security of our families. Unfortunately, even going through the hassle and finding the money to take such actions does not provide our families the same automatic rights granted to heterosexuals. The truth of the matter is that we lose access to our children on a regular basis. Most situations never hit the mainstream media or even our own queer media. They remain private, personal anguishes that rip up our families and our hearts. We cannot be complacent. Remember that laws affecting gay and lesbian relationships are changing rapidly. Because of the changing state of the laws, remember to review and update your documents regularly.

Fuel Your Desire to Affect Change

When you start to draw up these documents you may discover deep wells of fury and resentment within you about the fact that we have to jump through hoops to try to achieve safety for our families. Use these strong feelings as fuel to help further our civil rights.

On a local level we can work to change people's minds and attitudes. We can familiarize our straight friends and allies with the inequity of the situation and ask them to work on our behalf. Encourage them to contact their local political representatives to demand equal rights for all.

On a broader level we can contribute time and money to the organizations that are fighting the legislative battles. Do all that you can to secure your own family, and work to secure all of our families. We each must embrace this battle. Our civil liberties should not be optional or second rate. We, just as all people, deserve equal protection and equal rights. Working toward social justice for our families is one of the ways we can leave a safer, more secure world for our children and for everyone's children.

PART V

The Path of Pride

12

Family Activism

There is a long way to go before the world is a safe place for LGBTs, let alone a nourishing and supportive one for our families. It should be our constitutional right to have our relationships acknowledged as real, valid, and legal. It should be our constitutional right to create our families and have them honored. Securing equal rights for LGBTs is the civil rights movement of our time. We are not second-class citizens, yet, on a governmental level, we are still treated as if we are.

Staying in Touch with the Injustice of Homophobia

It is often difficult to stay in touch with the injustice of the discrimination against GLBTs. When you are out it is easy to become complacent and to feel like being queer is no big deal. When you are closeted it is easy to internalize the discrimination and to assume that is the way it is. It can help to remind yourself that our children are still taken away from us for no reason, we are not allowed to marry, in some countries we could be legally jailed or murdered for being who we are. This is injustice.

If we change the issue, it is impossible not to be outraged. If it were still illegal for interracial couples to marry, would you feel it was no big deal? When it comes to our own oppression it is more difficult to remember it is completely unacceptable. Forgiveness and understanding are very admirable qualities that we must teach to our children. Yet we cannot let forgiveness placate the pain of oppression or the desire and need to celebrate our lives and to commemorate the struggle. Every group of oppressed people commemorates their struggle, and so should we.

As LGBTs, we continue to create family in the face of adversity because we are strong. Those of us who are raising children are brave individuals on the cutting edge of change. As GLBT parents, we must continue to dream of a world that supports and nourishes our families. At this point in time, such a world remains a dream. There is a lot we can and must do to ensure the creation of such a world.

Being a Parent Is Being Political

Those of us who are choosing to parent are following a path of love and a path of pride. Parenting is a way of asserting our basic human right to love. In a society constructed to make us invisible, simply *being* a gay parent is a political act. No one chooses to parent because it is political. We choose to parent out of love and, like it or not, at this point in history, it is controversial. As our numbers increase, however, and we become a more visible form of family, the controversy will die down and our rights will finally be secured.

Many of us do not consider ourselves to be political people. We do not necessarily have any desire to be noticed or to stand out as different. Many of us hope that if we do not emphasize our differences, our sexual orientation will become a nonissue, as it should be. Quietly living as a LGBT family is a vital form of activism—silent activism. Activism does not have to be loud to be effective.

Others of us feel strongly that to make the world a safer place for our children we must be verbal, educate others, assert ourselves, and actively fight for our rights. This approach assumes that if *we* are not fighting for our rights, who will? Many people believe that "in your face" activism is the only way to make change. These people are the recognized social activists among us.

Love Alone Cannot Protect a Family

"Love Makes a Family" is a slogan used in the GLBT community to explain the validity of our families to ourselves and to the outside world. This slogan is very true: Without love we would not have children, plain and simple. This is only half of the picture, however. Love makes a family, but love is not enough to protect our families. It is only through our dedication, commitment, and activism that our families can be sustained. We must fight for our rights. This is what distinguishes us from heterosexual parents. Although this is a significant difference, it rarely is acknowledged.

There may indeed be times in your parenthood when you feel the luxury of not having to fight for your/our basic rights as people, families, children, and partners. Do not let this insular experience numb you to the greater truths. Do not allow yourself to become passive. Our families are being actively lobbied against in almost every U.S. state. LGBT teens are being murdered, we are losing custody of our children, we have no entitlement to make medical decisions for our own children, and queer children are committing suicide at alarming rates. As a whole, we are a targeted and oppressed people.

Commit to Social Activism

We must foster not only love in our families but a commitment to social activism, a commitment to social change. If you are spit on at an amusement park, as I was at Disneyland while walking with my daughter and partner some years back, do not try to take it in stride or internalize it: Do something. Talk to the management of the park about the discrimination you experienced. If they do not address the incident to your satisfaction then organize. Rally publicity, get your local gay group to boycott/picket the park. Write an editorial for your paper drawing attention to what it feels like to be treated this way and to have your children treated this way.

In the Bay Area there is a large and growing number of LGBT families. It is wonderful to see. Yet many of the LGBT parents I know remark that their straight friends and family frequently make comments to the effect of, "Don't you feel so lucky/grateful to live here?" When was the last time a straight person had to feel grateful to live in a place where they were accepted? Are we supposed to feel grateful for the feeling of being quarantined and the fear to move someplace where we may not be accepted? People are so well meaning in their liberal homophobia.

We must join our PTAs, we must become playground monitors, we must stay apprised of the local, state, and nationwide measures to protect or undermine our families. We must volunteer our time, money, and energy to fight for our right to be free and for basic human civil rights. This is not because love makes our family, but because our love is not enough to create a safe place for our families.

The more fiercely and directly we pursue justice, recognition, and equity, the more likely it will be that our children—and all people—will experience the benefits of a social transformation toward the acceptance of LGBTs. Follow the path that works for you, whether that leads you to the playground, the streets, the churches, the courts, your neighborhood, or into politics.

We have both tremendous power and responsibility to try to further social acceptance and understanding of our families and relationships. Regardless as to the way you would prefer to interface with society, at times, being a gay parent will call on you to be more public than you may feel comfortable being. Sometimes it becomes essential to draw attention to the changes that must be made so that you or your child need not continue to suffer unjustly. Parenting often makes it easier to do things that would have been unthinkable in the past. We find ourselves doing whatever we need to do to carve out a place for ourselves.

Modeling Activism

By living our lives as queer parents, we are modeling activism to our children. Children learn just as much, if not more, from our actions as from our words. Seize the opportunities as they arise to be a strong role model for your child.

We model activism and pride when we come out to other parents and children. When we present people with new language choices and address people's assumptions, stereotypes, and biases, we are teaching by example. As we work to build relationships across difference, we build bridges for others to cross. When we practice random acts of kindness toward strangers, we teach our children compassion. When we speak up in public when witnessing someone being oppressive, we teach our children bravery and justice.

When we do not point out bias as unacceptable, however, we do not stand for equity. When we do not stand up for others, we are modeling for our children that issues of equity, equality, and justice are not a constant priority, but an issue of comfort. Is that truly the message you want to give to your children? Speak up when it is convenient but otherwise let it slide?

As parents, we are activists in our lives. We are activists when we pose possibilities to children that they may not receive elsewhere. We do this as we tell them stories, as we play and talk with them, and answer their questions. We are activists as we fill out forms and cross out inappropriate entries or complain about their heterosexist assumptions. We are activists when we attend school activities as queer families and when we discuss politics at the dinner table.

Encouraging Activism in Children

Fostering children to become activists means fostering a strong sense of compassion and justice. When a child has a strong sense of justice, the skills of standing up for what is right become deep-rooted. Not all children are leaders nor do they need to be. Activism in daily life simply means taking action of any sort in the face of injustice. Encouraging a child to recognize stereotypes, prejudice, and bias on a regular basis lays the groundwork for compassion. Through activism and compassion, children from gay families can come to feel powerful and come to learn skills that will enable them not to personalize and internalize any oppression they experience in their own lives.

Once you have laid this groundwork, you can explore together what assumptions are being made at school, camp, on television, and in books. You can then brainstorm together ways that these could be changed. This form of reflection encourages your child to not accept life as it is presented, but to work toward change. By modeling activism, we teach our children that each person does make a difference.

One day love will be enough to protect our families, to protect queer teens, to protect all those who suffer from discrimination and oppression. Until that time comes, however, we must act and we must teach and inspire our children to work for social change. We cannot and will not rest until love is enough to make and sustain a family.

One day, love *will* be enough.

Resources

Multimedia

Both My Moms' Names Are Judy: Children of Gays Speak Out. 1994. 10 min. $25. Contact: Lesbian and Gay Parents Association of S. F. 415-522-8773.
A great short film for parents, kids, and educators; training materials included.

It's Elementary: Talking about Gay Issues in Schools. 1996. Seventy-eight minutes; or thirty-seven-minute classroom version. Contact: Women's Educational Media, 2180 Bryant Street #203, San Francisco, CA 94110. 415-641-4616.
Excellent documentary designed for adults; training materials included.

Love Makes a Family: Living in Lesbian and Gay Families. Contact: Family Ties, PO Box 975, Amherst, MA. 413-549-4886
A photo/text exhibit that brings gay and lesbian family images and voices to any school or community space across the country.

Organizations

Children of Lesbian and Gays Everywhere (COLAGE). 3543 18th Street #17, San Francisco, CA 94110. 415-861-5437. www.colage.org.
A great organization supporting our children with lots of support resources and information.

Family Pride Coalition. PO Box 34337, San Diego, CA 92163. 619-296-0199. www.familypride.org

A great organization that provides support education and advocacy for GLBT parents.

Gay, Lesbian and Straight Educators Network (GLSEN). 122 West 26th St., Suite 1100, New York, NY 10001. 212-727-0135. www.glsn.org. Or, GLSEN-Boston: 132 Boylstan St., 4th Floor, Boston, MA 02116. 617-451-1119. www.glsenboston.org.
A national organization with local chapters. GLSEN has phenomenal resources for teachers and parents. They are dedicated to ending homophobic bias in K–12 grades. GLSEN Boston has developed a comprehensive annotated bibliography for students and educators.

National Gay and Lesbian Task Force (NGLTF). 2320 17th St., NW, Washington, DC 20009. 202-332-6483. www.ngltf.org.
NGLTF is working to end violence, discrimination, prejudice, and injustice against LGBTs.

Parent, Families, and Friends of Lesbians and Gays (PFLAG). 1726 M Street, N.W., Suite 400, Washington, DC 20036. 202-467-8180. www.pflag.org.
PFLAG provides support, advocacy, and education for parents and supporters of LGBTs.

Teaching Tolerance. 400 Washington Ave., Montgomery, AL 36104, 334-264-7310. www.teachingtolerance.org.
A wonderful publication and source of videos offered to educators for free.

Additional Teachers Resources

The American Association of University Women (AAUW). 1111 Sixteenth N.W., Washington, DC 20036. 800-326-AAUW.

The Center for Research on Women at Wellesley College. Wellesley, MA. 617-283-2500.
Ask for information on the Seeking Educational Equity and Diversity (SEED) Project.

Consortium for Educational Equity. Rutgers University, Kilmer Campus, New Brunswick, NJ. 908-445-2071.

EQUALS, Lawrence Hall of Science. University of California at Berkeley. 510-642-1823.
Programs to increase the participation of girls and people of color in science, math, and technology.

National Women's History Project. Windsor, CA. 707-838-6000.
Teacher training and materials for home and school.

Organizations for Equal Education of the Sexes, Inc. Blue Hill, ME. 207-374-2489.
Posters of famous women.

Syracuse Cultural Workers. PO Box 6367, Syracuse, NY 13217. 315-474-1132. www.syraculturalworkers.org
Excellent resource for posters about women and famous gays and lesbians.

Legal Resources

ACLU Lesbian and Gay Rights Project. "The Rights of Lesbians and Gay Men: The Basic ACLU Guide to a Gay Person's Rights." 125 Broad Street, 18th Floor, New York, New York 10004. 212-549-2627

Gay and Lesbian Advocates and Defenders (GLAD). PO Box 218, Boston, MA 02112. 617-426-1350.

Lambda Legal Defense and Education Fund. 120 Wall St., Suite 1500, New York, New York 10005-3904. 212-809-8585. www.lambdalegal.org.
Lambda Legal Defense Fund and Education Fund has a number of free documents and publications available over the Internet.

A Legal Guide for Lesbian and Gay Couples
Curry, Hayden, Denis Clifford, and Robin Leonard. 1996. *A Legal Guide for Lesbian and Gay Couples.* Berkeley: Nolo Press.

National Center for Lesbian Rights (NCLR). 870 Market St. # 570, San Francisco, CA 94102. 415-392-6257. www.NCLRIGHTS.org.
The NCLR has a packet of documents entitled "Partnership Protection Documents."

Books

Kaufman, Kate, and Ellen Bass. 1996. *Free Your Mind: The Book for Gay, Lesbian, and Bisexual Youth and Their Allies.* New York: Harper Perennial.

Schultz, Steven, and Virginia Casper. 1999. *Gay Parents, Straight Schools: Building Communication and Trust.* New York: Teachers College Press.

Gender Awareness Books for Parents and Teachers

Chapman, Anne. 1988. *The Difference I Makes: A Resource Book on Gender for Educators.* Washington, DC: The National Association of Independent Schools.

Crawford, Susan. 1996. *Beyond Dolls and Guns: 101 Ways to Help Children Avoid Gender Bias.* Portsmouth, NH: Heinemann.

Day, Frances Ann. 994. *Multicultural Voices in Contemporary Literature: A Resource for Teachers.* Portsmouth, NH: Heinemann.

Hansen, Lorraine, Joyce Walker, Barbara Flom. The American Association of University Women. 1995. *Growing Smart: What's Working for Girls in School.* New York: Marlow.

Orenstein, Peggy. 1994. *School Girls: Young Women, Self-Esteem, and the Confidence Gap.* New York: Doubleday.

Pipher, Mary. 1994. *Reviving Ophelia: Saving the Selves of Adolescent Girls.* New York: Ballantine Books.

Pollack, William. 1998. *Real Boys.* New York: Henry Holt and Co.

Sadler, Myra, and David Sadler. 1994. *Failing at Fairness: How Our Schools Cheat Girls.* New York: Touchstone. (Includes chapter on "The Miseducation of Boys.")

Wellesley College Center for Research on Women. 1992. *How Schools Shortchange Girls: The AAUW Report.* Washington DC: American Association of University Women Educational Foundation.

Parenting Books

Becker, Gavin. 1999. *Protecting the Gift: Keeping Children and Teenagers Safe.* New York: The Dial Press.

Berends, Polly. 1987. *Whole Child/Whole Parent.* New York: Harper and Row.

Dodson, Shireen. 1998. *100 Books for Girls to Grow On.* New York: HarperCollins.

Eyre, Linda, and Richard. 1984. *Teaching Your Children Joy.* New York: Fireside.

Goleman, Daniel. 1997. *Emotional Intelligence: Why It Can Matter More than IQ.* New York: Bantam Books.

Kabat-Zinn, Jon, and Myla Kabat-Zinn. 1997. *Everyday Blessings: The Inner Work of Mindful Parenting.* New York: Hyperion.

Mathias, Barbara, and Mary Ann French. 1996. *40 Ways to Raise a Nonracist Child.* New York: Harper Perennial.

Prather, Hugh, and Gayle Prather. 1996. *Spiritual Parenting.* New York: Three Rivers Press.

Wright, Janet M. 1998. *Lesbian Step Families: An Ethnography of Love.* New York: Harrington Park Press.

Relationship Books

Hendricks, Gay, and Kathlyn Hendricks. 1990. *Conscious Loving: The Journey to Co-Commitment.* New York: Bantam Books.

Levine, Stephen, and Ondrea Levine. 1996. *Embracing the Beloved: Relationship as a Path of Awakening.* New York: Anchor Books.

References

Ahrons, Constance. 1994. *The Good Divorce: Keeping Your Family To-gether When Your Marriage Comes Apart*. New York: Harper Perennial.

American Academy of Pediatrics. 1997. Breastfeeding and the Use of Human Milk—Policy Statement. Chicago. *Pediatrics*. 100(6): 1035–1039.

Bottoms v. Bottoms. 457 SE 2d 102 (Va. 1995).

Both My Moms' Names Are Judy: Children of Gays Speak Out (film). 1994. San Francisco: Lesbian and Gay Parents Association of San Francisco.

Chamberlain, David. 1998. *The Mind of a Newborn*. Berkeley: North Atlantic Books.

Condon, W. S, and L. W. Sander. 1974. Neonate Movement Is Syn-chronized with Adult Speech: Interactional Participation and Lan-guage Acquisition. *Science* 183:99–101.

Corley, Rip. 1990. *Final Closet: The Gay Parents' Guide for Coming Out to Their Children*. Miami: Editech Press.

Crawford, Susan. 1996. *Beyond Dolls and Guns: 101 Ways to Help Children Avoid Gender Bias*. Portsmouth, NH: Heinemann.

Dodson, Shireen. 1998. *100 Books for Girls to Grow On*. New York: HarperCollins.

Harris, M., and P. Turner. 1986. Gay and Lesbian Parents. *Journal of Homosexuality* 12:101–113.

Hwang, Chris. 2000. (NCLR staff lawyer.) Personal communication. August 15.

Kendell, Kate. May 2000. Executive Director of NCLR. Personal communication.

Millot, J. L., J. C. Filiatre, and H. Montagner. 1988. Maternal Tactile Behavior Correlated with Mother and Newborn Infant Characteristics. *Early Human Development* 16:119–29.

Moss, H. A. 1974. *Early Sex Differences and Mother-Infant Interaction. Sex Differences in Behavior.* Edited by R Friedman, R. Richart, R. Van de Wiele. 149–63. New York: Wiley.

Patterson, Charlotte. 1992. Children of Lesbian and Gay Parents. *Child Development* 63:1025–1042.

Patterson, Charlotte. 2000. (Professor of Psychology at the University of Virginia.) Personal communication. August 15.

Peterson, Gayle. 1996. Communication and Problem Solving. Unpublished article.

Pies, Cherri. 1988. *Considering Parenthood: A Handbook for Lesbians.* Minneapolis: Spinsters Book Company.

Pomerleau, Andree, Daniel Bolduc, and Louise Cossette. 1990. Pink or Blue: Environmental Gender Stereotypes in the First Two Years of Life. *Sex Roles* 22:359–368.

Roberts, S., S. Dibble, J. Sanion, S. Paul, and H. Davids. 1998. Differences in Risk Factors for Breast Cancer: Lesbian and Heterosexual Women. *Journal of the Gay and Lesbian Medical Association* 2:93–101.

Turner, Pauline, Lynn Scadden, and M. Harris. 1990. Parenting in Gay and Lesbian Families. *Journal of Gay and Lesbian Psychotherapy* 55:57.

Wellesley College Center for Research on Women. 1992. *How Schools Shortchange Girls: The AAUW Report.* Washington DC: American Association of University Women Educational Foundation.

It's Elementary: Talking about Gay Issues in Schools (film). 1996. San Francisco. Women's Educational Media.

World Health Organization. 1995. *Division of Child Health and Development* 16. Geneva: World Health Organization.

Some Other New Harbinger Self-Help Titles

Family Guide to Emotional Wellness, $24.95
Undefended Love, $13.95
The Great Big Book of Hope, $15.95
Don't Leave it to Chance, $13.95
Emotional Claustrophobia, $12.95
The Relaxation & Stress Reduction Workbook, Fifth Edition, $19.95
The Loneliness Workbook, $14.95
Thriving with Your Autoimmune Disorder, $16.95
Illness and the Art of Creative Self-Expression, $13.95
The Interstitial Cystitis Survival Guide, $14.95
Outbreak Alert, $15.95
Don't Let Your Mind Stunt Your Growth, $10.95
Energy Tapping, $14.95
Under Her Wing, $13.95
Self-Esteem, Third Edition, $15.95
Women's Sexualitites, $15.95
Knee Pain, $14.95
Helping Your Anxious Child, $12.95
Breaking the Bonds of Irritable Bowel Syndrome, $14.95
Multiple Chemical Sensitivity: A Survival Guide, $16.95
Dancing Naked, $14.95
Why Are We Still Fighting, $15.95
From Sabotage to Success, $14.95
Parkinson's Disease and the Art of Moving, $15.95
A Survivor's Guide to Breast Cancer, $13.95
Men, Women, and Prostate Cancer, $15.95
Make Every Session Count: Getting the Most Out of Your Brief Therapy, $10.95
Virtual Addiction, $12.95
After the Breakup, $13.95
Why Can't I Be the Parent I Want to Be?, $12.95
The Secret Message of Shame, $13.95
The OCD Workbook, $18.95
Tapping Your Inner Strength, $13.95
Binge No More, $14.95
When to Forgive, $12.95
Practical Dreaming, $12.95
Healthy Baby, Toxic World, $15.95
Making Hope Happen, $14.95
I'll Take Care of You, $12.95
Survivor Guilt, $14.95
Children Changed by Trauma, $13.95
Understanding Your Child's Sexual Behavior, $12.95
The Self-Esteem Companion, $10.95
The Gay and Lesbian Self-Esteem Book, $13.95
Making the Big Move, $13.95
How to Survive and Thrive in an Empty Nest, $13.95
Living Well with a Hidden Disability, $15.95
Overcoming Repetitive Motion Injuries the Rossiter Way, $15.95
What to Tell the Kids About Your Divorce, $13.95
The Divorce Book, Second Edition, $15.95
Claiming Your Creative Self: True Stories from the Everyday Lives of Women, $15.95
Taking Control of TMJ, $13.95
Winning Against Relapse: A Workbook of Action Plans for Recurring Health and Emotional Problems, $14.95
Facing 30: Women Talk About Constructing a Real Life and Other Scary Rites of Passage, $12.95
The Worry Control Workbook, $15.95
Wanting What You Have: A Self-Discovery Workbook, $18.95
When Perfect Isn't Good Enough: Strategies for Coping with Perfectionism, $13.95
Earning Your Own Respect: A Handbook of Personal Responsibility, $12.95
High on Stress: A Woman's Guide to Optimizing the Stress in Her Life, $13.95
Infidelity: A Survival Guide, $13.95
Stop Walking on Eggshells, $14.95
Consumer's Guide to Psychiatric Drugs, $16.95
The Fibromyalgia Advocate: Getting the Support You Need to Cope with Fibromyalgia and Myofascial Pain, $18.95
Working Anger: Preventing and Resolving Conflict on the Job, $12.95
Healthy Living with Diabetes, $13.95
Better Boundries: Owning and Treasuring Your Life, $13.95
Goodbye Good Girl, $12.95
Fibromyalgia & Chronic Myofascial Pain Syndrome, $19.95
The Depression Workbook: Living With Depression and Manic Depression, $17.95

Call **toll free, 1-800-748-6273,** or log on to our online bookstore at **www.newharbinger.com** to order. Have your Visa or Mastercard number ready. Or send a check for the titles you want to New Harbinger Publications, Inc., 5674 Shattuck Ave., Oakland, CA 94609. Include $3.80 for the first book and 75¢ for each additional book, to cover shipping and handling. (California residents please include appropriate sales tax.) Allow two to five weeks for delivery.

Prices subject to change without notice.